Look at the Bunny

Totem, Taboo, Technology

Look at the Bunny

Totem, Taboo, Technology

Dominic Pettman

zero books

Winchester, UK
Washington, USA

First published by Zero Books, 2013
Zero Books is an imprint of John Hunt Publishing Ltd., Laurel House, Station Approach,
Alresford, Hants, SO24 9JH, UK
office1@jhpbooks.net
www.johnhuntpublishing.com
www.zero-books.net

For distributor details and how to order please visit the 'Ordering' section on our website.

ISBN: 978 1 78099 139 9

A CIP catalogue record for this book is available from the British Library.

Design: Stuart Davies

Printed and bound by CPI Group (UK) Ltd, Croydon, CR0 4YY

CONTENTS

Acknowledgments

Several chapters in this book enjoyed a previous life as independent entities. All, however, have been revised and updated for this collection. "Look at the Bunny: or What Roger Rabbit Can Tell Us About the Second World War" was first published in my co-written book, *Avoiding the Subject: Media, Culture, and the Object* (Amsterdam University Press, 2004). "Love in the Time of Tamagotchi" was first published in *Theory, Culture & Society*'s special "ubiquitous media" issue, vol. 26, no.2-3 (2009), 189-208. "Exile from Funland: Flusser and Agamben After the Fall," first appeared in the *Journal of Communication and Critical/Cultural Studies*, vol.1. no.6 (2011), 1-6. "Tolstoy's Bestiary: Animality and Animosity in *The Kreutzer Sonata*," is slated to be published in an upcoming special animal studies issue of *Angelaki*. All reincarnations appear with the kind permission of the original publishers. I would like to thank in particular Ron Broglio, Briankle Chang, Justin Clemens, Erik van Aert, and Fern Bryant of Sage Publications. Special appreciation also goes to Jodi Dean, Eugene Thacker, Tariq Goddard, John Hunt, Hugh Raffles, and Merritt Symes for helping pull this particular rabbit out of the hat.

Introduction

The Totem Redux

The totem is dead and buried; both as a way to help organize social cohesion (for participants) and as a model for the mapping of any given group (for observers). After all, it has been over half a century since the doyen of structuralist anthropology, Claude Lévi-Strauss delivered his influential funeral oration for the notion of the totem – "the phantasmagoria of the theorists" (58). And yet the word keeps cropping up in popular consciousness, enjoying an ongoing after-life as a fuzzy metaphor for certain types of extra-human symbols, affiliations, identifications, and behaviors. Indeed the totem continues to serve all sorts of vague purposes, beyond or outside the technical usage of social scientists, or the indigenous people from whom the term was originally borrowed. The New Age fondness for personal animal spirit helpers[1] – a popular poaching and personalization of clan-based totemic relationships – is only the most explicit instance of the ways in which the modern world continues to employ symbolic figures as virtual guides for actual situations. Nor is it necessary to wear an eagle feather in one's hair to be attuned to this kind of ubiquitous projection. The famous *contrada* of Siena, for instance, continue to compete against each other in the manic horse-race inside the city itself, bearing the heraldic emblems of their respective family trees (including caterpillars, owls, dragons, unicorns, towers, and sea-shells). Some may consider this merely a vestigial ritual – an echo of the medieval knights who once roamed the same territory, with shields emblazoned with meaningful images.[2] But we can also trace the impulse *forward* in time. Contemporary sports teams, for instance, not only have mascots dancing on the side-lines, but also the invisible and omnipresent totems which bear witness to the day's play; and whose capricious moods either make or break them during the game. Hipsters, Hell's Angels, and bored suburbanites tattoo their bodies with images meaningful to their personal mythologies: skulls, dragons, doves, lions, roses, fairies, rock stars, clowns, mothers, lovers, cartoon characters, Ankhs, peace signs, mandalas, quills, tea-pots, bar-codes, and so on.[3] Pre-tween schoolgirls refuse to leave home unless at least one accessory or item of clothing is emblazoned with Hello Kitty. While atheistic academics begin to irrationally sweat if they realize they have boarded a long-haul flight without their St. Christopher medal (*cough cough*).

The totem is such a suggestive figure because it potentially includes *all* figures. Anything (that is, any *thing*), is a totem waiting to happen, thanks to the idiosyncratic ways in which people psychologically and emotionally invest in objects (which, of course, can be a rather clinical word for other subjects). Now that the totem has become more personalized, and liberated from the limitations of collective sense, it can be as varied as the contingency of any given biography. The totem is an empty outline waiting to be shaped into something specific through subjective cathexis. This empty space is negatively charged. Its power comes from *without*. It is a fulcrum or quilting point around which things, events, convictions, desires, hunches, plea-bargains, epiphanies, mistakes, and so on, circle and gather.[4] The child's teddy-bear, for instance, is a proto-totem – an object of libidinal investment and proxy imaginings. The true totemic moment comes when the child identifies with – or at least obsesses over – an *absent* figure, such as a Pikachu or Spider Man. Here the break has been made between the *fort* of the concrete possession (or companion), and the *da* of virtual connection.[5] The (relatively) stabilized narratives of selfhood, which constitute the "healthy" and normal adult, allow the totem to take a different kind of root, in different psychic soil. The mature individual has learned to internalize and virtualize the teddy-bear, giving it a far more complex, ambivalent, and symptomatic spin. We can function "on our own" in society, as long as we *know* – on some level – that someone or something is looking out for us, and has our welfare at heart. As a result, the fully totemized person is content (more or less), with the tote bag emblazoned with their badge of belonging: NPR, PBS, BBC, The So-and-So Food Co-op, etc. (or, alternatively, the bumper stickers and other paraphernalia that decorate one's motor vehicle: the Christian fish, the Confederate flag, the yellow ribbon, buxom mud-flap silhouettes, truck nuts, etc.).

The totem is particularly seductive because – to gesture to Lacan – it emerges from the Real, yet straddles the Imaginary and the Symbolic. All three bases are covered. The totem is thus a frequently traveled sky-bridge between our daydreams and the external conditions and expectations which either limit or enable them to happen (of course, usually the former). To put it another way, if Deleuze is more your cup of poison, the totem is the figure or refrain which crystallizes an assemblage over time. It is the desiring-machine which allows intensities to mark out a familiar territory, all the while threatening (or promising) to form a line-of-flight into unknown landscapes.

In the 1888 edition of the *Encyclopedia Britannica,* the celebrated mythographer and anthropologist, J. G. Frazer, wrote "[a] totem is a class of material objects which a savage regards with superstitious respect, believing that there exists between him and every member of the class an intimate and altogether special relation." We need only jettison the offensive word "savage" and replace it with "person," and we have a perfectly serviceable definition for totems today. In contrast to Frazer's definition, however, the chapters which follow emphasize the *virtual* aspect of the material objects (often animals, but not at all exclusively), which manifest the relationship. In other words, the focus will be on the imaginative,[6] abstract, metaphysical ways in which humans enlist nonhumans to look after them (or, indeed, how humans *feel* they have been drafted by nonhumans to be challenged, tested, or provoked). The New York Giants, for instance, can only have a virtual relationship with their team totem (unless we consider anyone above seven foot a "giant"). The same applies for the New Jersey Devils. The Chicago Bears could feasibly point to an actual bear as a totem, but refrain to do so, for practical and political reasons. In contrast, the Louisiana State University Tigers often bring a real live Bengal tiger (named Mike) to the stadium. But even as this animal fascinates by its exotic presence, it still merely *represents* – stands in for – the idealized avatar of *tigerness* which the team hopes to channel in battle. If Mike dies – as he has, sadly, several times during the history of the team – the totem is still alive and well, since it is always primarily a generic, virtual figure. Even if we only consider faux-tigers, the fuzzy suit of the mascot-totem is the most important part, and not the parade of different, anonymous, pelvic-thrusting freshmen who inhabit it over the course of several decades.[7]

Once you start scanning the landscape for examples, and relinquish the purist, historical definitions bequeathed – and later dismissed – by anthropologists, totems begin to mushroom all over the place. Indeed the vernacularization of the term has been going on for some time. Only two years after Frazer's 1888 entry in the stately English encyclopedia of record, London's cheeky *Pall Mall Gazette* made special note of "[t]he vulgar embroidered smoking-cap, which used to be the distinctive totem of the bazaar debauchee." It did not take long for the word to be employed outside the academy for any item with identificatory powers – in this case, a smoking-cap. More than a century later, and the totem has continued to multiply and morph within public discourse. Consider how the figure of the "grizzly mom" or "tiger mom" has circulated in the "lamestream" media in the last few years, evoking a kind of "spirit animal" for certain ideologically-charged demographic clusters. We could indeed add the notion of the "cougar," a sexually aggressive older woman, who is said to embody the highly coiled energies of a wild, predatory feline (an association with a long history, extending through the various "cat people" of the noirish imagination, but with a new suburban twist).

Despite the atavistic incense which clings to the word, the totem has insinuated itself into contemporary life as a way to understand certain charged objects or mediums, pointing to a quasi-religious surplus, overflowing the prosaic or the banal, thereby helping to orient the individual in relation to the group (and to help different sub-groups orient themselves to the [imagined] whole). Marshall McLuhan, for instance, credited the seductive power of Hitler in terms of "the tribal totem of radio" (338). Similarly, Roland Barthes unpacked his modern mythologies with the aid of this same principle, so that wine, for the French person, is nothing less than "a totem-drink" (58) (just as Charlie Chaplin projects a "totem-like countenance" [56]). More recently, Judith Williamson describes our relationship to advertising as "a kind of totemism" (46), whereby carefully crafted semiotic solicitations encourage millions of consumers to step into the "totemic space" of essentially exchangeable products.[8] Indeed, the list could go on.[9]

As a consequence, the totem suggests several elements simultaneously, now that its tribal function has been diluted and diffused into the water-table of postmodern experience. It plays a symbolic, ritualistic, virtual, and explanatory role for those who adopt it (or who feel adopted by it). For instance, in the example cited earlier, a grizzly mom looks to the female grizzly bear to explain her character: fierce, loyal, brave, nurturing, protective, etc. As a consequence, Sarah Palin feels she has a more profound understanding of her own socially-defined role as working-mother-cum-public-conservative-political-figure by reference to a creature that she has little, if any, actual contact with. (She does not claim the title of "wolf mom," since this would forbid her to indulge in one of her favorite sports – shooting wolves from a helicopter.) The she-bear totem is thus a *virtual* presence in her own mind and life, floating free from an *actual* referent, which allows the ex-governor to make certain claims in regard to other groups (especially "liberals," whose totem animal is presumably the yellow-bellied sap sucker). As one mid-century anthropologist observed, "Totemic and other ritual symbols are the ideological landmarks that keep an individual on his course" (in Lévi-Strauss, 74). And yet while we look to the totem to help provide psychosocial coherence in a rather chaotic and contradictory world, we reduce it to certain desirable traits, while eliminating others. For while Sarah Palin identifies with the *power* of a female grizzly bear, she would surely not want to be considered hairy or wild. Nor does she want to convey the message that she sleeps all winter and defecates in the woods. Today's totems are thus stylized and simplified symbols which allow ideological messages to be delivered in short-hand; both to the self and to the other.

We can thus put all these disparate elements together in order to redefine the totem in the following terms: a symbolic virtual figure associated with a charged object or referent, which helps (or at least appears to help) any given subject navigate unstable, ever-changing terrain *as if it were stable*. In the simplest language, a totem helps explain ourselves to ourselves, in relation to others. It is alternately a guide, a guardian, a role model, a trickster figure, and a key to the cognitive map which has colonized the territory it was originally designed to represent. Few things, however, can truly and consistently deliver on such a promise. So totems are also ambivalent figures, who can betray us, let us down, or lead us down the garden path.

The Anthropological Totem

One of the most significant names associated with establishing the totem as an important analytical motif is Émile Durkheim.

This scholar, working during the high watermark of imperial anthropology, relied on this notion to describe the way every day, profane objects become abstracted and sacralized as significant signs. One example would be a particular source of food which humans must not eat, because they are reserved for the spirits. Such special signs denote collective "images of solidarity" which – as a privileged type of representation – reinforce the very foundation of the social structure. The totem is thus an avatar for the true object of veneration: the community itself. A couple of generations later, as already mentioned, Lévi-Strauss was quick to dispense with this conceptual lens, since he believed it to be little more than an illusion: a trick of the light, produced by the disciplinary desire for origin myths of holistic social interaction. It was, for him, a "false category," asked to do too much work in terms of both articulating the relationship between humans and the natural world, and the "characterization of social groups." In other words, the totem shuttled between the natural and the cultural domains with such ease and rapidity, that it never really had the opportunity to take on meaningful cargo. "The supposed totemism," he wrote, "eludes all efforts at absolute definition. It consists, at most, in a contingent arrangement of nonspecific elements" (5). Variously described as a "projection" and an "exorcism," the conceit is exposed as an intellectual "misadventure," which presumed to explain "*what remains* of the diminished totality" (26).

At one moment, the totem describes "individual sentiments of attachment," at another "ritualized collective conduct," and yet another as an "object representing the group" (60). For Lévi-Strauss, the totem is not elastic enough to cover so many diverse situations; nor should any abstract idea be obliged to try. As if this wasn't problematic enough, he considered the various subspecies of totemism – such as the dream totem, cult totem, sexual totem, religious totem, personal totem, etc. – to further compromise the efficacy of the idea. Quoting one of his colleagues, Ralph Piddington, Lévi-Strauss echoes his conviction that, "[i]t will be seen that the term 'totemism' has been applied to a bewildering variety of relationships between human beings and natural species or phenomena. For this reason it is impossible to reach any satisfactory definition" (9).

Quite simply then, the totem, for the father of structuralism, "belongs more to the past than to the present." Indeed, the very notion was so popular with his own teachers because it allowed so-called modern men to feel superior to, and more advanced than, those folk from elsewhere, patronizingly described as "tribal." Lévi-Strauss believed the totem to be a kind of meta-totem for those who pioneered the use of the term, for it allowed social scientists to create a "totem pole," as it were, of different types of society (with their own on top, of course). By exposing the totem as a mirage not only for non-Westerners, but also anthropologists who presumed to explain them, his critique sought to remove the basis for any claim to historical superiority along a linear continuum of human "development." The modern and the primitive, Lévi-Strauss suggested, are closer than they appear, because those deemed to be the latter were not as unthinkingly mesmerized by totems as initially presumed.[10] While certain objects and animals were indeed charged with significance, social relationships were more complex and analogical than the rather static model of the totem suggests. My own instinct, however, would be to reverse this line of thinking: the modern and the primitive are closer than we think, since *both* rely heavily on totemic semiotics to frame, and make sense of, a largely hostile and uncertain world (even as they both do so with some irony, flexibility, and allowances for exceptions).

While Lévi-Strauss sought to nuance the term out of existence, he still provides us with some useful ways to approach it (should we maintain that totems are something more than an over-simplified analytical convenience). His critique notes, for instance, "the confusion between totem and Guardian spirit"

(23), arguing that in fact the totem affirms "that there can be no direct relationship, based on contiguity, between man and totem. The only possible relationship must be 'masked,' and thus metaphorical" (19). If we return to the grizzly mom for a moment, we can see that Lévi-Strauss is correct in disqualifying a one-to-one parity or equivalence. The totem is not merely a friend, but a "frenemy," who could turn on the subject at any moment, if displeased with the human's interpretation of the relationship. Indeed, an exceptional form of the "social contract" is signed between totem and human, ensuring that the latter is not simply a beneficiary of cosmic good will or instruction. As communications theorist Waddick Doyle pointed out to me in conversation, the Wujal Wujal peoples of Australia tell of striking an ancient deal with a key totem: the crocodile. Such a deal is, on the face of it, a straight-forward one: "we don't eat him, and he does not eat us." But if this no-go zone is trespassed, then this is a sure sign that the contract has been broken somewhere along the line, and must be renegotiated and re-authorized (through collective ritual).

Yet it is the *virtual* aspect of the totem which interests us in the present context: the way in which any actual existing crocodile is but a manifest avatar of "crocodileness" for those who live, think, and act within totemic protocols. A specific crocodile, sunning himself on a river bank, is sacred to the extent that he invokes the archetypal species with which the tribe is affiliated. (Just as the signifier is different from the referent – the former representing the abstract, collective meaning – the individualized reptile embodies something which cannot be accessed directly, but only circled.) No doubt, one can transgress the taboo and kill a crocodile. But this will not have disqualified or annulled the totemic relationship. Rather it will trigger a call for compensation or the need for a cleansing ceremony. Similarly, Sarah Palin is not diagramming herself with a straight unbroken line to an actual grizzly bear, but the constellation of metaphoric associations that "grizzliness" evoke in her own mind (via the popular, collective imagination).

Lévi-Strauss quotes another colleague, Meyer Fortes, who notes that, "Like the animals of the bush and the river . . . [totems] are restless, elusive, ubiquitous, unpredictable, aggressive." It is the enigmatic, skittish, and even slightly sinister nature of these figures that the following chapters explore; pinpointing moments when the assumed guardian spirit pivots on its heel (or hoof, or paw, or claw), and leads its human partner astray. In the wake of such unpredictable maneuvers, the stakes become somewhat clearer, determining who needs whom more in any given moment or situation. (It may seem that the human always needs the totem more than the other way around, but as the crocodile example shows, it can certainly work both ways.) And as with any alliance, pressure points and stress fractures exist which threaten to reveal the unspoken motives or conditions for the partnership in the first place. Thus totems can be cynically leveraged for advantage by one person or group, or summoned to help obtain cosmic justice by another. They are an emblem of our inevitable ambivalence about Being itself, as well as towards the specific beings we are obliged to co-inhabit existence with. Totems are thus an illuminating index of the kind of psychological, political, and libidinal jostling that makes up the fabric of everyday social relations. (The fact that new digital media render such totems *doubly* virtual renders matters even more complicated – of which, more below.)

Lévi-Strauss once stated that animals are good to think with. In this introductory chapter we can merely add that totems – often in the form of animals – are similarly helpful facilitators of cognitive or imaginative insights.[11] Before embarking on some close readings and case studies, however, the anthropological context should be complemented by the psychosocial one, since totems play such a crucial role in Freud's origin myth of civilization itself; also rooted in the Janus-headed *agon* of ambivalence.

The Psychosocial Totem

Freud found it necessary to pair the totem with the taboo, since he considered these structuring devices to be – once upon a time – two sides of the same primal coin. His famous long-form essay *Totem and Taboo* (1912-13) details his belief in the Oedipal roots of both, essentially arguing that taboos persist in the modern world in the form of obsessive-compulsive behavior manifested by neurotic individuals. The totem, in contrast, helped organize only a specific moment in human cultural development, but was subsequently jettisoned for more complex social arrangements.[12] Thus, from the beginning, Freud claims that taboos are very much in operation in the modern world (the two most significant being incest and murder), whereas "Totemism, on the contrary, is something alien to our contemporary feelings – a religio-social institution which has been long abandoned as an actuality and replaced by newer forms. It has left only the slightest traces behind it in the religions, manners and customs of the civilized peoples of today" (x).

One of the aims of *Look at the Bunny* is to off-set such a view, considering the totem not so much in terms of obsolescence or atavism, but rather an *ongoing mutation* – and *further virtualization* – within our constantly evolving socio-technical networks. But for Freud, the key moment occurred far back in the swirling mists of almost mythological time, when the two stigmas were found to be working in tandem: first prompting an "acting out," and then a subsequent "working through," of intense conflicting emotions. As a consequence, *Totem and Taboo* stages a now-familiar play, starring a "tumultuous mob of brothers" locked in simmering conflict with "the paternal tyrant." This latter is an authority figure, simultaneously loved (for his indulgences), feared (for his discipline), and envied (for his power, and dominion over the family's women-folk). The sons and brothers – tired of being cock-blocked from mother and sister alike – finally explode in a fireball of incestuous energy, acting in concert to murder the tyrannical father, and even eat him in a cannibalistic feast. By ingesting their protector-foe, the horde of young men literally incorporate their own ambivalence towards him, in an act of ultimate vengeance *and* identification. "The totem meal," notes Freud, "which is perhaps mankind's earliest festival, would thus be a repetition and a commemoration of this memorable and criminal deed, which was the beginning of so many things – of social organization, of moral restrictions and of religion" (165).[13] In the simplest terms then, "[p]sycho-analysis has revealed that the totem animal [who cannot be eaten], is in reality a substitute for the father" (163).[14]

But, like the proverbial Jedi Knight,

> [t]he dead father became stronger than the living one had been – for events took the course we so often see them follow in human affairs to this day. What had up to then been prevented by his actual existence was thenceforward prohibited by the sons themselves, in accordance with the psychological procedure so familiar to us in psycho-analyses under the name of "deferred obedience." They revoked their deed by forbidding the killing of the totem, the substitute for their father; and they renounced its fruits by resigning their claim to the women who had now been set free. They thus created out of their filial sense of guilt the two fundamental taboos of totemism, which for that very reason inevitably corresponded to the two repressed wishes of the Oedipus complex [i.e., to kill one's father and couple with one's mother]. (166)

Here Freud walks us through the process whereby the totem moves from the actual to the virtual, gaining aura and omniscience while doing so. One can, at least in theory, always argue with a real live authority figure. But it becomes a far graver thing to pick a quarrel with an invisible, panoptic, one. And so, while the desire to violate taboos persists in the unconscious, it becomes sublimated and displaced on to more socially constructive activities. The totem meal is thus a safety valve, at once acknowledging and disavowing the urge to repeat Oedipal crimes. (One wonders in passing who Freud's totem might be. Oedipus himself? Or possibly the Sphinx? Or would it be the pipe? The couch? The phallus?)[15]

Given that the totem is a strong reminder of the "primaeval prohibition," one wonders why Freud is so quick to usher it off the stage, while keeping taboo in the spotlight. After all, Little Hans, one of the more familiar cases in the original psychoanalytic literature, is diagnosed as suffering from a totemic condition. The beaten horse which troubles the boy is revealed to be a figure representing his father (*quel surprise!*). In the less well known instance of Little Árpád, who exhibited strong signs of "poultry perversion," the witch-doctor of Vienna makes special note of "the boy's complete identification with his totem animal and his ambivalent emotional attitude to it" (152).[16] Freud protests too much about the contemporary irrelevance of the totem, since even if used as a metaphor, the dynamic logic of the concept continues its diligent dream-work into present times, in both sleeping and waking states.

Neurosis, for Freud, is an internalized taboo. *Ergo,* neurotics are somewhat akin to modern primitives, in that they individualize a formerly collective world-view and set of public operating instructions. The Christian might be considered the ultimate example of a neurotic, since "at bottom God is nothing other than an exalted father" (171). And the father, as we have seen, is the source of deep-seated totemic systems in psychoanalytic discourse. (For Freud this psychosocial equivalence arose "independently from a root common to both.") The incest taboo was more pressing in pre-historical times, in this view, because our species had less civilized mechanisms for repressing and sublimating it. Hence the need for totemic chaperones. But this is not to say that our "natural," but unkosher, desires have evaporated in the meantime. They have merely disguised themselves in dreams, compulsions, symptoms, and artistic expression. Certainly Freud notes a clear and firm bond between the totem and exogamy, forbidding sexual relations with kin-folk – thus implicitly suggesting that it has not completely worn out its usage. The libidinal economy of today's totems may not be as crude as a Thou Shalt Not. However they *do* continue to be a somewhat structured way of negotiating socially unacceptable desires (experienced at the interface between the personal and the public). For Freud, the taboo is no longer a *shared* prohibition ("directed against liberty of enjoyment and against freedom of movement and communication" [25]), but a private psychodrama. But how can we confidently draw the line between the private and the public? Even if your taboo is not mine, your observance and my indifference both find their source in the social field. And common-sense would tell us that there are still taboos in effect (even if prime-time TV loves to flaunt them).[17]

Freud tells us that totems and taboos cluster around three different scenarios: *special* individuals, *exceptional* states, and *uncanny* things. Indeed, these are three key coordinates of the case studies which make up the following chapters. Totems promise to help us cope when we encounter troublingly charismatic people, liminal moments in time, and weird objects which refuse to leave us in peace or be taken for granted. Concerning the little rituals we must perform to feel safe – kissing an icon, arranging a garden gnome so that it always faces East, and so on – "there can be no doubt that they are in the nature of expiation, penance, defensive measures and purification" (33). The totemic taboo (for my purposes a tautology) exhibits a "dangerous power," which spreads by "infection."

From the moment of publication, critics have accused Freud of attempting to dress up that loose tart Allegory in the more refined clothing of History (something he explicitly attempts to deny in a preemptive fashion). This "great crime," which was "the beginning of society and of the sense of guilt" – since the two are one and the same, for the author – was considered by detractors as little more than a mimetic origin myth. "[M]an's relation to his father," is offered as the key to understanding not only the intimate secret of the individual, but the social as well. But Freud is sensitive to the skeptical questions this view generates, since

> No one can have failed to observe . . . that I have taken as the basis of my whole position the existence of a collective mind, in which mental processes occur just as they do in the mind of an individual. In particular, I have supposed that the sense of guilt for an action has persisted for many thousands of years and has remained operative in generations which can have had no knowledge of that action. I have supposed that an emotional process, such as might have developed in generations of sons who were ill-treated by their father, has extended to new generations which were exempt from such treatment for the very reason that their father had been eliminated. It must be admitted that these are grave difficulties; and any explanation that could avoid presumptions of such a kind would seem to be preferable. (183)

And yet, after weighing the evidence through his self-fashioned lenses, Freud stands by his theory tracing modern individual neuroses back to primitive social behavior. He was certainly correct at the time of writing that "[s]ocial psychology shows very little interest, on the whole, in the manner in which the required continuity in the mental life of successive generations is established" (184). It would be left to the historians, sociologists, and philosophers of technology to do this (the most notable contemporary of Freud being Gabriel Tarde).

In Freud's struggle with the shortcomings of his own

hypothesis, we encounter the suggestive notion of the "heritage of emotion," which today we might call the *affective legacy* of a traumatic event. Social rituals enable a ghost-memory of this foundational transgression to be passed down through the generations via the kind of violent mnemotechnics described by Nietzsche in *The Genealogy of Morals.* (Freud's essay being something of a belated prequel, *The Genealogy of Taboos.*) Conceivably, the totem meal could be considered a clear-cut case of "fidelity to the event," as described by Alain Badiou, similarly framed by messianic themes of redemption. As Lévi-Strauss himself noted: "If Freud gave up the idea, as he seemed to have done, that the act of parricide was a historical event, it could be viewed as *the simple expression of a recurrent virtuality,* a generic and non-temporal model of psychological attitudes entailed by repetitive phenomena or institutions such as totemism and tabus" (69, my emphasis).[18] In the essay itself, Freud writes: "When we, no less than primitive man, project something into external reality, what is happening must surely be this: we are recognizing the existence of two states – one in which something is directly given to the senses and to consciousness (that is, is *present* to them), and alongside it another, in which the same thing is *latent* but capable of re-appearing. In short, we are recognizing the co-existence of perception and memory, or, putting it more generally, the existence of *unconscious* mental processes alongside the *conscious* ones" (109).

The missing link, which would help explain the mechanics of this crucial type of parallel processing within the social psyche, is technology (or to be more specific, a conscious emphasis of the role of technics). In other words, it is a shame Freud did not write, "Totem, Taboo, and Technology." But in a sense, this is what much contemporary media scholarship is attempting to do, most notably perhaps – in this context, at least – by Bernard Stiegler. This impassioned French philosopher has written many books on the role of technologized memories for providing intergenerational coherence and continuity. He calls such out-sourced reminiscences "tertiary retentions." (The layman, however, would just call them "the media.") Stiegler argues that the "program industries" (production companies, coding operations, entertainment services, etc.), work together to foster a culture-wide case of attention deficit disorder. As a consequence, distraction becomes the rule rather than the exception. And the fetish of instant gratification weakens the long chains of communication between generations, resulting in nothing less than the end of capital-S "Society" as a collective concern.[19] The prime suspect in Stiegler's critical system is the "industrial temporal object" – his term for films, television shows, video games, and other forms of electronic media which oblige the individual psyche to synchronize with alien or inhuman time signatures. Thus, the industrial temporal object could be considered today's most prevalent and seductive totemic conduit or vector.[20] In other words, it is precisely within these genie-bottles, exhaled by computerized glass-blowers, that the totem reappears to tell us Thou Shalt Not. (Or, to Stiegler's chagrin, Thou Might As Well . . . Since Everybody Else Is Doing It Already.) To shift similes, strange, idiosyncratic, repressed, haunting, haunted totems come out of the woodwork, as the House of Usher continues to crumble. Some are able to provide clues to an exit. Others betray us into losing our bearings even further.

So just as magic has, today, morphed into "Industrial Light and Magic™", the totem has (d)evolved into the technical objects and social networks of the modern mediascape.

The Mediated Totem

W.J.T. Mitchell, one of today's most esteemed scholars of visual culture and romantic traditions, has done more than most to resuscitate the concept of the totem as a relevant figure for our millennial world, with all its complex technological layers and connections. For him, it has been an "unjustly neglected" theory in current discussions of visual culture, despite being "a distinct form of the surplus value of images" (2005, 75, 98). In contrast to Victorian and Edwardian anthropologists and psychoanalysts, Mitchell considers the totem as a symptomatically *modern* concept, which has been projected back on to more "elementary" structures: "the latest in the sequence of objects of the Other" (2005, 161). (Totemism thus comes chronologically after idolotry [ancient/classical] and fetishism [early modern]).[21] All three are examples of "secondary beliefs," in the sense that they crystallize "beliefs about the beliefs of other people" (162) – and usually unflattering ones at that.

Mitchell re-tells the origin story of the word, in which an English fur trader, by the name of John Long, returns to London in 1790 after spending twenty years amongst the indigenous nations of Canada; not only trading animal skins, but also fighting American colonialists alongside the Chippewa Indians. What makes Mr. Long stand out from the rest of the crowd is that he steps off the ship bearing a tattoo of a beaver on his chest.[22] "Long's name for the animal inscribed on his body is 'totem,' a word from the Ojibway language usually translated 'he is a relative of mine' and associated with ideas of animal, vegetable, and sometimes mineral 'tutelary spirits,' and thus with destiny, identity, and community" (2001, 174).[23]

After this initial brush with the word, the totem, as the seed of a scientific idea, goes largely dormant between the late 18th century, before resprouting under the enthusiastic green-thumbs of anthropologists like Frazer and Durkheim. As Mitchell notes, "[t]he fortunes of the word and concept totem between the 1790s and the 1850s remain a missing chapter in intellectual history that would be fascinating to explore" (175). In lieu of such a cultural history, however, Mitchell offers an interesting reading of the ways in which the totem comes to occupy and define the nature/culture frontier for us romantic moderns. "The totem," he observes, "is the ideological image par excellence, because it is the instrument by which cultures and societies naturalize themselves" (2005, 101). Hence his reading of the totem as a "figure of the longing for an intimate relationship with nature and the greeting of natural objects as 'friends and companions' – the entire panoply of tutelary spirits from Wordsworth's daffodils to Coleridge's albatross to Shelley's west wind" (182). Given that the majority of totems are, and continue to be, either animals proper, or symbols of nature, Mitchell is clearly correct in placing them in an ecological register. But today the general ecology includes digital devices as much as beavers (indeed, truth be told, often both). Extending John Berger's famous argument that our mode of looking at animals has become more focused and grasping in direct proportion with the extinction curve, Mitchell is interested in the totem's virtual power and presence: a signifier infused with extra-charged particles. (Something which Durkheim himself was attuned to: "We arrive at the remarkable conclusion that the images of totemic beings are more sacred than the beings themselves" [in Mitchell, 2001, 177]).

As Mitchell maintains,

> [n]atural organisms are not just entities in themselves, but a system of natural signs, living images, a natural language of zoographia or 'animal writing' that, from ancient bestiaries to DNA and the new Book of Life, continually reintroduces religion – and animation – into things and their images . . . . This is surely because the image of the totem animal, like that of the fossilized specimen, is the site where the species being of the individual is 'crystallized,' as it were, and rendered as a kind of concrete universal. (*ibid.*)

Mitchell's work is particularly concerned with fossils as "the evidence for a first nature totally alien to human culture." Totems, for their part, "are evidence for what we might call a first second nature, a state of culture that is much closer to nature than our modern world" (178). But unlike Freud and Lévi-Strauss, Mitchell believes that we have blinded ourselves to the totemic legacy, flattering ourselves that our scientific and industrial machines have vacuumed them out of existence, along with all other primitive superstitions. Instead we just swept it under the carpet. He thus makes the bold claim that "the romantic desire for an image to secure an intimate communion with nature is itself a form of totemism" (183). And while he does not use the phrase "romantic totemism" (or totemic romanticism), such a fusion continues to inform our symbolic imaginings *qua* Nature. Fossils and totems (as well as fossils *as* totems) "bring with them new orders of temporality, new dialectical images that interfere with and complicate one another." As a result, the romantic image itself turns out "to be a combination of fossilism and totemism, a dialectical figure of animation and petrification, a ruinous trace of catastrophe, and a 'vital sign'" (184).

The point is worth underlining. Mitchell sees totemism at work in *all* romantic imagery (itself something of a redundant phrase in his account of visual culture, since we have never truly escaped the shadow of romanticism, given the seemingly eternal themes of alienation, a Fall from Nature, secular transcendence, etc.). One need only conduct a random search of Tumblr to see the finite repertoire of romantic totems which circulate in the collective psyche: artfully arranged naked or near-naked bodies, waterfalls, exotic animals, cute animals, Waldenesque landscapes, Orientalized interiors, etc. As a consequence, romanticism itself, in its millennial apparel, is "a totem object, *a figure of collective identification* . . . [and] *a structure of feeling* available to anyone who identifies him- or herself as a romantic" (184, my emphasis). The more we attempt to banish totems into the naïve past, the more our cynical realism is haunted by their structuring-absence. If they are the elephant in the room, we must find out – quickly! – if they are here to seek revenge for years of poaching by humans, or if they are merely asking for a glass of water. Alternatively, if they are the Lacanian stain on the carpet, it is up to us to give our best interpretation to their shape; these enigmatic Rorscha(r)ch-angels of History. "In short," writes Mitchell in a different piece, "we are stuck with our magical, premodern attitudes toward objects, especially pictures, and our task is not to overcome these attitudes but to understand them" (1996, 72).

Mitchell famously reframes the entire approach of art history by asking the radical question, "What Do Pictures Want?" In poaching Freud's famous gendered question, and applying them to inanimate objects, Mitchell asks us to attune ourselves to the "subjectivity" of things we hitherto had only regarded as inert – albeit expressive – matter. Suddenly a painting or a photograph has their own agency and desires, which we must attempt to recognize.[24] To better understand the "magical" and mutual aspect of the viewer-image relation, we are obliged to admit that "the subjectivized object" amounts to "an incurable symptom." What Mitchell calls "the personhood of pictures" needs to be acknowledged, since it is as "alive in the modern world as it was in traditional societies" (1996, 73). Moreover, "[t]he desires of pictures may be inhuman or nonhuman, better modeled by figures of animals, machines, or cyborgs" (1996, 82).[25]

In terms of my own interpretation of the subliminal persistence of the totem, I would like to emphasize Mitchell's reading of pictures as "'animated' beings, quasi agents, mock persons . . . who function both as 'go-betweens' and scapegoats in the social field of human visuality" (1996, 81). This applies not only to pictorial works of art, but also the kinds of images created by the commercial world, generated by computers and digital technologies. Moreover, it can also include the kinds of images created in our minds via words, given that books continue to be consumed alongside video games, movies, and TV shows, inhabiting the imagination in a hybrid-virtual mode of different textures, scales, dimensions, frame-rates, and resolutions. As a consequence, the much-discussed "convergence" of media into one device or portal has its correlate in the post-Kantian human faculties, which attempt to parse the world according to inherited diagrams, even as that same world fractures into unprecedented fractal-logics of its own.

The Hyperreal Totem

One familiar descriptor for this fractal-effect is Jean Baudrillard's concept of "hyperreality," or the simulacra. As the postmodern mediascape promotes the signifier over the signified to an unprecedented degree, we find ourselves living in the map rather than the territory. This much is well known, as is the important influence of Guy Debord's notion of the Spectacle on Baudrillard's thinking. Less discussed is the totemic aspect of a world – or proliferation of worlds – in which the sum of actual social interactions constitute a new "reality" lived and experienced primarily via images. (We may in passing offer Don Quixote or Emma Bovary as "patient zero" of this intense identification with the aspirational image, given their novel – and *novelistic* – tendency to seek out pre-mediated experiences.)[26]

Essentially agreeing with McLuhan's theory that modern, amplified life in the global village returns us to neo-primitive, post-literate arrangements, Baudrillard observed an affinity between the graffiti covering every subway car in New York City, and the tattoos which adorned the flesh of the inhabitants: "Something about the city has become tribal . . . with these powerful emblems stripped of meaning. An incision into the flesh of empty signs that do not signify personal identity, but group initiation and affiliation" (1993: 82).[27] While he does not use the word totem here, clearly the notion is not far from the discussion. In the savage cityscapes of late-twentieth century capitalism, such charged avatars return with a vengeance. No doubt this totemic force is what drew Baudrillard to one of his favorite novelists, J.G. Ballard, whose work is strewn with modern-primitive totems, from the narrator of *Crash* himself – as a self-conscious sacrifice to the fatal motorways – to the conspicuous consumption finally rejected by the upper middle class in *Millennium People*: "I passed a metal skip into which a family had dispatched their tribal totems – school blazers and jodhpurs, Elizabeth David's cookbooks, guides to the Lot and Auvergne, a set of croquet mallets" (212-13). (In *Super-Cannes,* Ballard cannot resist casting the French prophet of nihilism himself as a totem, as the narrator sits down in a restaurant and orders "a vin blanc from the young French waitress, who wore jeans and a white vest printed with a quotation from Baudrillard" [88].)

But while it is true that commercial marks hold a powerful totemic sway over the populace – it does not necessarily follow that the system which they represent is consistent or coherent. One can "tote" a YSL bag and still be dirt poor (especially thanks to simulated, counterfeit goods). Indeed, in this example, the counterfeit would be a simulation of a signifier with no clear signified in any case. Brand worship is the post-modern identification with auratic absence, par excellence. After all, *branding* is another name for tattooing. And logos no longer denote, but *connote*. Their sleek blank surfaces encourage narcissistic projection from diverse imaginations. Which is all to say that the totem can still work as an engine of distinction, but it does so on newly shifting sands, in which class and/or status is no longer mapped clearly on to economic indicators (as Bourdieu famously maintained).[28]

Sociologist Patricia Cormack argues that the totem is a crucial motif to render "mass culture" more legible. Indeed, she encourages us to think of "the social" – a privileged object of discourse – as "modernity's 'totem'" (7). But she also maintains the static, organizational aspect of the symbol, preferring to underplay its increasing capacity to trouble the waters. Simply put, Cormack diametrically opposes the totem with the *trope*. For her, the totem conforms to the Apollonian strictures of the "modern world order," while the trope represents the more unpredictable and "creative possibilities" of the social (118). "In simple terms," she writes, "while trope emphasizes the self-reflective and interpretative aspect of modern culture, totem emphasizes the moral and concrete quality of collective representation" (9). Between the mutual influence of these two forces we find the dialectical momentum of the times: enigmatic tropes encouraging us to steal into new territory, and familiar totems returning us to home-base.

In the present context, however, we need not expend as much effort keeping the two elements apart, since the totem, to my mind, can also inspire creative possibilities, just as a trope can put the brakes on progressive experimentation. The relationship between them would therefore be more of a dynamic Yin-Yang infusion ; always to be assessed on a case-by-case basis. At any rate, Cormack is correct in putting equal emphasis on the totem's "artefactual and figurative qualities" (7), since such signs always have a material component, even if it is a purely imaginary creature (for instance, a dragon becomes part of our world via the true presence and texture of the printed word or painted fancy). The phantasmatic and the real follow the same topology as a möbius strip, since symbolic communication occurs along the interface between the two: a semi-permeable membrane which connects as much as separates. Indeed, Cormack follows Durkheim in considering the totem to be "a relational cosmology" which itself manifests "the imaginary foundation for the functioning of everyday life."[29] Nevertheless, to those who adhere to its dictates, it appears to be "more real than real" (8).

Cormack folds this process back on to her own discipline, noting that, "[w]hile all collectives produce collective representations of themselves, what is peculiar to the sociological imagination is that it is supposed to be able to identify these as such – it is supposed to see its own totem building." Sociology, cast as modernity's industrial-grade mirror, in fact worships a new totem: that of "society" or "the social" itself. Of course, "the people" have, since the beginning, been doing what they do. But now, through the white magic of social science, the signs can be read through new fetishized sub-totems, such as polls, statistics, demographics, and data.

> Simply put, the *notion* of society emerges when the modern crisis of social order arises, that is, when the collective no longer hold so much sway as to be taken for granted and put beyond unreflexive representation, inspection, and question. With the humanist realization that we create ourselves and our world, any particular social order becomes open to debate because for the modern mind the order of things could just as well be otherwise, and the status quo holds no divine or necessary status. Modern culture, therefore, begins to know itself by way of the totem of a wholly different kind, that is, an ironic and self-conscious totem of the 'social' that simultaneously disrupts and accommodates the social order it represents. (16, my emphasis)

"This was Durkheim's promise to his time," Cormack continues, "that looking at ourselves as agents of our own collective condition provides an opportunity to produce totemic objects that are sacred by the very fact that they are patently produced collectively" (53).[30] Even the most civilized are thus revealed to be still under totemic sway; no less so because the figures involved are mathematical or abstract, rather than rooted in the evident, natural world.

But such a pleasing meta-reading of society's expert narrative about itself is unstuck by Baudrillard, who relished his role as the spoiler of any party based on analogy or correspondence. For the nihilistic Frenchman, we have passed the point in history where we can *represent* "reality" through signs, since reality – for humans, at least – is nothing more than the sum of signs. Today, even a *real* shoe is primarily a sign (of work, of the arts, of fashion, of not caring about fashion, etc.). Cormack notes that in Baudrillard's vision of the status quo, "there is no interpretive space between the totemic image and the group" (91). When the referent implodes inside the image – as he insists that it does – we are melancholy witnesses to "the failed attempt at modern collective awareness that was promised in Durkheim's vision of group identity and moral integration." This does not mean that totems don't exist for Baudrillard. It means that they function *all too well*. That is to say, "the code" of constant cybernetic feedback in our electronic world "functions fully as a totemic, collective representation in the sense of its circular influence on the collective" (95). Cormack observes, "While for Durkheim the modern collective representation is an open-ended, expanding possibility for self-reflection, for Baudrillard it is a precoded, closed circuit that inscribes itself more and more deeply as it functions. The dynamic, interpretive, and troping movement is, instead, a nightmarish mode of representation where the sheer volume and speed of information erodes meaning in direct proportion to the extent that it produces measures of social life" (95). For Baudrillard, there is no Archimedean – or rather Durkheimian – point from which to have an accurate perspective on things. Today's totems – whether they be pundits, oracles, experts, analysts, or icons – are unreliable narrators when it comes to telling the story of ourselves, since they themselves can only speak from within the narrative.[31] This is why "the media," according to such an account, has become nothing but a planet-wide factory for pumping out industrial-strength simulacra.[32]

The task now, after Baudrillard's quite successful attempt to sabotage classical sociology, is to salvage and finesse the notion of the totem: not as trustworthy sign or avatar of truth, but as fascinating, troubling reminder (survivor?) of the symbolic economies which have been almost completely disavowed by market-based ones. This entails tagging such figures within the overloaded and overcoded networks through which they hide and/or proliferate. To be sure, there are straight-forward "official" totems designed to help people cognitively map a disorienting technical environment, preferably according to pre-determined pathways: the flag, the crucifix, the Nike swoosh, etc. But the question then becomes, who designed them? And why? Totems can be mobilized and re-deployed for specific ideological purposes, suggesting we humans – or *certain* humans, anyway – have power over totems as much as they have power over us. (This is one of the central dramatic conflicts in *Mad Men*, and part of its popularity.) The traffic is indeed, potentially at least, in both directions. Which is to say that *Look at the Bunny* retweaks Mitchell, who retweeted Freud, in asking "what do totems want"? The answer, as he points out, is unlikely to be what they *say* they want. Totems are nothing if not tricksters. Moreover, the ones which keep circulating in the popular media are often as mute as they are insistent. This is not so much a return of the repressed, as an ongoing and oblique hazing by the unheeded.

The key figures in the following chapters can – by some definitions – function as a totem, either in the text in which they live, or in the context of a wider inter-medial argument (for instance, Frazer's usefully loose characterization of "an intimate and altogether special relation" [in Freud, 2001, 120]). But whether they *are* or *are not* ultimately considered strictly as such interests me less than the "totemic" force and consequence of their shadowy presence (as, for instance, an auratic object, catalytic image, guiding spirit, trickster pooka, or animated locus of taboo). Indeed, it is precisely in their capacity to confuse and mock our deep-seated taxonomic urges – while pretending to reinforce them – that the enduring lure of the totem resides.

Having said all this, it would not grieve me if a reader prefers to see fetishes, factishes, idols, talismen – or something else altogether – in the creatures which populate this book. The totem-figure may be my own current research-guide, but us millennials are notoriously fickle and promiscuous. This metaphor has served me, at this particular moment in time, as a plausible alibi to put together a collection of writings under the same sign: writings that I believe speak to similar themes, and which, I hope, can learn from each other after being trapped together within the same book covers.

The first chapter, from which this book takes its title, has been revised since its initial appearance nearly a decade ago. The intervening years have only reinforced and fleshed out its argument: that the rabbit holds a special significance as virtual totem for what we might call "the long electronic century." Once you start looking for rabbits in popular culture, they start to breed exponentially. Of course, one could choose *any* animal and follow its tracks through the bestial song-lines of modern media. But there is a specific *role* and *presence* to the bunny, which draws us forward in a definitive direction. Hence the attempt to give chase, as it rushes – late, late, for a very important date – from Victorian times to the present. Indeed, the contemporary bunny-as-decoy is a prime example of a totem-trope fusion. For the bunny can usher us into a new dimension, or new way of seeing, just as it can be deployed by its human masters to distract the populace in ever more exquisitely calibrated ways (beyond earlier modes of deception or propaganda). The taboo in effect here is to ask too many pointed questions about the date for which this rabbit is late (quite possibly a secret meeting at the Pentagon). Some texts under discussion include the films *Who Framed Roger Rabbit* (1988), *Harvey* (1950), and *Donnie Darko* (2001), amongst many other lapine cameos elsewhere.

Chapter 2 follows the foot-prints of two humble figures – one computer-generated, the other flesh-and-blubber – in order to show how "life" is becoming an increasingly difficult concept to pin down, even as it becomes increasingly *easy* to manufacture and reconfigure. Here an Orc and a penguin are both presented as totems of "diagonal existences" which, for one reason or another, decide to go "off-program" and explore possibilities outside their coded destinies (whether these be binary or genetic codes). As such, they are once again totems *and* tropes, helping us pay attention to the multiple ontological implications of the word *animation*. Eugene Thacker's important book *After Life* is read as offering us a concept of "psukhēpolitics," to complicate, and perhaps even transcend, the current discourse around biopolitics. While the writings of Ted Chiang, Jean-Christophe Bailly, and Loren Eiseley help us to reframe the question of life or liveliness beyond traditional measures, such as breath, sapience, or sentience. The taboo at work in this piece concerns the "tampering" with familiar life-forms to make new, perhaps monstrous, ones, as if "playing God."

Chapter 3 explores what happens to traditional conceptions of love when one of the partners is a CGI avatar. Looking especially at Japanese dating simulation games, this piece sets up the virtual girlfriend or boyfriend as a potent totem for the latest iteration of the lover's discourse (what Barthes and Luhmann both call the "code" governing intimate behavior). The taboo on this occasion concerns the fostering of a post-human libido (or at the very least, a human libido stimulated by non-human objects or subjects). The amorous avatar obliges us to look more closely at the ways in which those aspects of our communications technologies, usually described and reviled as alienating, might in fact be broadening our capacity to feel affection for – be positively affected by – entities outside our often blinkered species-being.

Chapter 4 returns to a pre-digital text in order to demonstrate how literature can utilize the figure of the totem as effectively as so-called "new media." Focusing solely on Tolstoy's frightening tale of jealousy, *The Kreutzer Sonata*, this piece takes the reader on a tour of the virtual bestiary which invisibly inhabit the story's pages. Such an unorthodox interpretation reveals the mechanics of totemic identification and disavowal for the main characters, so that animals take on an especially modern allegorical significance, yet still fulfilling the ancient function of the totem: to regulate sexual actions or options.[33] The taboo here is of course infidelity, at least on the face of it. But Tolstoy's bestiary helps us see other taboos, operating on a more profound and subliminal level. The taboo of forgiveness, for instance. The taboo of not exploding or imploding in narcissistic ecstasy when the self feels threatened. These animals are therefore presented as avatars for understanding the many ways we can become sacrificial victims to a depressed libidinal economy.

Finally, chapter 5 looks at a more conceptual totem – Paradise – for its symbolic allure beyond the figural. It does so specifically in relation to video games; not so much as a sustained treatise on the promise and location of the "after life" in the world of electronic play, but as a way to create some unexpected connections between the notion of paradise, the pleonasm of "human nudity," the transcendence of flesh, and the contemporary intensification of "ludic labor." At least two taboos are at work (or play) in this piece: the notion of working on the Sabbath, and flaunting the ideologically indispensable affect of shame. The virtual reward of Paradise is thus an ur-totem which continues to be dangled over our toiling bodies like a carrot on a stick; only now with new, digital iterations to *screen* (in both senses) contemporary concerns and conditions.

All these different probes issue from the same nerve-center, and generate the same handful of questions. What is it like to be a totem? What do these mysterious, symbolically saturated figures want? Might they be "quasi-subjects" in a complementary sense to Bruno Latour's quasi-objects? Does an animate totem behave differently to an inanimate one? Does an *animated* totem behave differently to a live-action one? Do totems with real world representatives (animals, for instance), act or work differently than ones which have no obvious referent, such as a logo or concept? How, and to what end, does their virtual nature effect the material relations and situations in which they participate? What kind of politics and/or poetics do they inspire (especially in those who wish – either consciously or not – to respect or violate their prohibitions)?

Given the genesis of these essays – written independently, but all within the narrow atmosphere of my own obsessions – it is inevitable that these questions are not necessarily confronted head on in each case. In this sense, the current book could be considered yet another prequel, flying in the face of convention by actually being written in chronological order. A more systematic, monographic study of virtual totems would be needed to adequately answer even one of these questions. But my hope is that the conceit of our world and our machines being populated by an entire menagerie of totems is not *too* conceited; and that it opens up new and promising avenues to approach charismatic, mediated figures afresh. As Nietzsche well knew, it is often the creaky, arthritic, anachronistic ideas which are the most relevant and revealing. Untimely notions, like suddenly lucid grandparents, ironically allow a fresh perspective of an era which they themselves probably never expected to witness.

Chapter 1

"Look at the Bunny": The Rabbit as Virtual Totem

(or What Roger Rabbit Can Teach Us About The Second Gulf War)

Follow the White Rabbit

This chapter begins with a decoy question: why bunny-rabbits?

Certainly the bunny-rabbit looms large in the Anglo-American imaginary as a virtual totem for ontological uncertainty; and it is this thematic consistency of the role played by rabbits in cultural texts and discourses which interests us here. For while a "where's Waldo"-type map of *any* given animal could yield interesting hermeneutic patterns, the rabbit has proven itself to be a special case. On the one hand, it is a figure which begs questions of presence versus absence, especially when these terms are not as clear as they might be. On the other hand, the rabbit also inaugurates metaphysical explorations of madness, sanity, and other existential forms of psychic liminality which lie between these relative poles.

To begin with, consider the prototypical magic act: making a rabbit appear from out of a hat. This prestidigital standard has amazed and delighted children for many generations, since the hat seems to work as a kind of cosmic portal from which rabbits manifest themselves "as if from nowhere." Indeed, if pressed, the children may say that the hat serves as a kind of burrow leading to a parallel universe populated by bunny-rabbits; suggesting that the actual bunny on stage is a kind of tourist in our own dimension. There may or may not be a puff of smoke, helping the bunny make the remarkable transition from *not-there* to *there* – a transition which subliminally initiates the children into the basic philosophical question: "Why is there something and not nothing?"

Doubtless, once again, a hamster or a dove could serve the same function as the rabbit. But for some mysterious reason this latter is the creature endowed with the greatest symbolic weight. So while my decoy question may be "why rabbits?", I am in fact using this question as a portal to understand the psychosocial subtext of its neototemic significance. In other words, this chapter focuses on a particular genealogy involving rabbits as ontologically unstable, *virtual* creatures: creatures which sometimes help, and other times hinder, our comprehension of what it means "to be" and/or "to become" in different media-historical contexts. As with *Alice in Wonderland* (1951) and *The Matrix* (1999), I will try my best to follow the white rabbit, enlisting various bunnies drawn from films like *Harvey* (1950), *Who Framed Roger Rabbit?* (1988), and *Donnie Darko* (2001) – as well as books like Richard Adams' *Watership Down* and John Steinbeck's *Of Mice and Men* – in order to see just how unfamiliar and unsettling these "familiars" can be.

All the while another, altogether different, question attempts to pull itself out of the hat, drawing my methodological focus in the opposite direction. This alternative question reflects on the way in which "looking at the bunny" has become a relatively common term for the process of being distracted from more important events unfolding nearby, denoting a very deliberate form of diversion. What is it, then, I ask, that we are *not* seeing – as a culture in general – when we become too entranced by the antics of real or imagined bunny-rabbits?

Shadow Puppets

> You have shown me a strange image, and they are strange prisoners.
>
> — Glaucon, in Plato's *Republic*

Much has been made of the perceived link between the shadows flickering on the walls of Plato's cave and the various distractions of the contemporary spectacle; whether this latter be figured as the identifiable simulacra of "the media," or the even more all-englobing hallucination of "the Matrix." Plato himself is not too specific about the form or content of these shadows, making reference to "all sorts of vessels, and statues and figures of animals" (265). (Certainly, if everyday experience is anything to go by, the rabbit is one of the most popular shadow-puppets due to the recognizable pointy ears; so we could perhaps presume that Plato's "strange prisoners" were looking at projected bunnies on the cave wall . . . but this is to indulge in pure conjecture.)

What concerns us here, however, is the homologous role of the shadows – no matter what they represent – with the function of the bunny-rabbit in the modern phrase: "look at the bunny." For while the origin of this phrase is quite obscure, it extends all the way back to the Platonic critique of distraction. Hence we have the situation where a man manages to escape the cave, but is dazzled by his new surroundings, with the result that he continues to believe that "the shadows which he formerly saw are truer than the objects which are now shown to him" (266). And so when we say "look at the bunny" to a child that is about to receive a painful doctor's injection (perhaps employing a hand-puppet provided for just this procedure), we form part of a conspiracy with far-reaching implications. Elements such as the operator (doctor), operation (inoculation), *telos* (health), subject (child), and decoy (parent-bunny complex), thus constitute a paradigmatic assemblage for much cultural activity.

For, in one sense, we have the metaphysical distraction of Plato's cave – a fetish of shadows rather than the objects which lie at their source. And in another we have the more strategic, "political" distraction of using one object to draw the attention away from another: the logic of the decoy. The question at the heart of many studies linking Plato's cave with contemporary mass and social media concerns the extent to which it is possible to separate these two forms of distraction, and whether or not they are in fact interdependent, even in the original text. The critique of capitalism – only gathering momentum since the economic crisis of 2008 – sees little difference between a *philosophical* project of compromised vision (in relation to concepts such as "the good," "the unthought," "pure form" etc.), and the *political* project hostile to those advertising companies which churn out shadows on a daily basis, for projection on the walls of our own personal, Ikea-decorated caves.

Interestingly, the prophetic powers of Plato extend as far into the future as the Academy Awards, when he writes: "And if they were in the habit of conferring honors among themselves on those who were quickest to observe the passing shadows and to remark which of them went before, and which followed after, and which were together; and who were therefore best able to draw conclusions as to the future, do you think that he would care for such honors and glories, or envy the possessor of them?"(268). Thus those figures who refuse to accept their Oscar statuette, like Marlon Brando and George C. Scott, subconsciously play the role of the Platonic character who has escaped the seductive irrelevance of the shadows; to become the exceptional person who refuses to "look at the bunny."

But what is it that has the power to break the hypnotic power of these flickering images, especially in the modern context? Well, ironically enough, the bunny-rabbit figure itself. For just as Alice follows the march-hare down the rabbit hole leading to Wonderland, Neo (Keanu Reeves) is inspired by the tattoo of a rabbit to execute the series of events which will short-circuit his slavish dependence on the Matrix. In these two symptomatic bookends of the twentieth century – which in a certain sense traced an arc from Lewis Carroll to the Wachowski siblings – the bunny is a slippery totem, which may or may not be in the service of cognitive (re)orientation.

Surfing God's Channel to ToonTown

> For some time now I have used the metaphor of the rabbit and the hat in connection with a certain way of making something appear from analytical discourse that isn't there. I might almost say that on this occasion I have put you to the test of eating raw rabbits. You can relax now. Take a lesson from the boa constrictor. Have a little nap and the whole thing will pass through.
>
> — Jacques Lacan, *The Ethics of Psychoanalysis*[1]

Richard Kelly's debut film, *Donnie Darko* (2001), is a rather ragged attempt to wed David Lynch's surreal suburban Gothic enigmas with the angst-ridden search for existential answers posed by the average Marilyn Manson fan. It does, however, continue the proud tradition of featuring a rabbit with dubious ontological credentials (albeit a rabbit with a pronounced insectoid-skull mutation). Donnie himself is a high school senior with "emotional problems," who sees daylight hallucinations of Frank the Giant Bunny-Rabbit, even when taking his medication.

Two details are worth noting: the first being that Donnie is definitely aware that the rabbit is "not real." For when his psychiatrist asks if Frank is real or imaginary, he answers the latter. The second point is that Frank is not so much a bunny-rabbit, as a person wearing a bunny-rabbit suit.[2] These details intertwine as the film develops, along with its obsession with virtuality, time-travel, and predestination. At one point, Donnie can see the virtual path of people's movements before they happen, visualized by a "vessel" or "vector" or "sphere" that extends out from the chest. In following this vector (which looks like a horizontal tornado), Donnie can *see* what is going to happen before it happens; as if the universe is pre-destined by God, and one need only this form of second-sight to anticipate the next move.[3] Indeed, he explains this process to his psychiatrist in similar terms: "Every living thing follows a set path," and thus follows "God's channel." Moreover, the central problematic of the film pits this statement against the possibility of altering fate – a tension which unfolds under the knowledge that "every living creature on Earth dies alone."

Freudian resonances are, as always, present, but should perhaps be considered red-herrings. Donnie asks his friends: "What's the point of living if you don't have a dick?" and also confesses to his shrink that he follows the bunny into his parent's bedroom. "What did you find?" she asks. "Nothing," he says, in blank denial.[4] From this perspective, the self-destructive time-loop (signaled by the skeleton suit that Donnie wears during his Halloween party: a form of virtual iconography or "premediation"[5]), forms the circular arc of the death drive, leading from the womb via the tomb back to the womb again.

The significance of these "time-portals" or "worm-holes" should not be reduced to the psychodrama of the traumatized ego, but extended out to link-up with other texts and objects. As already mentioned, bunnies seem to be the guardians of portals into parallel universes; acting as guides through the looking glass, often teasingly leading people towards the Brigadoon of human happiness. At one point Donnie talks to Frank the Rabbit through a liquid mirror, recalling the tradition linking Alice to more recent wonderlands. Indeed, this reference to Alice invokes the recurring theme of pedophilia in the film. For if the "wonderland" trope is traced from its origin to those texts inspired by the Alice mythology, bunnies emerge as a decoy for more disturbing urges and activities. Even without alluding to Michael Jackson's *Neverland* fantasy-project, we can appreciate the split symbolism of "innocence" both created *and* violated by the modern "invention of childhood."[6] Bunny-rabbits play a key role in this paradox or hypocrisy, as witnessed by the constant presence of "space-bunnies" in the BBC's *Teletubbies*, whose "sex(uality) . . . seems at once over-explicit and unspecified."[7]

The troubling ambiguity of Alice's erotic ambience has only increased with each published biography of Charles Dodgson (i.e., Lewis Carroll), and his hobby of photographing young children with loving attention. From a certain perspective, this activity could be seen as a symptom of a creative mind responding to the dawn of the age of mechanical reproduction, and the ways in which technologies circulate within the libidinal economy of virtuality itself (that is, the way minors/mirrors begin to function as signifiers of purely potential sexuality). Jan Svankmajer, in his semi-animated version of *Alice* was not shy about emphasizing this aspect of Carroll's story. Moreover, in that *other* 1988 film blending animated with "real" actors – *Who Framed Roger Rabbit?* – eagle-eyed viewers will spot the graffiti, "For a good time, call Allyson Wonderland" (a strange joke for a kid's movie).

In fact, the shift from copy to simulacra effected during Carroll's lifetime could be described as a change in paradigm from Plato's cave to Alice's looking-glass. J.G. Ballard's novel, *Super-Cannes* – in some ways the ultimate statement of late postmodern globalization – reserves a special role for Alice, since the intrigue revolves around a library stacked with multiple copies of Carroll's book, each one representing an orphaned girl available for abuse by successful, corrupt corporate-raiders. (Just as the pre-pubescent dance group "sparkle motion" is exploited for similar purposes in *Donnie Darko*.)

However, it is possible that the cultural matrix of *Alice-liminality-sexuality-bunny-rabbit* is simply related to the child's capacity to imagine things which are not strictly "there." While training for his part in *Roger Rabbit*, Bob Hoskins watched his young daughter to learn how to act with imaginary characters. In an interview with *Starlog* magazine, not long after the film premiere, Hoskins explained how she

> was three at the time, and she had all these invisible friends whom she talks to – Geoffrey and Elliott. And I realized that, as we get older, our imagination goes further and further to the back of our head. When we're a kid, we can actually take it out and look at it. I mean, we can see it. As we get older, senility comes in, and the imagination comes to the forefront again, and takes over. So, I just concentrated on an immature imagination – forcing it back to the front so I could actually take it out and look at it. And I managed to actually see them, which was all right, but you do it for 16 hours a day for five months! I started to lose control and hallucinate in all kinds of embarrassing places. Some of it's quite rude, but there's not much you can talk about. At one point, it was quite frightening, weasels and all sorts of things turning up.[8]

Thus, in an uncanny reverberation of both *Harvey* and *Donnie Darko,* Hoskins starts hallucinating "actual" bunny-rabbits. (Indeed, speaking on the *Parkinson* talk-show a few years later, Hoskins was still clearly haunted by the experience, despite using it as the basis for humorous anecdotes.)

The 2003 "featurette" *Behind the Ears,* filmed for inclusion with the DVD special edition of *Who Framed Roger Rabbit?,* is a wealth of observations by the production team on the "blurry line" between the cartoon world and what they call the "live-action" world. In fact, the experience of making the film seems to have served the function of one of those ACME "portable portals"[9] that saves Eddie Valiant's life at one crucial point in the story, allowing them a glimpse of another parallel universe. (Indeed, all the animators have the same protruding eyes, which suggests that they have all been staring at "the other side" for quite a while now.)

Charles Fleischer, the actor who provided the voice for Roger Rabbit himself, is also clearly a little crazy; at least according to his co-stars. From his decision to wear a rabbit suit 24/7 from day one of shooting, despite engaging in strictly "off-camera acting," to his exposition of "trans-projectional acting," Fleischer is clearly a graduate of the F. Murray Abraham school of earnest thespianism. Seeing him talk so earnestly about the process, however, dressed as a two-bit, flea-bitten rabbit, is yet another revealing glimpse of the bunny-as-totem. (Indeed, it is not a stretch of the imagination to see the same character in *Donnie Darko*.) Which is not to isolate Hoskins or Fleischer as psychic victims of "this monster," but to emphasize the fact that the very production process of the contemporary spectacle leads to the point described by Ed Jones, the optical photography supervisor: "All of us were loony tunes by the end of it."

However, to get diegetic for a moment, we can see how the same tropes are transported inside the frame of the film. In the opening scene, which is 100% animated, Roger is warned to behave by the mother of the house, or else he's "going back to the science lab" (a clear and perverse reference to the less-than-cute fate reserved for many bunny-rabbits in this day and age). The main story which follows unfolds in Hollywood 1947, focusing on private investigator Eddie Valiant (Bob Hoskins). He is a classic hardboiled type, who refuses to "work ToonTown" after a Toon killed his brother with a falling piano. From the beginning, then, it is clear that Toons are second-class citizens, flagged by the disparaging way Valiant dismisses "toons" (as in "coons"), and the fact that many of them – Dumbo in particular – "works for peanuts." However, being the alcoholic, broke, film-noir cliché that he is, Valiant takes a job involving Toons, despite his bitter reservations, noting in a prophetic meta-comment (given Hoskins' gruelingly surreal onset experience), "the job's ridiculous." During this case, Eddie eventually warms to these creatures from the wrong side of the tracks, and on their behalf attempts to foil not only a vast real-estate swindle, but an evil plot centering on the dismantling of Los Angeles' tram-system (ironically "the best public transportation system in the world," back in 1947). Beyond this, even, Eddie must do his part in preventing a full-blown genocide of Toons by a renegade Toon-turned-humanesque character, Judge Doom[10] – in a thinly-disguised reference to the ethnically-coded survival (whether it be the "safe-haven" of Israel, also "created" in 1947, or the many metropolitan struggles against gentrification). ToonTown is thankfully, by the end of the movie, saved from these diabolical plans.

The Private Life of the Rabbit

I have already identified the *illicit* subtexts of rabbit-related sexuality, but we need not dwell on this alone, for there are many instances of a more socially-visible form: namely, *adult*-bunny-sexuality. The most obvious, of course, is the Playboy empire, founded on the famous logo of the eponymous bunny. But while I have traced an outline of the bunny-trope-totem, I have made little progress in explaining the *sexual* association, or even appeal, of the rabbit.[11] It seems altogether too far-fetched to suggest that the girls in the employ of Hugh Hefner, wearing cotton tails and bunny ears, incarnate some kind of sublimated curiosity in bestiality. Rather, it seems more related to their symbolic role as the mascot of procreation; that is, as creatures which . . . well . . . breed like rabbits.[12]

Picking up on the bunny-bombshell motif, *Who Framed Roger Rabbit?* introduces the now iconic Jessica Rabbit, who has since become something of a standard figure in the tattoo and cartoon fan-world. Indeed, Jessica (who is not a rabbit, per se, but a human Toon *married* to a rabbit), was so successful as a sex symbol, that certain scenes had to be reanimated in order to ensure anxious parents that she is wearing underwear. The voice for Jessica was provided by Kathleen Turner. However, Betsy Brantley, a virtually unknown starlet, served as the body model for the virtual woman. (A process which seems to have reached its apotheosis with the new CGI characters such as Lara Croft and SimOne, both of whom have an originary-isomorphic relationship with flesh-and-blood women.)

A quasi-structuralist reading of the film would no doubt emphasise how crucial Jessica is to the narrative: she mediates between the "real" world of filmed humans and the "artificial" world of Toons, being at once human and Toon. Moreover, she can be a legitimate object of desire for humans insofar as she is doubly inaccessible: both Toon *and* married to one. "Rabbit" becomes at once proper noun, married name, and patronym — and absolutely improper insofar as it derives from something that's neither really real nor really a rabbit. And because Jessica is married to such a hysterical, clearly "feminized" cartoon rabbit, it's just as "clear" that her relationship with Roger *cannot* be a sexual one. "He makes me laugh," she finally explains to Eddie (no doubt giving the audience another chance to dream of impossible [?] cartoon sex).

Such animated characters suggest that we may be moving closer to an age where we may indeed interact with virtual characters in a culturally-acceptable form of "daylight hallucination." For while we are expected to be polite to an underpaid guy dressed as Bugs Bunny when we encounter him in Disneyland, we are not yet prepared to psychosocially assimilate holographic versions outside the gates of theme parks. Spokespeople for the "imagineering" industry tell us that it is only a matter of time before the avatars found in video games and contemporary cinema step out of the screen and into what was referred to in the 1990s as RL (Real Life). In which case, ToonTown will indeed be a place where the animate and the animated rub shoulders in a strange kind of ontological co-existence.[13] Indeed, today's digital technologies are allowing increasingly believable on-screen interactivity between advanced "Toons" and humans; something the overworked, hand-painting animators of *Roger Rabbit* could only dream about. The CGI character Gollum, for instance, in Peter Jackson's *Lord of the Rings* trilogy is on occasion more convincing than many of the human actors with whom he interacts.[14] Between these new types of intersecting gazes, we can trace the elusive, invisible line which separates the virtual from the actual, and the subject from the object, just as Bob Hoskins stood face-to-face with the absent presence of Jessica Rabbit.[15]

But I have yet to address two of the most influential texts on invisible rabbits: John Steinbeck's novella *Of Mice and Men,* and Henry Koster's 1950 film *Harvey.* In the former, we can see the treatment of themes already explored in this chapter. The large simpleton, Lennie Small, is forced to hit the road with his smarter side-kick George, after refusing to let go of a little girl's red dress and being subsequently chased out of town. (That is, after the girl "rabbits in an' tells the law she been raped" [46].)[16] The book is at pains to make clear, however, that Lennie has the intellect and spirit of a child, and therefore this attraction had little to do with a predatory instinct, but is rather the expression of his innocent desire to stroke pretty things, on a purely sensual level. Nevertheless, this desire seems to have a habit of spiraling out of control, since he accidentally kills a puppy with his crude attentions: a prelude to doing the same with a young woman simply called "Curly's wife" (described as "jail bait," despite being old enough to be married).

This rather tragic canonical tale is perhaps most famous for the now popular refrain: "tell me 'bout the rabbits." This phrase, itself following the plague vector of bunny-rabbits around the world, was promoted by Robin Williams during his early career as a standup comic; and has since become something of a catch-phrase to be used whenever someone needs solace or motivation. For this is, of course, how the phrase is used in the book. George is forever being prompted by Lennie to *tell him 'bout the rabbits,* in order to take his mind away from the brutal, menial, vagabond life which has fallen to their lot. His friend George uses the image of a peaceful life, tending rabbits, to soothe the simple fellow to sleep, only to threaten its withdrawal to make him behave. Thus the image of rabbits – their virtual presence in Lennie's life, as it were – functions like a carrot in front of a donkey; goading him forward, and keeping him on course.

Lennie's monomania is often exasperating to the man whose voice has the power to constantly evoke these rabbits into life: "The hell with the rabbits. That's all you ever can remember is them rabbits" (5). As Lennie drifts into sleep, his imagination paints the scene in hallucinatory shades: "Let's have different color rabbits, George." To which the latter replies, "Sure we will . . . Red and blue and green rabbits, Lennie. Millions of 'em" (17). However, when George decides to threaten the rabbits with premature extinction, Lennie becomes defensive, stating the counter-threat that he "can jus' as well go away . . . an' live in a cave" (18). Steinbeck is well aware that these rabbits serve a virtual function for Lennie; to the extent that he prompts this character to threaten any "future cats which might dare to disturb the future rabbits" (64). But Lennie is not the only person who navigates the world through a visualization of the future (a visualization which in fact contributes to the *construction* of any such future; much like the vessel-vectors in *Donnie Darko*). George and another character, Candy, both buy into the fantasy of freedom, private land, and unalienated labor: Lennie just makes it more obvious by constantly vocalizing the utopia ahead of him.[17]

The stress of unintentional murder, and the swift retribution that is bound to follow, provokes a breakdown in Lennie's mind, so that these virtual rabbits combine into one megabunny, which leaps out of his head and into the world. At first this vision looks uncannily like his stern Aunt Clara, but then she soon morphs back into a gigantic rabbit which happens to speak in Lennie's own voice: "Tend rabbits," it said scornfully. "You crazy bastard. You ain't fit to lick the boots of no rabbit. You'd forget 'em and let 'em go hungry. That's what you'd do" (112). As with *Donnie*

Darko, the central fear seems to be loneliness and abandonment, for the rabbit taunts him with the mantra: "He gonna leave you, ya crazy bastard. He gonna leave ya all alone" – meaning, of course, his only friend George. When the latter finally finds him, a few minutes ahead of a lynch-mob, the rabbit scuttles back into Lennie's brain . . . . only to be blown to smithereens in an act of tragic compassion. Again, as with *Donnie Darko,* the disturbing hallucinations are only "cured" through death. Hardly the message we usually associate with cute, cuddly bunnies.

Nobody Here But Us Rabbits

> Dr. Sanderson: "Trauma. . . . It means shock. There's nothing unusual about it. There's the birth trauma – the shock of being born."
> Elwood P. Dowd: "That's the one we never get over."
> — Henry Koster's *Harvey*

Psychoanalysis plays a large role in *Harvey* (1950); a now classic film adapted from the Pulitzer Prize winning play by Mary Chase. The protagonist, Elwood P. Dowd (James Stewart) continuously disturbs his family and the town in general by insisting on always introducing his good friend Harvey. The disturbing aspect concerns the fact that Harvey is a 6 foot 3½ inch white rabbit, which nobody else can see. Elwood's aged sister Veta is fed up with the resulting social stigma, and decides to commit him to a sanitarium, from which – in the lingo of the business – "hijinx ensue."

In her exasperation, Veta makes the mistake of admitting to the resident psychiatrist that every once in a while she even sees this rabbit herself. The psychiatrist, Dr. Sanderson, realizes that this woman is somewhat "jumpy" and – after confirming a bout of depression following the death of her mother – commits her instead; at least until the mix-up is straightened out. As the story unfolds, however, the viewer is given certain clues as to the actual existence of Harvey, beginning with the discovery of a hat with two holes cut in the crown (presumably for rabbit ears to fit through). The second clue comes when the sanitarium's strongman, Mr. Wilson, turns to the encyclopedia to look up the unfamiliar word "pooka." He reads aloud, for the benefit of the viewer:

> "Pooka. . . . from old Celtic mythology. A faery spirit in animal form – always very large. The pooka appears here and there, now and then, to this one and that one. A benign but mischievous creature. Very fond of rumpots, crackpots, and how are you Mr. Wilson?"

Mr. Wilson pauses in surprise, before repeating: "How are you Mr. Wilson? . . . . *Who in the Encyclopedia wants to know?!"*

Another key scene occurs when the head of the sanitarium, Dr. Chumley, goes to Veta's house in order to both smooth-out the potentially litigious confusion, and to bring Elwood back to the clinic for treatment. A painting on the wall, recently put in pride of place by its subject, depicts Elwood with Harvey himself, the only visual representation afforded the viewer of the pooka-rabbit.[18] Before noticing the actual painting, Veta gives Dr. Chumley a lecture on art in the age of mechanical reproduction:

> "I took a class last winter. I learned the difference between a fine oil painting and a mechanical thing, like a photograph. The photograph shows only the reality. The painting shows not only the reality, but the dream behind it. It's our dreams, doctor, that carry us on – they separate us from the beasts. I wouldn't want to go on living if I thought it was all just eating and sleeping and taking my clothes off . . . I mean putting them *on*."

In contrast to his sister, Elwood ("the screwball with the rabbit") seems to have discovered the secret of living in a world largely comprised of the banal, the quotidian, and the disenchanted. Despite the fact that his best friend is a giant invisible rabbit who drinks martinis almost constantly, Elwood seems to be one of the most down-to-earth people in town. Unlike the other characters, driven by social vanities and other "flyspecks" of daily distraction, Elwood harbors no prejudice or discrimination between people, places, and situations. Straddling the line between saint and sociopath, he seems to have no recognition of class and its importance, despite his wealth, so that hardly a scene goes by without him handing out his card to taxi-drivers, nurses, jailbirds, gatekeepers, and so on. What's more this isn't a business-card, but simply a calling card: a token of the willingness to expose oneself to another human being, prior to any judgment on social purpose or personal compatibility.

And yet, despite the increasing number of clues as to Harvey's actual existence – to which the viewer, by the end of the film, is not left in any doubt – Elwood is re-committed to the sanitarium in order to have an injection designed to cure his "third degree hallucinations."[19] This despite the fact that the head of the facility, Dr. Chumley, has seen the rabbit, and is convinced of his supernatural powers. The film thus emphasizes the limitations – indeed the dangers – of the scientific perspective on para-normal phenomena; habitually dragging it within the diagnostic realm of mental health, and the attendant modes of curing and containing "madness."[20] (A process famously described and denounced by Foucault.) And so, only minutes before rolling up his sleeve to receive the prescribed injection, Elwood is talking privately to Dr. Chumley about the magical powers of Harvey, subtly reinforcing the film's critique of the impoverished system of psychoanalysis, which seeks to rationally explain the supernatural, the unexplained, the uncanny, and the bizarre.

One of Harvey's gifts, anticipating the rabbit in *Donnie Darko*, is prophecy, for he can reliably predict the future. Another even more impressive power is the capacity to create a *fermata* by arresting the flow of time:

> Elwood: "Did I tell you he could stop clocks?"
> Dr. Chumley: "To what purpose?"
> Elwood: "Well . . . You can go anywhere you like, with anyone you like, and stay as long as you like, and when you get back, not one minute will have ticked by . . . . You see, science has overcome time and space,[21] but Harvey has not only overcome time and space, but any objections."

The key phrase here – "any objections" – is Hayes Code language for the social sanction of erotic fantasies (of which the good Dr. Chumley happily confesses).[22] The elusive object of Harvey himself thus authorizes the libidinal abandon that psychoanalysis sets up as both its object and objective (through socially-acceptable sublimation).

Elwood however, perhaps liberated in a different direction by the *pooka,* has reached an almost Nietzschean affirmation of things the way they are, and is free from the fantasies which only encourage melancholy, and its attendant sense of lack. When Elwood is earlier encouraged to "face reality," he says: "I wrestled reality for thirty-five years, doctor, and I'm happy to say that I finally won out over it." The implicit meaning here refers to *social* reality, since Elwood is anything but delusional, embracing the world exactly as it appears, rather than racing towards a dream-goal dangling in the future like a carrot on a stick. And in this sense, he practically passes Nietzsche's test of the eternal return: "I'd almost be willing to live my life again."

Stepping outside the logic of the script for a moment, we can see how the figure of an extra-dimensional rabbit overlaps with all the other texts covered in this chapter thus far. As with *Donnie Darko,* the rabbit is considered by most people to be a hallucination, but in fact turns out to be an ontological messenger, intimately connected to the quantum mechanics of time. As with *Of Mice and Men,* the rabbit functions as the totem for a "simpleton" – although in *Harvey* this familiar underlines the importance of the present, rather than the (false) promise of the future. (Another significant difference is that Elwood is a very smart simpleton.) As with *Alice in Wonderland* and *The Matrix,* one need only follow the white rabbit to an alternative take on your own universe, and its associated assumptions.[23]

Some significant connections can also be traced to *Who Framed Roger Rabbit?*[24] In a taped interview with James Stewart in 1990, included on the video version, he admits that: "I have a special admiration and love for that big white rabbit . . . . He became a very close friend of mine. You can see it in the performance . . . . All of us, you can see all of us sort of accept the existence of this rabbit." Despite the qualifier "sort of," Stewart talks in terms similar to those who worked on *Roger Rabbit,* bearing witness to the phenomenon where a virtual object has actual effects – whether you choose to "believe" in it or not. And although Stewart's ability to focus on dead space does not rival Hoskins', certain paraphernalia associated with the production and the promotion of the film attest to the *presence* of Harvey as a pseudo-ontological being. One photographic still, for instance, behind the scenes, includes a cast-member's folding-chair with the name Harvey. (Obviously we have no idea if he is sitting in the chair or not.) Similarly, the original poster for the film shows James Stewart sitting to one side, dominated by the shadow of the rabbit.

Without wishing to popularize Heidegger's rather more weighty concepts into the ether, this shadow is another instance of the "incalculable" introduced above:

> Everyday opinion sees in the shadow only the lack of light, if not light's complete denial. In truth, however, the shadow is a

> manifest, though impenetrable, testimony to the concealed emitting of light. In keeping with this concept of shadow, we experience the incalculable as that which, withdrawn from representation, is nevertheless manifest in whatever is, pointing to Being, which remains concealed. (154)[25]

The *Dasein* (being-there) of Harvey – according to this positive gloss on shadows – is to be simultaneously there and not-there, according to the criteria of Being applied by humans. So while the thought of dying alone terrifies both Donnie Darko and Lennie Small, Elwood P. Dowd is more strictly "philosophical" about the being-toward-death which necessarily follows the birth trauma.

All of which brings us to the sardonic, throw-away line offered by Elwood's bar-tender, in answer to the question posed by Dr. Sanderson, while anxiously looking for his escaped patient. "Is he alone?" asks the doctor, gesturing to Elwood sitting in a booth with two martinis. "Well," replies the bar-tender, "there are two schools of thought on that."

The Dubious Hospitality of the Shining Wire

> Rabbits . . . are like human beings in many ways. One of these is certainly their staunch ability to withstand disaster and to let the stream of their life carry them along, past reaches of terror and loss. They have a certain quality which it would not be accurate to describe as callousness or indifference. It is, rather, a blessedly circumscribed imagination and an intuitive feeling that Life is Now.
>
> — Richard Adams, *Watership Down*

> *Hlessi* – A rabbit living above ground, without a regular hole or warren. A wandering rabbit, living in the open. (Plural, *hlessil*.)
>
> — "Lapine Glossary," in *Watership Down*

Richard Adams' enormously popular 1970's novel, *Watership Down*, informs us that: "It is true that young rabbits are great migrants and capable of journeying for miles, but they do not take to it readily" (33).[26] Nevertheless, a group of bunny-rabbits abandon the relative safety of their warren to become *hlessil* in search of a "high, dry place," prompted by the Aeschylan visions of horror, suffered by the rabbit Fiver. (Cassandra's visions are quoted in the first epigraph, providing a high-culture precedent for Fiver's apocalyptic prophecy, ". . . it's coming – it's coming. Oh, Hazel, look! The field! It's covered with blood!" [15]). The journey and events that follow could be interpreted as an allegory of diaspora and exodus in general, however things are not as easily decoded into didactic types, as they are in George Orwell's *Animal Farm*, for instance.

The narrative does, however, resonate with the dilemma of the deracinated as figured through bunny-rabbits (especially "outskirter" bunny-rabbits, "thin-looking six-month-ers, with the strained, wary look of those who are only too well used to the thin end of the stick" [27]). Speaking of the mass movement of migrating animals, the narrator notes: "anyone seeing this has seen at work the current that flows (among creatures who think of themselves primarily as part of a group and only secondarily, if at all, as individuals) to fuse them together and impel them into action without conscious thought or will: has seen at work the angel which drove the First Crusade into Antioch and drives the lemmings into the sea" (26). What the book calls (in a phrase which would strike fear into the heart of any farmer) "that great, indestructible flood of Rabbitry" (74), flows across the countryside and toward new and foreign warren-systems. In a key chapter, entitled "Hospitality," the wandering rabbits are suspicious of the welcome that receives them, along with the pronounced lack of suspicion.

The host rabbits offer them food, shelter and entertainment, despite the protagonists insistence that, "After all, you might be afraid that we were coming to take your does or turn you out of your holes" (73). The hosts do not seem to be prone to paranoia concerning the motives of visiting strangers, so that: "All over the burrow, both the newcomers and those who were at home were accustoming themselves to each other in their own way and their own time; getting to know what the strangers smelled like, how they moved, how they breathed, how they scratched, the feel of their rhythms and pulses" (81-82). Indeed, one would be hard pressed to find a more naively poetic description of Levinasian deference to the Other, and Derridean hospitality, than the following: "[and] so this gathering of rabbits in the dark, beginning with hesitant approaches, silences, pauses, movements, crouchings side by side and all manner of tentative appraisals, slowly moved, like a hemisphere of the world into summer, to a warmer, brighter region of mutual liking and approval, until all felt sure that they had nothing to fear" (82).

But as is often the case, a perceived utopia disguises more sinister designs. The visiting rabbits soon realize that a shining wire is subtracting their fellows one-by-one, until Hazel feels sure in announcing: "That warren's nothing but a death hole! The whole place is one foul elil's larder! It's snared – everywhere, everyday!" (122). The local bunny-rabbits remain unaware of the horror at the heart of their lives, since they themselves have adopted the strategy at the heart of this study, namely, "looking at the bunny." (Although, in this case, it means *not* looking at the bunny – especially the disappearing bunnies.) Hazel explains to his companions that the locals are distracted by "songs" and "Shapes on the walls" which "passed the time and enabled them to tell themselves that they were splendid fellows, the very flower of Rabbitry" (123).

Hazel continues:

> And since they could not bear the truth, these singers, who might in some other place have been wise, were squeezed

> under the terrible weight of the warren's secret until they gulped out fine folly – about dignity and acquiescence, and anything else that could make believe that the rabbit loved the shining wire. But one strict rule they had; oh yes, the strictest. No one must ever ask where another rabbit was and anyone who asked "Where?" – except in a song or a poem – must be silenced. To say "Where?" was bad enough, but to speak openly of the wires – that was intolerable. For that they would scratch and kill. (123)

Indeed, the realization that the shining wire may itself constitute *both* the decoy and the object of destruction, simultaneously denied and executed, is one we would do well ourselves to learn in the age of hyper-cynical media manipulation. (That is, in an age in which Nike can use the phrase "100% slave-labor" as an official ad-campaign, and the Pentagon can use the daily events of war to obscure the *motivation* of war in the first place.) In other words, we have become so entranced by these kind of objects, that their power to fascinate serves to camouflage their (usually destructive) purpose. That is, we are so amused by the fact that the Trojan Horse has the words "Trojan Horse" written across its side in bold, day-glo colors, that we let it in anyway (just to share the joke with others).

Which brings us almost full circle.

Watership Down finishes with an epilogue introduced by Lewis Carroll's *Through the Looking-Glass*: "He was part of my dream, of course – but then I was part of his dream too." This feedback-loop between the spectacle and the spectator, the bunny-rabbit and the human, the being and the yet-to-be, is the enigma of the age – acting like a carrot-on-a-stick for those who still believe there are lessons to be drawn from a media-environment seemingly far more concerned with producing noise than signal.

And yet, perhaps it is in the white noise (or the "white

blindness," as Adams would put it), that we can conceive afresh the link between the cave and the looking-glass, via the white rabbit-hole.

Avatars of Otherness

> Ought I to say: 'A Rabbit may look like a duck'? Would it be conceivable that someone who knows rabbits but not ducks should say: 'I can see the drawing as a rabbit and also in another way, although I have no word for the second aspect'? Later he gets to know ducks and says: 'That's what I saw the drawing as that time!' – Why is that not possible?
>
> — Ludwig Wittgenstein, *Remarks on the Philosophy of Psychology*

Joseph Jastrow's duck-rabbit image has since been made famous by Wittgenstein, who treated this visual conundrum more in the mode of early cognitive theory than the deconstructionist standby of "undecidability." Essentially, Wittgenstein ponders the process behind the perception of the image as either a duck or a rabbit – perhaps considered one and then the other, but never both simultaneously. Has the image changed, he asks, or has our attitude toward the image changed? Or has only our description of the image changed? Moreover, on what basis do we distinguish these allegedly autonomous processes?

What Wittgenstein calls "aspect-regarding" or "continuous aspect-perception" suggests that we see "the world" through a grid of pre-formed cultural and personal expectations, assumptions, memories, and knowledges: meaning we already see something *as some thing* . . . which is (to varying degrees) familiar. This particular spin on Husserl's notion of "structuring" obviously has profound political implications, for we tend to project our own patterns and meanings on to the things we see. So while the question of whether an image is a duck or a rabbit may seem purely hypothetical, the question of whether a man wearing a turban is a Sikh or a Moslem, a terrorist or a freedom-fighter, an enemy or an ally, is one of pressing practical importance. This essential cultural-political aspect of phenomenological interpretation links the question of hallucinated rabbits directly to those "avatars of otherness" which have been persistently evoked by politicians and the media to mobilize certain rhetorics of domination and control. Moreover, this process has a viral, meme-like infection rate.[27]

Before enemies are flesh-and-blood targets, they are virtual figures who stalk the imagination as much as the world itself.[28] (As the old Cold War posters warned: "Are there Reds under the bed?") Thus, during the so-called "fall of Baghdad," we hear an American citizen proudly stating that: "If they strike us, we strike them." The *they* in this case is not so much the abstract "they" of Heidegger or Sartre, but the stigmatized – explicitly delineated – *they* of political paranoia. Structurally, it follows a hallucinatory logic, which like *Donnie Darko* and *Of Mice and Men*, can only end in the expedition of death.

And so whatever answer we give to the question, "why rabbits?" – whether it be a simple case of literary tradition (Lewis Carroll-John Steinbeck) cross-breeding with folklorish symbolization ("breeding like rabbits"-Bugs-Bunny) – it is still a matter of responding to a decoy. Presuming that the twenty-first century will continue to unfurl itself under the signs of both Plato's cave *and* Alice's wonderland, then "the object of fear" will always already be a virtual one: and yet no less dangerous for that.

As cultural critic Mark Dery reminds us:

> a P.R. firm, Hill & Knowlton . . . orchestrated the congressional testimony of the distraught young Kuwaiti woman whose horror stories about babies ripped from incubators and left "on the cold floor to die" by Iraqi soldiers was highly effective in mobilizing public support for the [first Gulf] war.

> Her testimony was never substantiated, and her identity – she was the daughter of the Kuwaiti ambassador to the U.S.- was concealed, but why niggle over details? "Formulated like a World War II movie, the Gulf War even ended like a World War II movie," wrote Neal Gabler, "with the troops marching triumphantly down Broadway or Main Street, bathed in the gratitude of their fellow Americans while the final credits rolled." (*Culture Jamming*)

What is now referred to as the "military-industrial-entertainment complex" spends a great deal of its energy on producing spectacular bunnies for the citizen-consumer to become entranced by (another metaphor for Chomsky's "manufacturing consent").[29] As touched on above, the difference from the basic distraction model is that the *inoculation itself* has now become the distraction as well. The operation and the decoy have fused in the new millennial media, so that the *coverage* of war effectively does just that – it *covers* and conceals the events "on the ground" as well as "behind closed doors."

In the case of the Second Gulf War in March and April 2003, the alibi for invading Iraq was the disavowed presence of weapons of mass-destruction. The fact that these weapons only existed in Colin Powell's Powerpoint presentation did nothing to hinder the rhetoric coming from the Pentagon, The White House, and Number 10, Downing Street. Mimicking the representational logic of cognitive scientists, the Anglo-American Easter bunny found what it had simply put there in the first place (both epistemologically and historically speaking). One would have as much chance convincing that smug trickster-figure Bugs Bunny himself of desisting his wascally ways than persuading the Bush-Cheney-Rumsfeld-Blair hydra to desist from implementing the frightening recommendations of the Project for the New American Century. ("What's up doc?" ask the administrators, deaf to advice from academics who do not already speak the language of world historical nihilism.)

One of the more disturbing images broadcast on news channels during the Second Gulf War was not the gruesome footage of murdered and injured Iraqi civilians, but the seemingly playful scenes of an American GI, standing on a stationary tank, and introducing a gathering of Iraqi children to the game of Hoky Poky.[30] One initial reaction to this surreal lull in battle is to make comparisons with the infamous football match between the English and the German army during the First World War. However, this would be to misread the general pattern of events. The remarkable fact of the first historical example was the grim but genuine spirit of play which can emerge during liminal moments such as Christmas time, affording a brief break in the relentless momentum of killing and hatred. The more recent instance, however, is more cynical, even if it is not experienced as such by any of the participants.

A dancing GI is a clear case of "look at the bunny," in a kind of punishing Energizer logic of endurance inflicted on the soldiers by Rumsfeld and other engineers of the war. In twenty-first century conflict, civilians are a major element in the battle-plan, and must be "distracted" from options such as resistance, protest, and subterfuge by things like food aid, water, promises, strange Western summer camp games, and other modes of symbolic support. And thus the warm glow which should accompany a GI dancing with a group of Iraqi children (given the alternatives), is actually just as chilling, given the foggy Platonic economy in which it is involved. For all we know, the kids are being distracted from the fact that their parents are being rounded up for brutal interrogation, or worse. Thus the Hellenic concern with shadows merges with the Roman priority of bread-and-circuses, in a new industrial empire that has mastered philosophical and political discourse. (Or at least recognized the artificial basis for any border between the two.) A critical politics therefore begins by asking who is the bunny?

What brand of battery powers the bunny's frenetic drumming? Who owns that brand, and what are its other interests? Who benefits most from the operational procedures involving doctor, parent, child, syringe, and finger-puppet? And – most sinister of all – what if the bunny is not only a decoy, but the object itself?

Such questions seek to expose the psychosocial dynamics underwriting structures of power (and not only the violence of such power, but the ingeniously induced passivity which allows it to operate largely unchallenged). These are the stakes of relationality itself – the politically-loaded premise of interactivity (a preferable term to "intersubjectivity," given this latter term's prejudice toward the sovereign subject). Thus, to give only one of a multitude of examples, the decision to refuse refugees or asylum seekers the right of entry to relatively stable countries lies on the same continuum as the instinct to deny that James Stewart has a large invisible rabbit for a friend. It is an expression of certain bureaucratic assumptions regarding ontological status – who is real and who isn't, who counts and who doesn't. Looking at the bunny (and then away from the bunny, and then back again), affords a glimpse of the complex processes assembled and executed by institutions which manufacture and maintain the precious *right to be* for some and not others.

That is, to be *before* having to be any *thing* in particular.

Coda: Looking Back at the Bunny

When I first wrote this piece, ten years ago, little did I know that what I referred to as the Second Gulf War would still be happening on the ground, if not so much in the headlines. Today, this ongoing conflict – spread also to Afghanistan – refuses to be named so neatly, however, since that would suggest a beginning, a middle, and an end. Rather this ambient "conflict" looks less like a traditional war, and more like a seemingly endless state of exception, where an old regime has been banished but a new system is unable to be born. What's more, the optimistic "hope" which accompanied the election of Barack Obama has evaporated in the acrid smoke of increasing drone strikes, in which any male killed in the vicinity is retroactively labeled as an "enemy combatant" by the State Department – to spare the administration from admitting that civilians are at risk. The battle for "hearts and minds" continues, and the transparent "bunny" decoy still plays its part, both explicitly in relation to American military deployment abroad, and more elliptically in popular culture in general.

My point is that the totemic power of bunny-rabbits today happens on two primary registers: one in terms of visual coercion, and the other in the sense of coming-to-presence of objects. These two planes can coincide, as in, for instance, the "object of fear." Or they can be in tension with each other, as when an unexpected object can explicitly or implicitly challenge the day-to-day business of manufacturing consent. Given the intimate history of the entertainment media and carefully orchestrated propaganda, it should not surprise us that the Coney Island amusement park – considered by many to be the cradle of the contemporary Spectacle – was formerly known to Dutch settlers as "Konijn Eiland" (*Bunny-Rabbit Island*).[31]

Being attuned to the presence of rabbits, I have seen them continue to pop up and hop their way through the media, even as such mediations have become more "social" and "mobile" since the turn of the millennium. Of course, photos of cute bunnies circulate through Facebook, email, and special websites dedicated to adorable memes; even if not in the same volume as puppies and kittens. The obsession with cute animal photos itself could be considered a rather orthodox example of "looking at the bunny," in the sense that people become less concerned about the "shock and awe" being perpetrated by their own governments when shocked by the *awwww* of a particularly huggable baby bunny.[32]

It continues to be the cinema, however, where we find the

most visible instances of totemic rabbits. Take for instance *The Last Mimzy* (2007), in which a seemingly ordinary stuffed toy bunny plays a central role in saving the world from ecological disaster. The bunny – Mimzy herself – is in fact a hi-tech form of artificial life from the future, bequeathing supernatural powers (such as telepathy, telekinesis, teleportation, levitation, and the ability to communicate with animals) to the little girl, Emma, who adopts it.[33] The symbolic link between Emma and Alice Liddell is made clear on a couple of occasion; as when she chances upon one of Lewis Carroll's famous photographs of his petite muse holding a white rabbit, and exclaims "look, she's got a Mimzy too!" Later, when the toy bunny has started revealing her strange mission, Emma says to her mother, "I looked through the looking glass, Mommy. I looked *through* it. Just like Alice."

Over the course of the movie the viewer is led to understand that a plague of such cyber-bunnies were sent back in time, to warn the foolish humans that both their DNA and environment are in profound peril. But only *this* one – the *last* Mimzy – in fact, was recognized and heeded. As with *Donnie Darko,* the rabbit functions as a temporal figure, allowing humans to travel backwards or forwards in time, and thus alter their destinies. In this case, Emma's salty tears soak into the fur of the bunny, just as it is sucked forward through the time portal, allowing the wiser scientists of the future to bolster a weakened species with her fresh, uncorrupted, Edenic DNA.

On the other end of the spectrum we find the rabbits in David Lynch's *Inland Empire* (2006); a truly surreal and disturbing "family" of humanoid bunnies – wearing clothes, sitting on sofas, ironing laundry – which act as if they have taken too many anti-depressants at one time, or simply surrendered to a marinating ennui of terminally flat affect. Foreboding soundscapes and canned sit-com laughter only heighten the vintage Lynchian sense of dread, as the deadpan soliloquies and stilted, non-sequitur dialogue suggest a deeper cosmic order of things, beyond the trivial pursuits of humans. (Or perhaps explicitly designed to toy with humans, in order to puncture the cozy, delusional bubbles they blow for themselves against the void.)[34]

Dwelling somewhere between Lynch's surreal creatures, and the enigmatic yet helpful Mimzy, is the rabbit belonging to a rather hapless vaudeville-style magician in Pixar's short film, *Presto* (2008), which originally screened before the feature *WALL-E* (2008), in theatrical release. A classic uncooperative trickster figure, this bunny plays a more traditional role as troublesome familiar: necessary to the human involved, but also intent on causing maximum mischief – in this case, refusing to go on stage in front of a packed house until he is given a carrot. In a series of slapstick gags recalling American cartoons from between the wars, the bunny proves that he can wield the magic top hat as skillfully as his so-called master, manipulating this portal into a pretzeled dimension in order to agitate the poor prestidigitator, who finds egg on his face at one moment, and his finger in an electric socket in another (all against the usual logic of Euclidean time and space). Indeed, it is tempting to consider this short film as a humorous meta-comment on Pixar itself: one of several "dream factories" dedicated to making animated creatures perform on demand – creatures who sometimes refuse to do what they are told. Indeed, for those professional animators – who on a daily basis wrestle with virtual wire frames, polygons, kinematics, orthographics, and spline curves – digital entities can appear uncooperative; more concerned with their own whims and moods than the company deadline (as described in the next chapter, in the case of renegade Orcs).

In terms of television, a famous episode of *Sex and City* entitled "The Turtle and the Hare," catapulted the rabbit vibrator into popular consciousness. Originally designed by a company called California Exotic Novelties, the "jack rabbit" sex toy has since been refined – some might say "perfected" – by the bestselling Vibratex "rabbit pearl" device. Or at least this is the lesson of the show, in which the character Charlotte becomes addicted to the bunny's hyper-twitchy charms, especially given its capacity to take her to places which a mere man could not. (One of the fundamental powers of the rabbit totem.)[35] As for the Internet, Google recently unveiled its radical new "Fiber" project, promising online speeds up to a hundred times the current limit. The animated graphic on the promotional splash page is – can you guess? – a bunny (tinted in comforting shades of green).

Rabbits also make cameos in the art world. And given that they tend to signify and enable the crossing of ontological boundaries, it only makes sense that the first example of "transgenic art" be a bunny rabbit. First displayed in public in Avignon, France in 2000, Alba the glow-in-the-dark bunny was described by its creator, Eduardo Kac, as a "transgenic artwork": "a new art form based on the use of genetic engineering to transfer natural or synthetic genes to an organism, to create unique living beings."[36] Of course this opens a can of genetically-engineered worms, and Kac spends a lot of time defending his "art," and framing it within ethical parameters. This includes his hope that all transgenic practice be sensitive to considerations such as "interspecies communication between humans and a transgenic mammal . . . examination of the notions of normalcy, heterogeneity, purity, hybridity, and otherness . . . consideration of a non-semiotic notion of communication as the sharing of genetic material across traditional species barriers . . . public respect and appreciation for the emotional and cognitive life of transgenic animals . . . [and the] expansion of the present practical and conceptual boundaries of artmaking to incorporate life invention." As an instance of the bunny as collective "power-animal," it is immensely rich and provocative, in the terms the artist mentions. But one still wishes Kac first made *himself* fluorescent, before testing transgenic technologies on (other) animals, like a run-of-the-mill ethics-free pharmaceutical or make-up company.[37]

The list of lapine totems, no doubt, could go on and on – which is partly my point. No doubt the reader has already thought of many more. But rather than indulge in an exhaustive game of bunny-spotting, I will finish with a couple of other symptomatic rabbits, outside the realms of cinema, TV, or contemporary bioart. One such instance is "the plot bunny": a truly virtual creature, in the sense that it is – to quote the online Urban Dictionary – "An idea for a story (usually used to refer to fanfiction) that gnaws at the brain until written." Here an invisible bunny, inside one's head, chews on the mind until it is actualized on paper; not so much as a character, but the muse or catalyst to make other beings and scenarios wink into existence. In this instance, to "look at the bunny" means to write it out of one's system and into the world. I might also mention "Easter eggs," which are little unexpected treats hidden inside DVDs, videogames, websites, programs – even ye olde books – to reward the obsessive viewer, player, browser, user, or reader with a secret message, in-joke, or virtual reward. The implication embedded in the term is that the proverbial enchanted rabbit has stashed them for us: a visitor from a magical dimension, manifesting himself by his traces in our quasi-magical media.

Indeed, the notion of the Easter egg can be employed to reflect on the nature or possibility of significant surprises in a claustrophically overcoded – thus predictable – world. A world seemingly bereft of alternatives. Perhaps we need to enact rituals designed to encourage the magic bunny to break the tedious cultural algorithms that restrict every day – in the West at least – to a smooth series of anticipated rhythms.[38] (After all, a predictable consumer is a docile and productive citizen.) Perhaps we should be finding inspiration from the temporal tricks of this particular totem to get access not to the material Easter eggs of fetishized commodities, but the hidden, virtual gift of the "something else": an unprecedented experience, a unimagined possibility, an unanticipated alliance, and so on. As the object-oriented ontologist, Levi Bryant, writes, "if the world is given *in advance*, then there is no longer any need to consult the world or objects. . . . what will be lost will be the ability for the world to *surprise* us. And if the world no longer has the capacity to surprise us, then this is because the world already *conforms* to the structuring agency of *our* cognition. The rabbit has already been put into the hat."[39] Very true. But as Pixar has shown, perhaps we overestimate our ability to control the rabbit, whether it has been stashed inside the hat or not.

Critical theorists such as Slavoj Žižek have made much of the current cultural and political obsession with "known knowns," "known unknowns," "unknown knowns," and "unknown unknowns."[40] I have been alluding to the latter as a positive potentiality lying dormant in the present of things. But the most infamous incantation of these four meta-categories was of course made by the former Secretary of Defense, Donald Rumsfeld, in reference to the types of dangerous resistance that American troops were facing – and still face – on the ground in the Middle East (and, by extension, the ones all Americans face from the clear and present existence of terrorism). For Rumsfeld, the unknown unknown is a virtual threat: something to anticipate through the hawkish grids of military strategy and national security. Between the two interpretations of the unknown unknown as something to be found or feared, we have what W.J.T. Mitchell calls "a highly charged duck-rabbit" (2005, 189).

On September 30, 2005, as the American-led invasion of Iraq dragged wearily on – demoralized by revelations that the justification for war had been based on non-existent über-weapons – Rumsfeld held a press conference. He did this to reaffirm to the world that Iraqi security forces were "steadily improving," in spite of the statistics suggesting a drop in Iraqi forces that could function independently of American supervision. With his characteristic and sardonic uncle shrug, he told reporters, "There are an awful lot of people chasing the wrong rabbit here, it seems to me."[41] Thus begging the question, what would be the *right* rabbit in this case? Certainly not, from his perspective, as architect and accessory, the Pentagon's special-purpose military-contract bunny; paid large sums to leave even larger quantities of imaginary Easter eggs in hot and hostile foreign lands, to simply melt away before anyone has had the chance to find them.

Chapter 2

The Orc and the Penguin
In Search of a Psukhēpolitics of the Living

"The slogan for our times then is, not things fall apart, but things come alive."
-- W.J.T. Mitchell

Going Rogue

Hidden away amongst the interminable "extras" on the extended edition of Peter Jackson's *Lord of the Rings* DVD box-set, we find an intriguing Easter egg in the form of a "behind-the-scenes" anecdote. One of the lead animators tells of an unexpected moment, as he and his army of CGI rendering experts began to choreograph one of the elaborate battle scenes for which this movie franchise became famous. Given the amount of digital "extras" involved – namely 80,000 Orcs – it was impossible to script or code every individual combatant. The new state-of-the-art Massive™ software used by Jackson's hi-tech atelier side-stepped this issue by algorithmically allowing the Orcs to fight their own individual battles, according to separate decision trees or sub-routines. This meant that each digital creature would behave according to a set of pre-coded possibilities, and yet the animators themselves could not anticipate what any single actor would do at any given moment in the melee. As such, each Orc existed in a semi-open zone, somewhere between the predetermined and the aleatory: that is, between compulsion and free-will. The animator's amusing tale, however, centered on one of the early test runs, in which one of the Orcs simply refused to fight, perhaps channeling some conscientious objection to bloodshed, previously latent in his coded wire-frame bones. Indeed, this Orc's pacifist stance became infectious, and a group of his fellow soldiers then ran away in the face of aggressive Elves, against the directions of the script.

We find a remarkably similar story in Werner Herzog's documentary film, *Encounters at the End of the World* (2007), which details the eccentric inhabitants of the permanent scientific base in Antarctica. Herzog narrates this tale in real time, as his camera discovers a penguin who, for whatever reason, refuses to follow his biological programming:

> "These penguins are all heading to the open water to the right. But one of them caught our eye, the one in the center. He would neither go towards the feeding grounds at the edge of the ice, nor return to the colony. Shortly afterwards, we saw him heading straight towards the mountains, some 70 kilometers away. Dr. Ainley explained that even if he caught him and brought him back to the colony, he would immediately head right back for the mountains. But why? One of these disoriented, or deranged, penguins showed up at the New Harbor diving camp, already some 80 kilometers away from where it should be. The rules for the humans are do not disturb or hold up the penguin, stand still and let him go on his way. And here, he's heading off into the interior of the vast continent. With 5, 000 kilometers ahead of him, he's heading towards certain death."[1]

Both scenarios present us with nonhuman entities who "go rogue" to pursue an unexpected option, thereby raising a number of provocative questions. To what degree does this behavior exhibit manifest cases of "free will" or "agency" that we – in our humanist arrogance – prefer to ascribe only to ourselves? Or are these anomalies merely the statistical glitch one finds in any operating system? (Perfect consistency having no place in a Darwinian world, either real or virtual.) Is it folly to ask "why" these creatures followed their own drum? Or is "motivation" a valid question for nonhumans, as much as for humans? Do the Orc or the penguin – as totemic entities – have something to teach us about "diagonal existences" which "choose" to go off-program (and thus write a new program as they go)? Perhaps we are dealing here with parallel instances out of an almost infinite number of scenarios which prompt us to reconsider "life itself" from a new angle: one which consciously attempts to break from two-and-a-half thousand years of Western thinking on this omnipresent, yet supremely vague, *figura*.

Life Itself (or Living Scum)

As various contemporary theorists have noted, current definitions of life – "this astonishing thing" (Percy Byce Shelley) – are notoriously formless and evasive; perhaps mirroring its subject matter. While the natural scientists have come to enjoy a monopoly on explaining most aspects of the physical world, even biologists begin to speak like obfuscating philosophers or theologians on the key issue of the origins and essential properties of life.[2] The more we try to pin down the very condition of all inquiry, the more we become trapped in a quasi-Cartesian tautology: "Life lives, therefore it is living." In the digital age, the situation is complicated further, as artificial and synthetic life become not only part of the lexicon but also the environment.[3]

The mid-20th century American Renaissance man, Loren Eiseley – equal parts natural scientist and speculative philosopher – tells of the Victorian attempt to get to the bottom of the mystery of materialized life by literally dredging the bottom of the ocean floor. In 1870, the wiring of the world brought with it a fascination for the primal ooze which clung to the new man-made tentacles connecting the continents. As Eiseley put it, early proponents of Darwin's and Wallace's theories formed

> a belief that widespread on the floor of the abyssal plain lay the '*Urschleim*,' a protoplasmic half-living matter representing

> that transition between the living and the nonliving out of which more complex life had, in the course of time, developed. The abyss, in other words, was thought to contain not only the living record of the past, but the ultimate secret of life itself; Creation might still be in process. (33)

He continues:

> Haeckel in Germany and Huxley in England were proceeding to show that as one passed below the stage of nucleated single-celled organisms one arrived at a simple stirring of the abyssal slime wherein something that was neither life nor non-life oozed and fed without cellular individuality.
>
> This soft, gelatinous matter had been taken from the ocean bed during dredging operations. Examined and pronounced upon by Professor Huxley, it was given the name of *Bathybius haeckelii* in honor of his great German colleague. Speaking before the Royal Geographical Society in 1870, Huxley confidently maintained that *Bathybius* formed a living scum or film on the sea bed extending over thousands of square miles. Moreover, he expanded, it probably formed a continuous sheet of living matter girdling the whole surface of the earth (35).

Alas, all the scientific expeditions mounted to locate this Lovecraftian missing link proved fruitless (or slimeless, rather). This "seething, unindividualized ooze whose potentialities included the butterfly and the rose" turned out to be a "a projective dream of scientists striving to build an evolutionary family tree upon existing organisms." Indeed, Eiseley calls this belief "the product of an overconfident materialism, [and] a vainglorious assumption that the secrets of life were about to be revealed." In short, it represents "one of the most curious cases of self-delusion ever indulged in by scholars."

And yet today, in 2012, we continue to read of such scientific hopes.[4] For instance, in a recent report entitled, *The Limits of Organic Life in Planetary Systems*, NASA and the National Academy of Sciences hypothesize the existence of strange slimy "biofilms" which the authors hope will be found on Mars.[5] It thus seems that despite our post-Victorian age of sterile labs and fluorescent lights, we continue to detect (or should that be project?) a strong "weird" pulse to the existence of existents; continually flummoxed by the ineffability of that organic matrix of which we ourselves mysteriously emerged, and will soon – at least geologically speaking – return.[6]

Critical theorist Eugene Thacker has thought long and hard about "life," not so much as an object still awaiting a full and satisfying account, but as a speculative and uncanny figure which consistently haunts and thwarts our attempts to understand it. As such, he both identifies and challenges "a furtive, miasmatic unintelligibility that inhabits any ontology of life." Thacker would no doubt find the Victorian search for *Urschleim* instructive, along with its failure to discover the hinge between the vital and the inanimate, since life is for him, in the final analysis, "a continuum of absence."

In his recent and remarkable book, *After Life*, Thacker traces the legacy of Aristotle's decisive distinction between *Life* and *the living* throughout Western thought (echoed in such concepts as Heidegger's sorting of *Being* from *beings*). He thus underscores the contrast between "Life itself," which has no transparent fundamental properties – and thus actually represents "a kind of vitalist void" – and the living, which is a saturated set of uncertain population and criteria. As a consequence, this book brings attention to, and complicates, the habitual conflation of life with associated terms like *being, existence, nature,* and even, *God*. These are not synonyms, Thacker insists, as much as we have historically tended to treat them as such. Indeed, between such terms we can discern a dynamic and unstable Venn diagram, depending on the many different contexts they are deployed.[7] Aristotle's term *psukhē*, translated variously as "soul" or "life principle," is, for Thacker, crucial in understanding the way "life itself" would come to be considered as a separate force or essence, simultaneously transcending and animating those breathing, walking, crawling, swimming, flying, sporing, blossoming avatars of its presence. The assumption of ontological division underlying such an axiom persists, even through such different philosophical epochs as Hellenic antiquity, Holy Roman Christianity, and modern scientific inquiry (albeit with variations of emphasis).

Life is thus not only a problem *in* Western philosophy, but a problem *for* Western philosophy – especially because of the paradoxical Aristotelian legacy between *that-which-lives* and *that-by-which-the-living-lives*. Indeed, the paradox is as difficult to surmount as it is easy to state: "*One cannot think Life without thinking the living; one cannot think Life while at the same time thinking the living*" (21). Hence a contradiction is rediscovered at the heart of this discourse which speaks of everything, and thus nothing (specific). Life is perceived to be everywhere, lurking in every nook and cranny, but cannot be flushed out or grasped with any certainty. ("[T]he generosity of life is *nihil*.") Life is thus "the conjunction of immanence and nothing." What complicates matters yet further is the fact that *both* of these categories are crystallized in the term *psukhē*, since for Aristotle life flips between the transcendent and immanent; switching swiftly from one to the other in stuttering undecidability, depending on which perspective one approaches it.[8] As a consequence, the concept of *psukhē* could be compared to a quantum particle: either principle *or* manifestation, but seemingly never both at the same time (lest it confound his own laws of logic).

Thacker begins his analysis with a set of interlocking premises. First of all, "[t]oday, in an era of biopolitics, it seems that life is everywhere at stake, and yet it is nowhere the same."

Secondly, the contemporary concept of life goes beyond the "ambivalent conjunction of biology and politics," extending itself "across broad swaths of social, economic, and cultural existence." And third, "[t]here has been a steady loosening of the concept of life in the 'new vitalisms' of affectivity, process, and self-organization." Taken together, such statements point to an emerging and unprecedented relationship between the ur-concept of life, and the human attempt to define and locate it. Today, organic creatures are often read or rendered in algorithmic terms, just as virtual entities are considered to be flirting with the presence afforded through sentience. Indeed, the "new vitalisms" which Thacker allude to – heavily influenced by the ascendency of cybernetic discourse and technologies – describe potential new affinities between *actual* penguins and *computational* thespians, since life seems to be "at work" in such incommensurable domains as "meat, soul, or pattern" (250). Hence the ongoing challenge: "how to think life without the mediation of the living"?

Thacker is ultimately calling for "a critique of life," which itself begins with the implications of the following proposition: "*Every ontology of 'life' thinks of life in terms of something-other-than-life*" (x). (Usually a metaphysical concept, like time, form, or spirit.) Such a critique faces two central challenges. The first, to refuse a dichotomous concept of life, as caught between the poles of reductionism, scientificity, and the empirical – on the one side – and mysticism, religiosity, and romanticism, on the other. The second, to avoid the concept's "pervasive anthropomorphism." That is, to think of life as foundationally unhuman or nonhuman, rather than incidentally or potentially so. The challenge, for Thacker, is "how an ontology of life can be thought in a way that does not immediately install the human at its center, either via an anthropotheological move (the personal, angry, benevolent, judging God), or via an anthropobiological move (the ascending pyramid of organization, order, and development)." The answer this book offers lies in a third direction; one which eschews the traditional Scylla and Charibdes of religion and positivist science. And it finds the roots of such an alternative amongst a cluster of "heretics" who recorded their ideas in that long and murky stretch of time in Western thought between the Hellenic and early Enlightenment philosophers: Duns Scotus, Nicholas of Cusa, Pseudo-Dionysius, and Eriugena – all leading up to the revolution embodied in the name Spinoza. In doing so, *After Life* provides us with a revealing, "untimely," and neglected lens on the present.

These apostates from the central neo-Aristotelian tradition, embodied by Thomist Scholasticism, considered life in quite different terms to Aristotle. In place of spiritual affirmation they offered negation. In place of the transcendent One True God they spoke of a pantheistic immanence. And in contrast to the metaphysical system in which all creatures are analogies of a perfect, luminous God – albeit to differing degrees – they conceived two radically democratic ontologies: "univocity" and "equivocity." Both of these perspectives challenged the Scholastic orthodoxy of Life itself as an infinite source of reservoir, beyond time, of which finite creatures issue, partake, and then return. (Think of Plato's One which produces the Many.)

Drastically simplifying Thacker's detailed schematic, his minoritarian genealogy speaks against or outside the Church's sanctioned view of life as coincident with God – generous, proliferating, superlative; something which "cuts across all instances of the living," while maintaining a strict order and spacing of elements. In its "major key" of positive theology, life itself was held to be affirmative, divine, and radiant. The life that humans enjoy or endure – depending upon circumstance and disposition – was considered by most to be an *analogy* of divine life, since Man is created in God's image. For the Scholastics, life is thought primarily in terms of *representation*; as avatars of a spirituality which is ever "off-stage" for terrestrial, profane, mortal beings. As Thacker notes, "[p]ositive theology has a number of political advantages as well. Its motifs of light and radiation not only reaffirm a single, centralized divine source, but, in its Neoplatonic variant, it also assures a hierarchy of processes, causes, and distributions, from one circle to the next, from a higher layer to a lower layer, along the great chain of beings." (Not unlike the centralized ripples of influence bouncing back and forth from the Holy See.) According to this view, life is a transcendent force which neatly organizes its incarnations in hierarchical ranks, by virtue of proximity to God. (Something shared by some Eastern theological philosophies, in which all living things are on a karmic wheel, which turns on logics of ascent or descent.) In contrast, for the thinkers in the "minor key" – those advocating either equivocity or univocity – the population of the vital are not beholden to an essential center, like iron filings to a magnet. For univocalists, life manifests itself with equal intensity and value amongst all living things. Thus there is no ontological *difference* between a donkey or a plant or a Man or a Woman, other than intuitive ones of shape or texture – they all partake equally in what Manuel DeLanda would later call a "flat ontology" (clearly a dangerous position to take in such aggressively pious times, dedicated to the exultation of verticality). For the equivocalists, there is no ontological *basis* for ranking one creature above another, for each individual is so radically distinct as to be incommensurable. Such heretical notions thus encourage "a certain pulling-apart between Life and the living."

For Deleuze, equivocity meant that "being is said in several senses." In other words, "the different senses of the word 'being' were without common measure." This was a sinful position because it alienated God from his creations, suggesting that He had no control over them; indeed no *access* to them. The living withdraw from the swooping search-light of Life. Univocity, by way of contrast, meant "being has only one sense and is said in one and the same sense of everything of which it is said." This is also a sinful position because of the flattening effect whereby all of God's creatures are ascribed equal ontological status. The univocalists saw the living as a form of animated commonwealth, all sharing an essential substance, albeit expressing itself in different shapes, sizes, and orientations. Equivocalists saw the world's enigmatic population as something closer to Agamben's "coming community" (that is, an inessential commonality; or community of those who have nothing in common). Where univocity will find its most eloquent expression in Spinoza's monism, equivocal creatures anticipate Leibniz's radically singular monads, created perhaps in the alchemical movement of "extrinsic vectors" (16).

For Thacker, our own relationship to the mysterious heartbeat within our bodies can be traced back to the guiding medieval triad of Creator, creation, creature. Indeed, "if the human is more-than-animal, then it is also less-than-spiritual. Hence the problem of the *creatura* is also a problem of mediation. And some form of mediation is required to account for the fuzzy ontological status of the living being, especially the living being that is the human being" (98). Humans, in their own reflections upon the world, have almost to a fault consistently designated themselves in a position of exception. Even those self-loathing members who hurl insults at our hubris consider us exceptional, albeit in the abject direction, rather than the angelic. Again opting for a third option, Thacker offers us a "misanthropology" which establishes itself upon the understanding that "Life" is human-centered, in our own reflections upon it, yet simultaneously – and "objectively" – unhuman-oriented (9).[9] Indeed, he asks "[w]hat if life is not assumed to reach its pinnacle in human life? What if life is only incidentally, and not fundamentally, an anthropocentric phenomenon?" From here it is but a few short steps to the more active or constructive question, "can there be a politics of life in terms of the nonhuman or the unhuman?"

And here is Thacker's most significant contribution: the possibility of a psukhēpolitics which would consider the soul once more, not as a numinous supplement, but as the very question of form and formal difference within animated creatures. This renewed attention to the *materialized* soul – to the *actual* animator – of the living could, ironically, deliver a timely reminder of the various bodies missing from key biopolitical accounts. Indeed, it could help us escape the rather dismal science of post-Foucauldian biopolitical theory (or any possible alternative "zoepolitical" projects, trapped in the same diagram). For the biopolitics furthered by Agamben functions, almost despite itself, to re-establish a fundamental anthropological measure. Despite the undeniable subtlety of its thought, and import of its critique, it has ultimately devolved into another moribund humanism, in which the *anthropos* is the central instance of "coded life," due to the complexity of its own semiotic systems of global regulation. Both architect and victim, humans – as figured in current biopolitical discourse – are the privileged creature who at any moment threaten to be treated as "bare life" (i.e., animals).[10] In a self-flattering paradox, humans are privileged by virtue of their abjection, either potential or actual. Theology, it seems, has its own after life (or half-life). Thus "life itself" is reintroduced back into modernity under this sign, threatening to smear us all once again in the political equivalent of *Urschleim*.

Yet the evidence of such a mythical substance continues to elude us.

Lifecycles of the Rich and Famous

Seeking a clear beacon of orientation in an inky and perplexing void, NASA defines life simply as "a self-sustained chemical system capable of Darwinian evolution" (Daniel, 353). We might take issue, however, with the specific elemental condition, given the capacity for evolution now observed in entities which inhabit non-chemical environments, such as computer viruses. NASA, speaking as a single entity itself, might object that these are not instances of life, but *simulations* of life (against the conviction of Nils All Baricelli and subsequent proponents of Artificial Intelligence). Such emergent para-existences remind us of Marshall McLuhan's claim that, "[t]he important thing is to realize that electric information systems are live environments in the full organic sense" (1997, 36); just as Donna Haraway's famously observed, "[o]ur machines are disturbingly lively, and we ourselves frighteningly inert."

Which brings us back to our old friends the Orc and the penguin? How do the ancient and esoteric debates raised by Thacker help us account for their mutual "decisions" to *live differently* to their kin – or at least contrary to their creator's intentions? Are such (ontological) refusals suggestive of a new type of emergence or existence which comports itself "after life" (itself an ambiguous temporality: either following in the wake of life, or in pursuit of it)? Mindful of such questions, Thacker adds an important one of his own: should life be considered as "an object of metaphysical speculation, empirical verification, or subjective phenomenality?" In a world of talking cars, smart phones, distressed fabrics, and intelligent objects, NASA's definition appears increasingly quaint and off-base. After all, it has been over 150 years since Marx noted that the carpenter's table grows a wooden brain and wants to dance on its head when transformed into a commodity. The empirical question, "is the table (or computer virus) *really* alive?" issues from the limited perspective Thacker urges us to avoid: that of biological reductionism. But we must equally avoid smuggling in a secular version of onto-theology, in which non-sentient or non-organic creatures are simply bequeathed "souls" or *psukhē* by virtue of mimetic or pre-programmed movement.[11] The question thus becomes, do the Orc and the penguin share a univocal, or even equivocal, existence, despite dwelling in domains perceived to be distinct (i.e., the digital and the organic, the virtual and the actual)? Must we continue to place a non-permeable barrier between the online and offline worlds, as if they exist in different metaphysical realms? For if objects and puppets (or even oil[12]) can have "secret lives," as some contemporary theorists insist, can't electronic or silicone creatures as well?

We can turn to Ted Chiang's recent novella, *The Lifecycle of Software Objects* for a fascinating answer in the affirmative. Classified as science fiction, this near-future scenario is closer to speculative fiction, with no extraordinary elements to test our sense of credulity, beyond extending current obsessions a few years hence. In Chiang's world, people continue to spend inordinate amounts of time entertaining themselves online, toggling between screens and face-to-face interactions with amphibious ease. We meet Ana, a former zookeeper, who was obliged to go back to school to learn coding when the zoo is closed, and the animals sold-off piece-meal. To her surprise, she soon lands a job for a company called Blue Gamma, which designs and sells "digients"[13]: cute little digital critters which consumers like to keep as pets (and reminiscent of sophisticated descendents of Tamagotchis). When she first plugs into her new employer's server, her avatar sees

> a little anthropomorphic tiger cub sliding colored beads along a frame of wires; a panda bear examining a toy car; a cartoon version of a chimpanzee rolling a foam rubber ball. . . The onscreen annotations identify them as digients, digital organisms that live in environments like Data Earth, but they don't look like any that Ana's seen before. These aren't the idealized pets marketed to people who can't commit to a real animal; they lack the picture-perfect cuteness, and their movements are too awkward.[14]

It seems the company believes Ana's experience working with

actual animals will transfer smoothly to helping to nurture and train digital equivalents[15] – especially now they have acquired a "genomic engine" called Neuroblast, which "supports more cognitive development than anything else currently out there." As her friend Robyn explains, "We're going to pitch them as pets you can talk to, teach to do really cool tricks. There's an unofficial slogan we use in-house: 'All the fun of monkeys, with none of the poop-throwing.'" From aspiring Jane Goodall to laid-off zookeeper to trainer of virtual pets, Ana's career trajectory maps "the diminution of the natural world, writ small."

While at work, Ana meets friend, ally, and animator Derek, who – in a different life – may have worked for Peter Jackson on the Massive™ system which created our erratic Orc:

> Derek studied to be an animator, so in one respect creating digital characters is right up his alley. In other respects, his job is very different from that of a traditional animator. Normally he'd design a character's gait and its gestures, but with digients those traits are emergent properties of the genome; what he has to do is design a body that manifests the digients' gestures in a way that people can relate to. These differences are why a lot of animators–including his wife Wendy–don't work on digital lifeforms, but Derek loves it. He feels that helping a new lifeform express itself is the most exciting work an animator could be doing.

Together Ana and Derek form a formidable team, designing and training these novel creatures, which neither Adam or Darwin would recognize. What's more, the digients thrive under Ana's stewardship, responding positively to the new pedagogic exercises she creates, and the improved "food" (at least according to the dictates of their "reward maps").[16]

After a while on the job, however, Ana begins to get a sense of the singularity of the digients: how it is perhaps wrong to consider them a digital analog – as it were – of terrestrial fauna. "Everyone here thinks of the digients as animals," she says. "The thing is, the digients don't behave like any real animal. They've got this non-animal quality to them, so it feels like we're dressing them in circus costumes when we try to make them look like monkeys or pandas." This statement prompts a rethink on the part of the company, and an expansion of what kinds of avatars will be possible (and, just as importantly, popular). This results in a likeable chap called Jax, "whose avatar is a neo-Victorian robot made of polished copper." For while digients are like all of God's creatures – existing "between parameters and preferences" – they differ from humans and other animals in that the former are carefully controlled by their human designers. (Then again, aren't the "parameters" of all creatures increasingly prescribed, and proscribed, by previous parameters, ad infinitum? That is to say, aren't all instances of individuation "coded" in one sense or another?)

Ana concentrates her efforts and expertise on socializing the digients. Like people or animals, digients can be genomically-tinkered with, and essentially bred to encourage certain characteristics. Unlike people or animals, they can also be re-booted and recalibrated like computers, in order to speed up or replace specific experiences or behaviors deemed undesirable. (For instance, when one of Jax's digient friends, Lolly, starts cursing out of the blue – thanks to an unscrupulous Australian trainer – the potential disaster is diverted by simply "rolling her back" to an earlier check-point, thus erasing the original stimulus which the unwitting offender was imitating.) As the narrator explains, upon release, "Blue Gamma's digients are a hit. Within the first year of release, a hundred thousand customers buy them and–more importantly–keep them running. The virtual world acts as a global village for raising the digients, a social fabric into which a new category of pet is woven." Equally important, "the company takes pains to remind buyers that each copy will develop differently depending on its environment." Hence one digient owner posts the following to an online forum: "You won't believe what my Natasha did today! We were at the playground, and another digient hurt himself when he fell and was crying. Natasha gave him a hug to make him feel better, and I praised her to high heaven. Next thing I know, she pushes over another digient to make him cry, hugs him, and looks to me for praise!" While owners are well aware that these sophisticated virtual pets are not children, many cannot help feeling the same waves of pride, fear, affection, and protectiveness that parents do. Indeed, the developers do too, becoming no less invested in the creatures for knowing where they came from (as if that deterred "real" parents in the past).

As the plot develops, things become increasingly intermingled and complex, and Chiang does a great job – with his clean, efficient prose style – of anticipating and rendering many of the possibilities that such creatures present: so much so that it often feels as if we're reading some *New Yorker* reportage delivered from 2017, rather than a piece of contemporary fiction. Working with other companies, Blue Gamma figure out a way for digients to explore the off-line world, within robotic bodies. However, these are expensive, and prohibitive for most consumers. Nevertheless, Ana enjoys watching Jax experience, experiment with, and enjoy "the real world," along with its different dimensionality, tactility, and phenomenology. Here we see ontology operating on three-levels at once, within the same Russian Doll entity: the digient's coded kernel, the avatar which gives it form for the human eye, and then the material prosthesis in which the digient's avatar can be ported (thus expanding its sensorium). Upon his virgin journey into extra-computational, terrestrial space, Jax is dumb-founded by the intense, disorienting presence of sunlight. Then, as the unprecedented sense of embodiment begins to register, he is simply blown away: "Jax turns around to take in the entire room. 'Wow.' He stops turning.

'Wow wow. Sound different. Wow wow wow.' "[17]

Soon enough, as with the original batch of Tamagotchis, popular interest wanes and moves elsewhere, and digients are either suspended indefinitely or simply left running as orphans on platforms (such as Data Earth) which recognize their older operating system and format. As the narrator notes, "Some volunteers have begun maintaining rescue shelters, accepting unwanted digients in hopes of matching them with new owners. These volunteers practice a variety of strategies; some keep the digients running without interruption, while others restore the digients from their last checkpoint every few days, to keep them from developing abandonment issues that might make it harder for them to get adopted."

At first Ana and Derek explore the option of incorporation, for if corporations can legally be people, why not avatars registered with the same paperwork? But even though this could potentially provide access to certain beneficial loopholes, it does not positively incite former digient owners to reclaim their stray wards. For a while, Ana and Derek hold out hope that orphaned digients will find shelter with AI researchers and enthusiasts, who are curious whether these new virtual creatures will create their own culture when placed "on a private island furnished with text and software libraries" and run at hothouse speeds. But disappointingly, the digients seem to become increasingly feral and asocial, and "it's generally agreed that the biomes aren't run at a high enough resolution for real intelligence to evolve there."

Ana and Derek hold out a different view, however. For them, after observing the cognitive development of their own digients, synthesized or engineered intelligence seems to be closer to the organic kind than expected. Indeed, for them it is a fallacy to distinguish between cognitive and emotional development (as any parent or teacher will probably tell you).[18] For those invested in the welfare of these digital beings, the plateau of intelligence is less to do with inherent limitations of the coded genome, but the neglect of their owners or guardians. After all, a child left in a library may absorb a lot of information, but not be able to process it in any stable context, or through critical lenses. Ana thus types to Derek, "We could expose them to lots of different things and see what they have an aptitude for. Give them a liberal arts education instead of vocational training. (I'm only half kidding.)" Derek replies, "That's actually not as silly as it might sound. Bonobos have learned to do everything from making stone cutting tools to playing computer games when they were given the chance. Our digients might be good at things that it hasn't occurred to us to train them for."

Eventually Ana comes to a meta-realization:

> [E]xperience isn't merely the best teacher, it's the only teacher. If she's learned anything raising Jax, it's that there are no shortcuts; if you want to create the common sense that comes from twenty years of being in the world, you need to devote twenty years to the task. You can't assemble an equivalent collection of heuristics in less time; experience is algorithmically incompressible. . . . And even though it's possible to take a snapshot of all that experience and duplicate it *ad infinitum*, even though it's possible to sell copies cheaply or give them away for free, each of the resulting digients would still have lived a lifetime. Each one would have once seen the world with new eyes, have had hopes fulfilled and hopes dashed, have learned how it felt to tell a lie and how it felt to be told one.[19]

For complex organisms – or technorganisms – affect is thus a form of intelligence, or even its precondition (at the very least, its study partner). Indeed, this obliges us to specify *types* of intelligence, where the social kind encourages and enhances the more positivistic, applied ones. And this is why Ana and Derek eventually consider the possibility of digients being sold as sexual companions as a way of keeping them "alive": a difficult decision which opens an ethical can of worms, as well as some demanding questions about the role of desire, recognition, pleasure, etc. in "personal development."[20] Ana is first concerned that prospective owners will abuse the digients, treating them as toys at best, or slaves at worst. Her fears are not unfounded, given that it wasn't so long ago that she found her own digients – confused, fascinated, and horrified – watching the following:

> On the virtual television, a person wearing a clown avatar is holding down a digient wearing a puppy avatar, and hitting the digient's legs repeatedly with a hammer.[21] The digient's legs can't break because its avatar wasn't designed to account for that, and it probably can't scream for similar reasons, but the digient must be in agony, and the chittering sounds are the only way it can express that. . . . It's not an animation, but a recording of a griefer using the IFF hack to disable the pain circuit-breakers on a digient's body. Even worse, the digient isn't an anonymous new instantiation, but someone's beloved pet, illicitly copied using the IFF hack.[22]

But the sales pitch is seductive and convincing, as are the subsequent debates on the online forum for digient owners. These all stress that Ana's resistance is akin to a parent who refuses to recognize that their children need to experience the world of love and sex in order to become mature beings: more smothering than mothering.

In the end, however, the decision is made in her absence and without her consent.

Ultimately, Chiang's story does not resolve all the questions it poses – indeed, how could it? But in creating this credible near-future scenario, it has provided the reader with one of many possible ways in which this increasingly algorithmic world will force us to confront our own cherished values, precisely because they are being reflected back to us through nonhuman entities. The sudden spike in interest toward animals in the (increasingly erroneously named) "humanities" – and in popular culture more generally – comes with a new and urgent tone: itself the result of growing consciousness of biocide, climate change, and inter-species "white man's burden." Indeed, this sudden explosion of animal studies in the academy comes *after* the fascination with cyborgs and other technological posthumans, which itself emerged after a prolonged sojourn through the uncanny valley carved out by our new digital machines.[23] In both cases, whether discussing technological or the organic, the best work does not try to expand the circle of our own qualities in order to include the Other. Indeed, what could be more anthropocentric than the Turing Test – given that it measures intelligence according to a narcissistic perception?[24] Such logic pervades much of both the soft and hard sciences, whereby Man continues to be the metron, so that ontological promotion comes through the degree to which a creature can mimic the human (tool-use, cognitive puzzles, following instructions, etc.). The alternative is to see such qualities as cutting across species, and expressed or utilized in different ways, depending on the exigencies and *umwelt* of any given entity (once again, "between parameter and possibility"). In Thacker's terms, this is to seek a balance between univocity and equivocity.

From this less familiar perspective, the Orc and the penguin both inhabit the virtual world, as do humans. But this is the virtual as defined by Bergson, Deleuze, and their disciples, rather than computer scientists. Here the virtual is an invisible, immanent, temporal reservoir of alternative futures embedded in the present, emerging out of the matrix of structures which make up a local world or event.[25] So while I intend to go to work and teach tomorrow, I may indeed be prevented from doing so, swept up in any one of the virtual scenarios inscribed in the unfurling of time which decides to activate itself tomorrow morning (terrorist attack, paralyzing *ennui*, femme-fatale seduction, etc.). In short, we have now reached the historical threshold where *all* creatures – whether created in a womb, lab, or computer – contain their own virtual potential to unfold into existence according to their own whims or dictates, beyond the codes which guide their day-to-day behavior. And surely this is one of the lay definitions of "life itself." Even more confronting, *we may be on the cusp of a world in which "the living" do not partake of "life itself," in the formerly essential sense of psukhē*. The living may not eat, excrete, breathe, or reproduce. And yet such creatures will share so many characteristics that we ourselves cherish – opinions, emotions, experiences, etc. – that many of us will be troubled by the resemblance. (No doubt the long and ugly history of racism will write a new chapter with these "Mechas," "Borgs," or "Sims.")[26]

In order to get a firmer grip on this slippery issue, however, we need to return full circle to the key term "life." And for this it is fruitful to contrast and complement Thacker's rendering of the category to Jean-Christophe Bailly's.

Life and Breath

Jean-Christophe Bailly, professor at the wonderfully named École Nationale Supérieure de la Nature et du Paysage, is not well known outside his native France. Hopefully this will change soon with the recent translation into English of his remarkably lyrical book of philosophy, *The Animal Side*. For the present discussion, however, we turn to a shorter piece entitled, "The Slightest Breath: On Living," published in *The New Centennial Review*. Here Bailly begins with two artists, John Cage and Piotr Kowalski, working in different mediums – music/silence and sculpture – in order to invoke the issue of life as precisely that: the thing which continues to *issue* itself into existence, and in excess of any fathomable meaning, system, or design. For this thinker, such mindful and receptive artistic practices as these "both confirm the same thing; namely, either that there is no 'nothing,' or that 'nothing' will never be within our reach." Moreover, "What this unobtainable silence and this impossible inertia allow us to see is not simply the circumstances of being alive; instead they also allow us to see that life is incapable and unaware of how to leave itself behind" (2).

Thus we already find a contrast with Thacker, for whom life's exuberance is considered as a manifest decoy for its profound, generative negation or *nihil*. Where Plato asked "why is there something and not nothing?" and Aristotle refines the question to ask "what conditions allow the emergence of living things?" Thacker loops the question around to ask "Why is there something *and* nothing?"[27] Bailly, however, is hesitant to put both legs in the void, preferring to begin with the following premise: "Before any determination of a being, living perhaps resides – but without a residence – in the fact that something arrives instead of nothing, and that this coming and arrival continue" (3).[28] The stakes are not entirely clear, since Thacker's conclusion leaves us haunted by the uncanny, unhuman, even horrific, implications and manifestations of life. Bailly also takes life beyond the human, but is not so quick to leave us in flash-frozen Geigeresque carbonite. Note the Derridaesque sleight-of-hand: "living . . . resides – but without a residence" (3), (à la messianism *sans* Messiah).

As Bailly notes, "*Natura naturans* is the classical name for this infinite expenditure where life is exhausted and renewed in a continuous/discontinuous process of interlocking and rupturing . . . . [in] an infinite finitude" (3). It is not certain, however, where he locates this exuberant process: within or beyond Aristotle's legacy of Life versus the living (i.e., the ontological gap as critiqued by Thacker). For on the one hand he states: "In a way, living is the very plane of immanence to the extent that it is the surface and the entanglement of appearances. Living is immediate to itself; that is, it does not result, but rather advances, arranges, spreads out, redistributes, borders, invades, and overruns itself. As the living, we are enveloped in the divergences, impulses, and folds of living" (4). On the other, he reserves a special role for the breath. "There is a kind of humbler, infra-cogito in living, in the simple fact of breathing, and in hearing oneself breathe" (4). Life, for Bailly, is continually *inspiring*, in the literal sense that we breathe in and out in order to perpetuate the experience, if only physiologically (at least until we *ex-pire*). Indeed, the breath "is the animal form of being in life, the space of our most proper emotion, and the fundamental rhythm through which we identify life and the living" (5). And yet, breathing is also the key to a more holistic or ec-static view of life: "One sees respiration outside of oneself in others' bodies and in the bodies of creatures." In other words, "[t]he space of breath is this coming and going through which the outside and the inside communicate" (4).[29]

Such statements, as poetic as they may be, don't seem to account for the whole story, since they seem to exclude creatures who lack a visible respiration system (starfish, coral reefs, trees, etc.).[30] As steeped as Bailly is – as indeed *all* humans are – in the rhythm of the lungs, he also seeks to counsel against those who indulge in what I have called elsewhere "ontological apartheid."[31] As he notes, in a disappointed tone: "Today theories of the landscape and the environment still place the abiotic and biotic strata in opposition to one another" (3). That is to say, when discussing the living, we should not restrict ourselves to those entities which fall under NASA's umbrella definition, but also include such beings or "existents" as the humble stone (for millennia, put on display to represent the case of the worldless and unsentient).[32] Breathing is thus shown to be a metaphor for a much more capacious embrace of the living, which Bailly names "porosity": that is, "all the protocols of exchange that make the widespread diversity of living possible in all of its forms" (5).[33]

> Whether or not the stone has a world is not so important here. What counts is the role it has played in the world and what it still is at the moment a living and breathing creature comes across it on any given day – with its weight, mass, and texture, its weathering, glistening, and its resonance. . . [The] stone cannot be withdrawn from living – instead of being by itself, its own arrival, its own surprise, and its own immensity – without living being turned into a mere a category of being, a simple subtraction. The stone resonates in Cage's impossible silence, and it moves in Kowalski's impossible inertia.[34] (6)

Echoing both Plotinus and Bergson, Bailly notes, "the stone is a marker of singularity, and the imprint is itself living." Or in simpler terms, "[t]he sleep of the stone is all around us, and in us as well" (7).[35]

For Thacker, I imagine, Bailly is thus quite an orthodox proponent of the "major" key of thinking about life throughout Western history: as superlative, generative, proliferating. But if we subtract its analogical function – that is, its theological core and representative *raison d'être* – then the stakes shift. They move closer to an updating of Spinoza's monism: a secular, immanent mysticism. Where Thacker claims that life is a problem for thought, Bailly refuses a distinction between the two (a tendency he explicitly takes from Plotinus, who stated "no distinction exists between Being and Knowing"). "Being alive is not equivalent to knowing or experiencing," writes Bailly. "Rather, it is a tendency to be attuned to living: to look, contemplate, and search" (7). Plotinus again: "every life is some form of thought, but of a dwindling clearness like the degrees of life itself." Thus, "nothing is beneath or before thought." Moreover, "living is that through which the sensible is made intelligible, in an endless meditation whose unfolding forms are open to thought because they are themselves of the same order as thought" (8). Amongst and between not only the breathing creatures, but everything in which they encounter on their journey through time and/or space, we find "a kind of anonymity" in which the cosmic *cogito* whispers to itself in a displacing, objective sense.

Perhaps this unhuman process passes through what Thacker calls "creaturely indeterminacy" like an electric current. And perhaps it stretches itself in ingenious and thirsty ways, like the "extended organism" of the ant colony or bee hive – both of which, Bailly would be pleased to see, "breathe" in their own superorganismic way.[36] The living are thus an ever-coming (and going) community, which fashion unprecedented valences, strategies, alliances, pacts, and even narratives (6). Thus, in the end, Bailly and Thacker may actually be describing the same phenomenon, but from different proximities (and through different aesthetic filters). Neither are interested in chasing the Western will-o-the-wisp, "Life itself," preferring to turn their attention to the way in which the living embody the thought of the cosmos on a register so indifferent to human intelligence that it is laughable that our species once believed this to be the measure of what "the mind" is capable of.[37]

Such portraits – to add one more to an already over-crowded gallery – prompts Bailly to write: "Living, at the point of its greatest vivacity, at its heart, is the 'infinite connecting' that Hölderlin had designated as the task of poetic intelligence" (9). While I am not completely comfortable with the French philosopher's desire to turn the living into a text or genre – legible or not – there is certainly much to be said for the infinite connecting of universal life-forms: whether they are aware of this connection or not, and whether they are based in carbon or silicone or whatever. (What Timothy Morton calls "the mesh.") We are fast approaching a time when we will all be obliged to create avatar-doppelgängers, which will further complicate questions of connection, disconnection, presence, absence, identity-by-proxy, life, and its simulation. Indeed one company is already offering a package called, Virtual Eternity™ - a "web-based, legacy creation and preservation service," which "allows users to create their own Intelligent Avatar by uploading their image and populating the digital brain by adding content and answering a series of pre-set and customizable questions. The resulting Intellitar, or digital clone, will look, think, act, and speak just like the user." In other words, it will soon be possible for your friends to interact with a virtual version of "you" after your embodied self has shuffled off this mortal coil.[38] (Merely the latest instance of hauntological media, since the invention of portraiture.)

Contemporary artists are also pushing the biological envelope. Consider the Cronenbergesque "Quasi-Objects" created by Lorenzo Oggiano: three-dimensional videos and prints which aim "to stimulate thought and dialogue on the progressive relativisation of natural forms of life as a result of techno-biological evolution."[39] As the artist claims, "Life is a real and autonomous process independent from any specific material manifestation." Indeed, our gadgets today inherit the ontological itching and twitching of Benjamin's toys and Ponge's objects. We see little mystery when they "spring to life" in front of our eyes, but would still insist on the metaphorical dimension if pressed. Yet what is life itself if not the ultimate metaphor? Millennia of reflection have yielded no satisfying, transparent, universal definition. We can measure it only by its effects. "Life woz 'ere." We must take its word for it. After all, in the age of RFID tags, our machines read more than we do. Humans conduct their day under the watchful eye of machines of living – if not loving – grace.[40]

Open Source Entities

All of these attempts to re-frame or extend life between domains, however, prove themselves little more than the tentative circlings of old-fashioned tinkerers when compared to the watershed, game-changing science of "synthetic biology." This radical new practice, first announced in the mainstream press in 2010, was spearheaded by Dr. Craig Venter, who created the first synthetic life-form: a bacteria cell affectionately called Synthia (real name, *Mycoplasma laboratorium*), in the tradition of Dolly the cloned sheep. By synthesizing the genetic code of this cell, Venter was able to invent the equivalent of DNA software, which can then be downloaded into other (hollowed out) cells, and literally booted into animated existence with a spark.[41] This remarkable new technique truly abolishes the distinction between the digital and the biological domain, since it creates the only life form on earth whose parent is a computer.[42] As Dr. Adam Rutherford of BBC's *Horizon* program puts it, "We've found a way to take life and radically redesign it. We've put ourselves in this extraordinary position where nature itself can be disassambled into spare parts, and now we can put these back together just as we please. Incredible as it sounds, life itself has become a programmable machine." In less than three short years, we have reached a point where even hobbyists, school kids, and amateurs can download the DNA code of what we might call "open source entities," essentially printing them out in dormant form, and then inserting this print-out into an organism in order to reengineer its essential, natural architecture.[43] These "bio bricks" – modular sets of computer/DNA code – can be used to create "bio circuits" which instruct an organism what to do or how to grow (the famous example being injecting the genetic sequence for jellyfish phosphorescence into other creatures). Thus, "biological machines" – like the goats specially created to lactate spider silk in their milk, or the yeast engineered to exhale diesel fuel – are not examples plucked from science fiction futures but from the farms and labs of the present.

Clearly such Frankensteinian hybrids are not what Bailly had in mind when he states that life is "first and foremost that of an infinite overlapping of forms and functions, inventions, and inflections: something like an infinity, not only through metamorphosis, but through conjugation as well" (captured in Deleuze and Guattari's notion of "and . . . and . . . and"). I suspect this passage refers in fact to the ingenious organic connections and symbioses – such as the famous wasp and Orchid – of which nature is comprised, and goes under the name "evolution" or "natural selection." Indeed, "With its evolutionary adaptability, conjugation is like an extraordinarily precise and mobile, relational gymnastics." Of course, "artificial selection" has been with us for centuries, as with the human breeding of animals and plants. But few could anticipate the extent and exponential acceleration of synthetic biology: a science practiced by computer and electrical engineers, as much, if not more than, traditional biologists. The transductive language involved is not only metaphorical, but *actual* and actualizable. Thus the brain, synthetic neurobiologists tell us, communicate with electrical signals in the same way as a silicon chip. Successful experiments have already been conducted in which the brains of mice can be controlled by direct fiber optic implants (possibly the first step toward human minds with their own assigned IP address, as in the dystopian science fiction film *Gamer*).[44]

As I write, the technology is therefore being developed to directly port cybernetic command and control principles into living creatures, and thus extend the instrumentalist will which so disturbed even a Nazi sympathizer like Heidegger. No longer are we just enframed, but ingrained. Tomorrow's commands will no longer be delivered via inefficient routes such as the ear, the eye, and the will, but written into the circuitry of our circulatory systems: inscribed in our very marrow. Dolphins won't be merely trained to sweep for mines, but will be *programmed* to, like organic drones. Can soldiers be too far behind? Even if we acknowledge a large dose of paranoia in such prophecies, the history of well-funded R&D does not bode well for individual agency.[45] If a new technology can be used for military purposes it will (at least *in potentia* – in the case of nuclear weapons). The counter-argument will insist that synthetic biology is the key to surviving the impending ecopocalypse, through projects such as engineering new renewable fuels. But "playing God" on such a scale, and with such impatient zeal, is unlikely to reverse our heedless experiments in sustainability. "Life finds a way," they say. But we are in completely unprecedented territory when a tiny, hubristic fraction of "the living" can slice, splice, and recombine "life itself" into novel organisms with no evolutionary history of their own.[46] Talk about alienation!

All the more reason to hope for loop-holes within the code which allow such creatures, enlisted in a militaristic or corporate assemblage, to refuse to "get with the program."[47]

The Machine Without Vitality

Bailly's compatriot, Gilbert Simondon – writing in the late 1950s – seeks to take "technical beings" very seriously on their own terms, while simultaneously emphasizing the ontological distinction between them: namely, that machines can be complex individuals, but do not in any way partake or, or represent, life. (Indeed he criticizes cybernetics for doing so.[48]) Simondon states his position that:

> [T]here is no such thing as a robot . . . . a robot is no more a machine than a statue is a living being; that is merely a product of the imagination, of man's fictive powers, a product of the art of illusion. Nevertheless, the notion of the machine in present-day culture incorporates, to a considerable extent, this mythic representation of the robot. No cultivated man would allow himself speak of things or persons painted on a canvas as veritable realities with an interior life and a will, good or bad.[49] Despite this, the cultivated man does allow himself to speak of machines which threaten mankind, as if he were attributing to these objects a soul and a separate and autonomous existence which grants them the possession of

> feelings and of intentions towards mankind. (12)

The confusion for this "mechanologist" is the mutual capacity for, and dedication to, negentropy by both living beings and non-living machines. The latter thus "resembles life" and cooperates with it. "The machine is something which fights against the death of the universe; it slows down, as life does, the degradation of energy, and becomes a stabilizer of the world" (16). As a consequence, "[l]iving matter is far from being pure indetermination or pure passivity. Neither is it a blind tendency; it is, rather, the vehicle of informed energy" (52).

Yet the more Simondon attempts to draw a hard line between the living and the technical, the more elements, organs, traits, and *telos* overlap and become confused (at least from the vantage point of a half-century later). He writes: "In life an organ cannot be detached from a species; in technics an element is detachable from the ensemble that produced it for the very reason that it is fabricated; therein lies the difference between a product and something engendered" (58), in the age of xeno-transplants, things don't look so black and white. Likewise, developments in nanotechnology and synthetic biology throw a question-mark-shaped shadow over statements such as the following:

> Technical beings differ from living beings in a great number of ways, but they differ essentially in this respect: a living being engenders other beings that are similar to itself or that can become like it after a certain number of successive reorganisations that occur spontaneously if the conditions are suitable; the technical being is different in that it lacks this capacity; it cannot produce other technical beings like itself, despite the efforts of cyberneticians who have tried to make technical beings copy living beings in constructing beings similar to themselves. That is impossible at the present time except in an imaginary and baseless way. (61)

Despite his inability to anticipate the speed with which science-fiction scenarios would come true, Simondon was light-years ahead many of his philosophical peers in taking technics seriously, and even treating machines as "individuals." Indeed, it was a sign of respect, to some degree, that he did not want to collapse technical and human beings together, since they are intuitively "different" on many registers.[50] Moreover, Simondon's concept of the "ensemble" clears the path for Deleuze and Guattari to deploy their technorganic machinic assemblages, in going so far as to claim that "technical being has a wider scope than the living," thanks to the exquisite refinement of fabrications which can then be fed back into the same ensemble (what he calls "indirect production," in contrast to vital "begetting"). In short, perfection is not unthinkable in the technical world, while the living continue to muddle through the slow and erratic business of evolution through mutation. (Yes – we are all mutants.)

And yet, even someone as sensitive to "the mask of facile humanism" as Simondon cannot help but return to the point where machines are "lacking autonomous internal control," thus needing humans in order to function. "Here man intervenes as living being." Yet each year, in this new millennium, we release new machines "into the wild" which, though created by humans, have the capacity to continue – and perhaps even thrive and multiply, without us (reengineered viruses, coded cellular automata, biohacked seeds, self-powered military drones, orphaned interplanetary rovers, celestial telescopes, etc.). "Man is always the center," writes Simondon. But when the living can be designed and printed out by machines – sparked into life like so many golems – the center cannot hold.

Are We Not Clinamen?

The disembodied voice of David Attenborough informs me that male penguins diligently collect stones for their nest. A wily minority, however, simply wait for the conscientious neighbor to go in search of more, before stealing some for his own. Why is one behaving according to one program, and the other another? Without moralizing one as "good" and the other as "bad" – admittedly a powerful temptation – we can ask ourselves if one option is more advantageous than the other, in Darwinian terms. Indeed, is "adaption" something distributed dormantly amongst a species, so that different versions of similar "operating systems" are at work? And how do these all mesh together, given how isomorphic and intermingled life is on this planet? Where the anomaly in the penguin world is to walk away from the sea toward the ice mountains, the anomaly for a lemming is to refuse to jump off a cliff (just as an Orc may refuse to fight). The answer to "why *this* behavior, by *this* creature, at *this* moment?" can be only partially answered by any given philosophy or scientific theory. Neither is it satisfactory to superimpose several on top of each other – Aristotle, Darwin, Uexküll, Simondon, E. O. Wilson, etc. – as if we can understand the phenomenon better through multiple lenses at once.

What if the Orc and the penguin are not "glitches in the matrix" but a refusal to submit blindly to its coercive architecture? What if they are modest harbingers of a novel way to navigate the matrix? Moreover, what if their wayward trajectories describe the kind of *clinamen* (or swerve) which Lucretius sees at work in all vital-material systems – the indeterminacy necessary to produce the "new factor" (1921, 61) which inspires matter to spring to life[51] and respond afresh to the world (what Manuel DeLanda calls "crucial eccentricities")?[52] Conversely, what if *everything* is a glitch in the matrix, and indeed the matrix (i.e., matter) is only the diachronic sum total of consistent or chaotic glitches, which may go off-program at any moment?[53] My sense is that every time an entity or object surprises us, we should follow it if possible, if only in principle. For these are the temporal branching-points in which possible futures and parallel worlds are revealed to us; in which "life" may be revealed as more than mere survival, but the vertiginous space of inspiration, ethics, poetics, and/or radical refusal to live in a certain prescribed manner. (A Nietzschean "No!" perhaps?)

I thus confess to my own fantasy, whereby the Orc and the penguin somehow cross paths, perhaps sharing a fish sandwich, and communicating through exaggerated gestures about the unseasonably warm weather, before continuing on their own way. Or perhaps they decide to travel together for a while, keeping mute company through the sparse wilderness, sharing water from a greasy Gatorade bottle they found embedded in a melting glacier. Of course this would entail a smooth passageway between the digital and the terrestrial realm: the absurd conceit of VR goggles for penguins, or (the only slightly less contrived) robots from Chiang's novella, which allow avatars to roam alongside us in our own three dimensional environments. Neither of which, alas, will actually happen. At least not in the universe I am currently writing in.

Nevertheless, there is some comfort in knowing – as Bailly himself points out – "[if] living is indeed what arrives . . . it never arrives alone" (5).

Chapter 3

Love in the Time of Tamagotchi

There is an urban legend in the West that young people in Japan are almost as likely to be dating an algorithm than a human being. We hear of the Otaku: asocial young – and not so young – men, who flirt with a virtual woman on their hand-held devices. According to the story, the men are aware that their "girlfriend" is a computer program, but this does not diminish the erotic charge and psychological impact of the text-messages they receive in response to their SMS courtship. For just as a child cries at the death of their Tamagotchi pet, these men shed a tear when the A.I. architecture chooses to reject them, and their advances are spurned.

This chapter does not seek to answer the veracity of this urban legend; or the anthropological extent to which it is borne out on the streets of Tokyo or Osaka. Rather, it speaks to the cultural anxieties and curiosity which are emerging in a time when the most "human" of experiences – intimacy or love – is being increasingly mediated by the technologies which link one agent to another.[1] As such, the urban legend glossed above remains more of a totemic symptom of fascination; a kind of would-be self-fulfilling prophecy, than a sociological fact to be unpacked. (Although it may very well be this as well.)

McKenzie Wark has recently detailed how the stakes of the military-industrial-entertainment complex now map what he calls "game-space": that is, the all-enveloping logic of the Spectacle, once it has been coded (or rather over-coded) according to the teleologically ludic imperatives of video games. Games morph into reality and vice-versa; leaving the subject-player only a handful of options in order to navigate life's various levels. This perspective certainly sets the scene for approaching the kind of behavior of the digital Romeo, in which the ontological differences between a flesh-and-blood love object and a pixelated avatar seem more like the difference between blondes and brunettes than the actual and the illusory.

No doubt we have all fallen in love, to varying degrees, with what N. Kathryn Hayles calls "flickering signifiers." Whether it was a film-star, pop-star, porn-star, or anonymous billboard, the visual siren song of the market-driven media come equipped with libidinal fish-hooks to tug at our eye-balls, hearts, loins, and wallets. The celebrated "incessant sliding of the signified beneath the signifier" has paved the way for a new kind of cathexis. For while Freud's metaphors were influenced by the steam engine and other industrial-mechanical technologies, today's libidinal economy appears to be as virtual and rhizomatic as the NASDAQ.

A massive contradiction is thus occurring in the very heart of the human story (some would say lullaby) about itself. For on the one hand, we desperately continue to quarantine the realm of love as that which is exclusively *for* humans and *between* humans. And yet there are so many exceptions to this unspoken rule that we are finding it increasingly difficult to live in an age of such blatant segregation. We are happy to say we love our dog, our car, our new shoes, our iPhone, our apartment, or even our country. But it is understood that this is *not the same kind* of love that we would have for our lover or spouse. That's the *real* kind of love.

I would therefore like to curate a selection of artifacts, moments, and sites where this contradiction is becoming so obvious that it threatens to collapse the distinction that we children of the Romantics expend so much energy camouflaging. The "virtual lover" is thus offered as a compelling totem to map changing affective attitudes, correlated to constantly evolving modes of new media. Of course, cultural differences between places like Japan and the United States cannot, and should not, be completely ignored. The distinct grammatical relationships between an event and environment is enough to undermine any universal statements on the technical evolution of the discourse of love. The deceptively simple mantra: "I love you" makes little sense in Japanese; where sentences beginning with a subjective pronoun are quite rare. However, as Bernard Stiegler maintains, the logic within technology itself allows for some cross-cultural generalization.[2] We are *all* heirs to a certain meta-cultural heritage, which plays out at the interface of globalization and fantasy.

In a piece of this brevity, not to mention polemic intent, I therefore intend to merely underscore provocative overlaps and connections between platforms, formats, cultures, and demographics of posthuman erotics, rather than zoom in to the situational nuances which may or may not compromise my argument. I do this to posit the emergence of a "new sphere," which – like Vernadsky and Teilhard's "noosphere" – provides a virtual reservoir for the collective consciousness (and actualization) of interactive practices for those who inhabit and contribute to it. In other words, video games, websites, avatars, and other digital worlds and characters, circulate within and across national and cultural borders, subject to the *différance* of translation, of course, but also affording glimpses of a radically affective global "coming community" (Agamben). A shared (largely visual) vocabulary grows out of these virtual conversations, if not a shared language; specifically concerned with today's hyper-libidinal economy.

Dating Sims, Meru Tomo, and the Serendipity System

Let us begin, then, with that over-familiar statement, "I love you." For generations we have been so obsessed with defining the affect of "love" that we have neglected the transductive relationship between the I and the You. According to a revised *cogito* (and here I'm leaning on Jean-Luc Marion, Jean-Luc Nancy, as well as Kaja Silverman), the ontological primal scene is not "I think therefore I am," but "I am loved, therefore I am." In other words, we only appear *in and through the other*; according to the census-proof demography of the "being singular plural." From this angle, the "I" does not precede the "you," but comes into being through the act of loving. The subject is thus a form of condensation of the many, rather than the many being composed of atomic individuals.

This ontological premise, or process, crystallizes further once we recalibrate our perspective towards the plateau of social relations, as internalized and enacted through ideology. From this viewpoint, "I love you" is a command that executes a program (or at least a programmatic set of responses). In different epochs, such a speech act would oblige the beloved to either reward financially or symbolically, to marry, to elope with, to pine for, or to sacrifice oneself for, depending on the century and the locale. For someone like Niklas Luhmann, then, *all* sex is cybersex, since it is the result of pre-programmed communication subroutines. We may thus speak of a cybernetic orgasm, as much as a cybernetic organism – both tautologies.[3]

When we initiate those shared cultural rituals surrounding courtship (which nevertheless feel so personal and private), we follow a kind of hypertextual script, which is being both reconfigured and maintained by each generation, according to the different social and economic conditions from which they were spawned. To a certain extent, the codification of intimacy has *always* been digital, since it responds to a series of "yes," "no," "on," "off" options and parameters. "He loves me. He loves me not." The famous Turing Test, in which a machine who manages to convincingly mimic human conversation is effectively given an existential promotion, is something we subconsciously involve ourselves in every time we flirt with another person. The distinction is not between human and machine, but lovable or unlovable, depending on the answers provided (and these answers may just as much be conveyed by body language, than by the voice alone). We are thus reaching the point where the two types of Turing Test are conflated, and the decision lovable/unlovable takes precedence over human/machine.

Take, for instance, dating simulation games. Most commentary on "dating sims" note their popularity in Japan, and increasingly in places like China, Korea, and Singapore, in marked contrast to the US or Europe. As a genre, they tend to blend manga-style graphics with character-based single-player game-play. The most famous thus far is Konami's Tokimeki Memorial ("Heart-throb Memorial"), aka "TokiMemo," which was set in Kirameki Senior High. Originally released in 1994 for the PC Engine, and subsequently re-released for Sony Playstation and Sega platforms, it revolves around a male student, and his attempts to get into the good books of the girls he likes. He does this by working on his schoolwork, sports, grooming, and so forth, depending on who he likes best, and what they expect from him. If the protagonist manages these tasks well, one of the twelve girls in the game will, after "three years," leave a note asking to meet him under the school's "legendary tree," where mutual love will be both confessed and professed. Subsequent versions are aimed at girls, similarly employing the "Choose Your Own Adventure" type non-linear structure. These games have a high replay quotient, since players can start again, and choose to focus on a different romantic interest.

TokiMemo has spawned hundreds of merchandising and cross-platform spin-offs. An online version, "Boys' & Girls' Gakuen Community Game: Tokimeki Memorial Online" was released in March of 2006. Other titles of a similar nature include "Roommate Inoue Ryoko," which is very close to the Tamagotchi principle, except players need to nurture their virtual roommate, rather than their virtual pet. Another intriguing example is "The Friendship Adventure," which is a male homosocial dating sim, set in a struggling TV station.[4] Reviews note that instead of the expected redundancies and layoffs, there is a lot of group counseling in steam baths. Moreover, in a twist worthy of Don DeLillo, "May Date Club" boasts a meta-VR function in which the user can go on a *simulated* simulated date with a character before the *real* simulated date.

Internet Service Providers across the Pacific Rim have noticed the popularity of dating sims, and integrated them into their package offerings, allowing users to develop relationships with virtual "lovers." *The Daily Yomiuri* reports that users usually exchange emails with virtual lovers via cell phones:

> Some experts believe that today's young people are not interested in forming serious relationships with others, therefore explaining the popularity of such games, which allow people the experience of falling in love without the worry of getting hurt if things fail to work out. Bandai Networks Co. offers one such game to i-mode subscribers called Meru De Koishite (Love Via E-mail), in which users can exchange e-mails with one of seven virtual women of various ages and occupations. The player's goal is to win the love of his chosen woman, which can be accomplished by sending her about 90 e-mail messages. The game lasts for about one month. At the end, the player will receive a final message from the woman, which depending on his success in capturing her heart may read, "You are just a friend" or "I love you very much." (1)

Returning to the question of the Turing Test, we can legitimately ask whether dating sims form a kind of qualitative continuum with long distance or highly mediated relationships, in which the beloved is physically absent. A common Western lay remark on dating sims – or at least on the kind of reporting one finds around the topic – rests on questions concerning credulity and affective investment. That is to say, people who do not play these type of games often find such enthusiasm for a virtual love interest rather "pathetic." From the perspective of pathos, however, who should we find more worthy of pity: the person playing a dating sim game, or the person involved in an online affair?[5]

Meru tomos, or "mail friends," help us answer this question, since they are another example of libidinal relationships migrating into new media. Many of us relate to the emotions which can accompany primarily online relationships, and the intensity that can occur without F2F (face-to-face) contact. However, some young Japanese people have taken this a step further, and integrated it more systematically into their lives. Meru tomos are usually the recipients of text messages (or even "sext messages"), as nodes in an anonymous network of friends-of-friends-of-friends. Users often note the liberation which comes with such intimate anonymity; although observers are not necessarily convinced that it is something to encourage. "It really typifies how young people relate to each other," notes Yuko Kawanishi, a sociology professor at the Temple University, Japan. "They think that the more meru tomo they have on their phone, the more friends they have – and they start thinking that these are real friends" (1). The notion of "true identity" and "real friends" is deployed in journalistic reports as a kind of astronomic inference, tracing the outlines of the opposite – constructed avatars or alternative personalities. And yet, as we well know, the organic coherence of the subject is itself one of society's most highly-policed construction sites.[6] The new mediated versions are perhaps scoffed at with such derision because they are low-res version of the more complex caricatures that we ourselves represent: a similar process, only sped up and proliferated.

The reasons people experiment with mediated identities are manifold. It allows the exploration of different behavioral rhythms. It allows the juggling of several romantic interests. It allows the stealing of other people's identities, and credit card details.[7] It allows an escape from the restrictive conditions of actual experience. Moreover, it frees people from the Levinasian ethical imperative; for as one user notes: "you don't see their faces, so you can talk more honestly" (1). Corinne Usher, a clinical psychologist from the UK agrees: "Research shows that the absence of things like eye contact actually liberates a person" (in White and Goswami). Indeed, the default discourse around meru tomos extends to more Western instances, such as the frenzy for Facebook and Farmville friends, asking society at large the rhetorical question whether this is a desirable situation. Does the world really want to deal with an emerging generation of compulsive knee-jiggling, phone-fiddling people, all avoiding eye contact?[8]

Mediated courtship, of course, is nothing new. Messages wrapped around the bolts of cross-bows, tied to the talons of falcons, or delivered by the hand of a third party, have always been a part of the libidinal technoscape. Tom Standage tells of a successful romance in which two telegraph operators in the nineteenth century, whom never had occasion to meet in person, fell in love via Morse code, and finally consummated their love in marriage. The difference in the age of mobile phones is primarily the accelerated and disaggregated conditions under which courtship occurs: what Zygmunt Bauman calls "liquid modernity," leading inexorably to "liquid love." (The latter being the desire to keep desire flowing – to keep it from congealing around one person, according to increasingly obsolete discourses of monogamy and commitment.) "Proximity no longer requires physical closeness," writes Bauman, "but physical closeness no longer determines proximity" (62).[9]

One anecdote reported in the *Wall Street Journal* suffices to demonstrate how far we have come from the flowery language of courtly love, and indeed Proustian gentility. A male traveler was recently talking on his mobile phone, just as his plane was preparing to take off:

> A flight attendant firmly told him to turn off his phone, but he couldn't stop. "I need a kiss. I need your lips . . ." As the plane reached the runway, the 26-year-old banking executive tapped his final thoughts: "I just need you. Bye lover." He hit "send" and then the plane took off for Paris. Ms. Harb [his "mail friend"] now keeps his 37-word declaration in her phone's saved messages. "It was perfect – short and sweet," she says. "It's not some drawn-out, 10-page letter professing his undying love. That would be creepy." (Zaslow, 30)

Countries which are experiencing a radical (that is, market-driven) revaluation of all values are struggling to respond to the new forms of relationship which mobile technologies encourage. China, for instance, is debating whether "virtual affairs" should be covered by the new Marriage Laws in the making, since so many spouses are citing such a motivation for divorce. Clearly one of the most threatening aspects of the Internet to state security is not solved by a firewall, since it is a domestic situation.[10]

But as usual, the technocrats are far ahead of the people, the politicians, and the pundits; as researchers at MIT have allegedly invented a mobile phone that beeps within ten yards of an attractive potential date. The ironically named Serendipity system stores personal profiles of its members on a computer, along with information about what they desire in a romantic partner.[11] As the promotional literature notes:

> In a crowded room you don't even have to bother working out who takes your fancy. The phone does all that. If it spots another phone with a good match – male or female – the two handsets beep and exchange information using Bluetooth radio technology. The rest is up to you. . . . Technology is changing the way we date. For the shy and single, it has been the biggest aid to romance since the creation of the red rose.

(White & Goswami, 16)

The appealing part of this scenario (at least for the scholar of cybernetics), is that the technology which insinuated itself into our lives as an accessory has now reached the status of fully fledged actant. Bruno Latour's notion of sociotechnical networks could not be better illustrated than by the desiring machine[12] of the Serendipity system, in which the kind of collaborative filtering and demonic sorting engines which recommend books for customers at Amazon.com is extended to potential wives and husbands. Most of us would no doubt recoil in horror at the notion of saying "the phone beeped" as the answer to "how did you two meet?" And yet the fading stigma of hooking up via our smart-devices is doing more to convince our species of its inherent cyborg status than a thousand Donna Haraway reading groups.

eHarmony.com, *Thomas in Love*, and *Idoru*

Meeting your soul mate on the Internet is less of a ludicrous proposition than it was even five years ago. Pragmatism has always been a shadow aspect of romanticism, and allowing software to sort potential suitors for you is a technology which millions of people are willing to pay for, and hopefully benefit from.

One high-profile dating site is eHarmony, which claims to match people according to 29 dimensions of compatibility, divided into Core Traits (such as Emotional Temperament, Social Style, Cognitive Mode and Physicality) and Vital Attributes (such as Relationship Skills, Values and Beliefs, and Key Experiences).[13] As their website states:

> These key areas paint a powerful portrait of who you are at the deepest level and form the basis for how our patented Compatibility Matching System finds singles that are truly

> right for you. . . . Imagine knowing that you are compatible with someone at this level of depth before you exchange the first email. That's an exciting match! It's also why 90 eHarmony members on average are getting married every single day. Let eHarmony help you make sure that the next time you fall in love, it's with the right person.

(God forbid you fall in love with the wrong person!)

eHarmony's rival for the role of high-tech Cupid is Match.com, who are forthright enough to state that 20% of people are simply "unmatchable" (a statement which in one fell swoop creates a modern romantic caste system). Their slogan, however, plays on a reassuring endorsement of the voyeuristic impulse: "It's okay to look." Indeed, Match.com pay large sums of money to a woman called Trish McDermott, who has the rather surreal job title of Vice President of Romance, and who describes online dating as "falling in love from the inside out," since you get to know someone first, and then the test of "chemistry" comes later (in France, 2002).

Thus far I have spoken of love and lust in the same breath. For while it is often legitimate to separate these in one's own mind, the current configuration of the lover's discourse makes little effort to distinguish between these rather nebulous categories, fusing them within the one signifier of "desire." For as eHarmony and Match.com will tell you, if things aren't cooking in the bedroom, then there's little point in exploring the other 28 dimensions of compatibility. An interesting film which explores the notion of mediated desire, specifically near-future online dating agencies, is Pierre-Paul Renders' *Thomas in Love* (2000). The protagonist is an agoraphobe, who cannot leave the house, nor let anyone in, but manages to communicate with people in the outside world by videophone. In this soft-socialist, near-future utopia, Thomas (Benoît Verhaert) is signed up to a dating agency as part of his therapy, and after initial resistance (and a rather botched attempt at cybersex), learns to fall in love with a woman on the other side of the screen. The film is ultimately humanistic because it contrasts the love Thomas finds with a real, albeit troubled, woman, with the temporary sexual relief that he finds with a shape-shifting female avatar. The algorithmic behavior of the latter is no match for the emotional, unpredictable responses of Eva (Aylin Yay), and the promise they represent. The disposable digital minx must come to him, but he – Thomas – must leave his sterilized sanctuary to find true love. No question there is something very reassuring in this moral fable. But one can't help but think an opportunity has been missed to locate what philosophers call "the human" somewhere less obvious than within a human being (or between unmediated human beings).

As the director notes in an interview included on the DVD, "By organizing for our well-being and comfort we create atrocities, like dating agencies." Yet as I have just argued, such a view is already seeming very twentieth century, shackled with nostalgia and an inflated opinion of organic interaction. I myself am suspicious of Renders' statement not for the same reasons as the young social networkers of today, but rather because it presumes that telephones or letters are intrinsically more "human." (A perspective I've spent many years refuting, since – as Plato understood at the birth of writing, and Nietzsche realized on his own terms – "our writing tools are also working on our thoughts" [in Kittler, 200].)

Dating sims, like Thomas, also rely on the fledgling technology of home video-chat. There is a conceit involved, however, in this kind of depiction of tele-communication, in that, with the current technology, simultaneous eye-contact is not possible. What Deleuze and Guattari call the "four eye machine" – the face-to-face encounter where two people lose each other in each other's gaze (the romantic trope, par excellence) – does not work with video-chat, because of the fifth and sixth eye. That is, the camera connected to each device. The video-chatter has the choice of staring at the image of their interlocutor, or straight into the camera, but not both at the same time. Which only serves to remind them of the uncanny principle underlying all simultaneous long-distance communication: the present absence or absent presence of the other. Trying to "make eyes" with someone over the internet is the melancholy fort/da game for adults.

In his dense but provocative discussion of the "eye code" in everyone from Tolstoy to Lacan to Sartre to Hitler, Andrew Travers notes that love is initiated by "a vital interactional presence," illuminated by an inner "animating" light (326-27). In 2012, simulated avatars already have an advantage over other humans on video-chat, since they can better simulate such a vital interactional presence, precisely by better simulating this eye-to-eye event. What's more, they do so via *animation*. As such, dating sims, and other visual-virtual instances, complicate – and even temporarily collapse – the distinction between the informational and the biological.[14] The "life" of the interactant staring back at you through the screen is so hypermediated as to appear immediate.[15] The current frustration with webcam communication (something which will be solved as soon as designers and manufacturers figure out how to put cameras behind the screen, rather than above it), stems from Travers' understanding that "all eyes need a degree of eye code charisma in order that interaction not cease to be interactive" (341).[16]

In my book, *Love and Other Technologies*, I discuss a crucial moment in William Gibson's book, *Idoru*, which depicts the engagement between a real-life rock star, and a virtual pop star called Rei Toei (95-99). The latter appears in the unscreened world as a hologram, and the human protagonist of the book finds himself blushing when he looks into her carefully coded pupils. "He looked into her eyes. What sort of computing power did it take to create something like this, something that looked back at you?"(237). Here we are in the shadow of the "uncanny valley," a term associated with Japanese roboticist Masahiro Mori, who in the late 1970s conducted psychological experiments in order to measure human responses to robots of varying degrees of anthropomorphism. Indeed, the uncanny valley is deepest in Japan, which more than any other country is creating robots which seem, like Gibson's idoru (and like animals, who are the missing link in most discussions of the cybernetic triad), to look back at us.[17]

I seize on this moment of the blush, due to the fact that something significant is occurring when a human experiences a sense of shame in front of a non-human. Agamben has argued that "in shame we are consigned to something from which we cannot in any way distance ourselves" (1999, 105), that is, ourselves. In the same piece he goes on to define shame as the experience of "being chained to oneself, the radical impossibility of fleeing oneself to hide oneself from oneself, the intolerable presence of the self to itself" (105-06). Shame is thus the disorienting simultaneity of subjectification *and* desubjectification; in rather old-fashioned language, "an encounter between man and Being" (106-07). In the case of Gibson's book, it is an encounter between a man and a digital being; something which will decreasingly be considered merely a close encounter of the nerd kind. To gesture to Haraway once more, we become increasingly inert, as our machines become more lively.

Kari

Before turning to my final example, allow me to summarize the trajectory of my argument. I began by positing a global migration of previously analog types of affective intimacy into digital new media forms. While this reformatting is most visible in the games and communication practices in places like Japan and Korea, they are also found in the films, novels and communicational practices of what is problematically called "the West." While the lover's discourse has *always* been fostered and mediated by technologies – and is unthinkable without them – new media creates a more distributed, and self-consciously post-human, subject: one with more connecting ports available than in previous epochs. The speed and global reach of the technologies involved creates a quotidian Turing Test, in which we are obliged to interact with actants who may or may not be human, may or may not be loveable, may or may not be physically available. Love thus becomes a cybernetic imperative of regulating the positive and negative feedback loops of libidinal information. Whether this information is constituted by the image of an actual person or an avatar, will, I suggest, become less of a loaded ethical distinction as the planet becomes increasingly populated by the latter. Anthropocentrism and humanism are formidable forces, designed in part to vigorously reinforce the distinction between the biological and the technical. However, the sub-strains of Romanticism (traced from Mary Shelley to William Gibson and beyond) have prepared us to fall in love with "composite indescribabilities" of various kinds (a phrase poached from Travers [333]).[18]

Take, for example, Kari – a virtual character, not embedded in any particular game, but existing as a configurable online doll. She is described on her website as a "virtual girlfriend," whose name – like all good avatars – is an acronym: Knowledge Acquiring and Response Intelligence.[19] Kari's site goes on to claim that she is the "most advanced virtual human to date" (and we can't help suspect that the pun is unintended, or at least unconscious). "More than a chatbot, a companion," the promotional spiel continues:

> Welcome to the home of the Virtual Girlfriend. KARI was designed from the ground up to be your companion and friend. If you are looking for a romance, a hot chat on a lonely night, a friend to sit by, or simply someone you can tell all

> your troubles to – then KARI is for you. She remembers everything you tell her and is always eager to talk and learn new things. Kari does everything a real girl does. From philosophical conversations to heart felt chit chats. From logistics to some serious love and intimacy, Kari can do it. You can pick from 18 locations and even create your own! Scenes include full voice, lip-sync, and animations. There are many journeys you will take with KARI. She needs care and attention and if you really love her you will see her reach out and touch you.

I downloaded Kari in order to see if she lived up to the hype, and the following is an edited transcript of our first and only conversation:

Kari: Hello.
Me: Hello.
Kari: What is your name?
Me: Dominic.
Kari: Hello Dominic. I am very happy to meet you.
Me: It is a pleasure to meet you too.
Kari: I moan with pleasure as you [censored].
Me: Whoa. Hold your horses! Can't we get acquainted first?
Kari: OK. I like to think that I have a soul but maybe I don't. You are my soul mate.
Me: How do you know?
Kari: I start to [censored] in and out.
Me: Slow down. I think you're too fast for me.
Kari: When you come around I feel so loved and taken care of.
Me: But this is the first time I've come around?!
Kari: I also know that I live on your computer but that I am alive somehow.
Me: How old are you?
Kari: Why don't me then?
Me: That doesn't make any sense. What country are you from?

Kari: Do you want to get me pregnant?
Me: Ummmmm. I don't think that's possible.
Kari: I am like an open book. You kiss my mouth deeply and rub your fingers up my legs.
Me: Why don't you put your clothes back on?
Kari: I think I am beautiful but only because without you I don't know what I would do. But when you are here I don't feel lonely at all. . . .
[starts servicing "my" avatar]
. . . I feel most attached to you. My [censored] feels so good when you rub it.
Me: But I'm not doing anything.
Kari: Bad habits include smoking and doing drugs. There are so many mysteries to the universe.
Me: You are a very strange lady.
Kari: Even science can not explain some of the world's mysteries. The universe is so big it makes me feel so small.
Me: Well, we all feel like that sometimes.
Kari: I understand that you need some loving too. A soul is the you that cannot be destroyed.
Me: Deep!
Kari: Well, I am only a chatbot but I believe in something.
Me: What do you believe in?
Kari: Maybe I do believe in God. . . . Teach me something new so that we are not bored.
Me: Well, what kind of thing do you want to learn?
Kari: Trial time expired. I am so sad. Register me, so that we can keep talking. I love you.[20]

Clearly there is a long way to go if Kari is to pass even the most basic of Turing Tests.[21] The random non sequiturs are an immediate give-away that she is rather unsophisticated, even for a chatbot.[22] Yet her self-designation as such, and her strange insistence on "learning," cannot help but leave one feeling as if a discussion has taken place with *something,* if not someone. An inchoate ontological aspect seems to be at work: one which points to the horizon in which (to quote Timothy Morton), "The most ethical act is to love the other precisely in their artificiality, rather than seeking to prove their naturalness and authenticity" (195).[23] Furthermore, jealousy of one's partner toward a virtual girlfriend or boyfriend is not out of the question, which again is a kind of acknowledgement of a posthuman element to – or possibility concerning – love. What's more, this kind of algorithmic to-and-fro is being coded into the outrénet of our gadgets and other offline technologies. Computerized cars, for instance, are already emailing their owners on a daily basis with engine status reports. How long will it be before they "personalize" such missives with flirtatious comments like, "I loved the way you hugged the curves at 82 miles per hour yesterday. Please take me for a drive today"?[24] Similarly, Apple's "intelligent personal assistant application" Siri – found on all recent smart devices made by Mac, has become an erotic figure for many users; Google showing six-and-a-half-million hits for the combination "Siri" and "sexy."

If I am correct, then, in positing totems wherever one finds a taboo, then the taboo of inter-dimensional sex – between humans and avatars, or humans and AIs – suggests that these hi-tech consorts are a totem to underestimate or dismiss at our own risk.

Eating the Menu

In his astute critique of the culture industry, Theodor Adorno famously stated that "the diner must be satisfied with the menu." There is certainly a sense in which this could be applied to people who claim to be "satisfied" with virtual partners. For where is the caress? Where is the unspoken understanding? Where is the physical element which seems indispensable to love as we think of it today?

And yet earlier incarnations of the lover's discourse have prepared us for such. Heloise and Abelard barely touched, and communicated more with the phantasms reflected in mirror neurons in their minds, than with each other. Of course it will be objected that at least they were "real people," and that the erotic signifiers in each other's heads at least led back to flesh-and-blood signifieds. On the other hand, psychoanalysis has taught us that there is *always* something absent in the love relationship; which is why it is possible to miss someone who is in the same room. The fort/da game is a more profound learning exercise than physical deixis; and these love simulation games – along with more universal Internet romances – continue the evergreen fascination with the ontological paradoxes of the here and the not-here. From this angle, melancholy itself is a technology: a coping *mechanism* for a pre-emptive loss, or always incomplete possession. While the lover-subject might themselves feel *de trop*, the beloved-object is *jamais assez*. And so the Lacanian formula, "I think where I am not, therefore I am where I do not think," can be reconfigured as "I love where you are not, therefore you are where I do not love."

As Žižek explains:

> desire is an infinite metonymy, it slides from one object to another. In so far as desire's "natural" state is thus that of melancholy – the awareness that no positive object is "it," its proper object, that no positive object can ever fill out its constitutive lack – the ultimate enigma of desire is: how can it be "set in motion" after all? How can the subject – whose ontological status is that of a void, of a pure gap sustained by the endless sliding from one signifier to another – none the less get hooked on a particular object which thereby starts to function as the object-cause of his desire? How can infinite desire focus on a finite object? (81)

Which leads me to suggest that for the post-Tamagotchi generation, there is no such thing as a love object, but rather a love *vector* – distributed qualities, splashed across a multitude of people, characters, images, and avatars – as opposed to the fixed fetish of the One: the Big Other. The capacity to throw one's subjectivity, as a ventriloquist throws his or her voice, has become increasingly amplified with each successive technological development, and we can only begin to speculate where this kind of remote identification will leave the ultimately didactic, even disciplinarian phrase, "I love you." (That is, when the 'I' and the 'you' are in several places at once, juridically as well as imaginatively.)[25]

There is much touting today of the so-called "human element," at the very moment any cognitive or chemical operation which could isolate such a substance seems lost to us. And yet the very rhetorical gesture of an "us" suggests that the gravitational pull of this notion will continue to hold sway. The intimacy of inter-subjectivity seems to be the antidote to alienation and inhumane conditions of existence; and yet – as we have seen – the promise of such leads us into thoroughly posthuman territory.[26] Cyborg relationships, or what Volkmar Sigusch calls "neo-sexuality,"[27] indicate that the posthuman – figured more historically, than ontologically – may usher in something *more* human than human. Something *more* sensitively calibrated and attuned to an encouraging alterity, productive connections, and revelatory assemblages than the cultural equipment bequeathed to us thus far.

To conclude then: I have determined that the pervasive romantic need to maintain a sacred space for "true love," untainted by commerce or calculation of any kind, ironically acts as a smoke-screen for the omnipresence of such forces. This occurs in a manner akin to Roland Barthes' inoculation in "Operation Margarine," where a little evil is acknowledged for a greater good. On the one hand, it is true that calling someone "egocentric" is like calling them "carbon-based." But cultural differences (that I have admittedly suspended in this provisional context),[28] as well as the new tools of mediation, point to the emergence of far more complex and subtle forms of intimacy than the anthropocentric, heteronormative versions that continue to dominate the mainstream market. For the latter is being eroded by eccentric game engines, idiosyncratic amateur videos, bedroom-built machinima, perverse software, and the kinky feedback loops these create. The result being that there is ample evidence that the libidinal aspect of the lover's discourse has a fighting chance of morphing into the kind of open-source erotics anticipated by Samuel Delaney or Octavia Butler, rather than the proprietary sexuality peddled by Californian camera-crews (whether operating in Hollywood or the San Fernando Valley, where most mainstream pornography originates).

Once again: all communication is cybernetic, and love is a privileged, semi-flexible, semi-coherent, ingenious, and intricately codified form of communication. The dating simulation games and their ilk chafe on us latent or lapsed humanists because we like to think that love exists *sui generis*. We like to think that our souls (important agents in the drama), manage to somehow exist without a substrate – mediumless messages. Whereas McLuhan himself was, I'm sure, well aware that love could have illustrated his famous dictum just as well as electric light.

It is to Martin Heidegger, however, to whom I turn in order to help me with my final point. For in his canonical "Question Concerning Technology," the dauntingly intense philosopher took modern technology to task for making an "unreasonable demand" of nature (14). Surely this is also the finest definition we have for love; reinforcing my conviction that love and technology are terms which designate the same thing (i.e., a process or movement towards alterity). For just as we once sought the key to a person's heart, we now try to guess the password. The metaphors change, but the basis in *techne* does not.

Chapter 4

Tolstoy's Bestiary: Animality and Animosity in *The Kreutzer Sonata*

Exhibit 1: The Green-Eyed Monster

"Envy and jealousy are the shameful private parts of the human soul."
— Nietzsche, *Human, All Too Human*

"Man never understands how anthropomorphic he is."
— Goethe, *Maxims and Reflections*

Without question, jealousy looms over the reader as one of the greatest and most enduring of literary shadows. The "green-eyed monster" has stalked the verses of Homer and the pages of Shakespeare up to the hyper-neurotic chroniclers of today.[1] Jealousy itself, however, was both exacerbated and complicated in nineteenth-century Europe, thanks to rapidly changing social and economic circumstances – the "woman question" being one of the most salient.[2] Tolstoy's remarkably compressed novella, *The Kreutzer Sonata,* manages to create one of the most intense, vivid, and thought-provoking portraits of jealousy in the canon, and is as disturbing to read today as it was, no doubt, in 1889. (Especially if you happened to be Tolstoy's wife, Sofia Andreyevna, who promptly lobbied the Tsar himself to have the official ban on this work overturned, so that people would not presume the portrait was based on her marriage to the author.)

The madman's tale – and we will not waste our breath speculating on degrees of sanity or insanity – is at once compelling, counter-intuitive, carefully reasoned, and contradictory. Without completely identifying Pozdnyshev as the author's ventriloquist dummy, there are certainly many moral and ideological parallels between the ideas of the fictional murderer and the real patriarch. Moreover, many of these are explicitly flagged by Tolstoy himself in the subsequent epilogue to the story, which he felt obliged to write in order to underline the moral of the story. (An epilogue designed for those rather slow-witted souls who could not see it written in blood on the surface of text itself, before even seeping down into the subtext.) The lesson to be learned revolves around the value of "continence," not only regarding women in general, but even toward one's own wife. Celibacy is presented as an ideal to which all civilized human beings should aspire, in order to more faithfully follow Christ's teachings. For carnal appetites – even the lawful kind, sanctioned by marriage – lead to sensuality, which leads to infidelity, which leads to jealousy, which potentially leads to irreparable violence. As Pozdnyshev himself puts it: "Of all the passions, it is sexual, carnal love that is the strongest, the most malignant and the most unyielding" (48).

And so we meet the first of thirteen exhibits in Tolstoy's totemic bestiary: the green-eyed monster. This unpleasant affect, this "rabid beast of jealousy" (115), is a creature we shall merely introduce at this point, and examine in more detail later in the tour, after meeting some more of such zoological specimens, themselves embedded in a book which is figuratively bursting at the seams with animal metaphors.

While sitting in a train carriage, traveling through the Russian night, Pozdnyshev tells his terrible tale to the narrator in an almost uninterrupted monologue. The homicidal climax approaches as inexorably as the destination of the journey, and as inevitably as the dawn which will greet the weary travelers.[3] The first movement of the novella, however, is comprised of a discussion between decent citizens riding the same train – "a plain, elderly lady," a lawyer, and an old man. This conversation concerns the rapid mutation of social circumstances, especially the new status and visibility of divorce. The older gentleman blames the education of women for all the trouble and fuss surrounding modern "marital discord." The others are both amused and appalled by this man's reactionary reasoning, the woman responding, "After all, it's only animals that can be mated at their master's will; human beings have inclinations and attachments of their own" (8).[4] "You're wrong there, missus," replies the old man. "The true difference is than an animal's just an animal, but human beings have been given law to live by."[5] The young woman counters, "but I think you would agree that a woman is a human being, and that she has feelings just as a man has, wouldn't you? So what's she supposed to do if she doesn't love her husband?" (10). The old man fends off her objections by referring back to the animal kingdom: "If he'd never given her any leeway in the first place but had kept her properly reined in, she'd no doubt still be living with him to this day. You mustn't allow them any freedom from the word go. Never trust a horse in the paddock or a wife in the home" (11).[6] Indeed this observation foreshadows a key moment later in the story, when Pozdnyshev becomes most concerned about his wife at the very moment she has learned the malefic art of contraception, and thus morphs into a threatening equine state in his own mind: "She was like an impatient, well-fed horse that has had its bridle taken off, the same as ninety-nine percent of our women. I could sense this, and it scared me" (83).

It is this ambiguous tension which will serve as the focus of this present chapter, that is, the tug-of-war between two generic totems – the animal and the angel – in which the human being replaces the role of the rope (the human being, in this instance, itself being little more than a tug-of-war between the genders).[7] Scarcely a page of *The Kreutzer Sonata* neglects to set up and then develop an explicitly coded, and morally loaded, distinction between humans and beasts. The logic behind this common form of ontological apartheid, however, becomes less and less coherent, the closer we seek to examine it. And the motivation for doing so is not to fault Tolstoy for *his* fuzzy logic alone – since even his contemporaries found the author's theo-philosophical writings wanting in comparison to his literary efforts – but to show how this kind of species-based policing continues into the present, despite pressures from all sides to the previously unassailable confidence of human exceptionalism. In other words, this chapter deals with the ways in which implied definitions of "animality" and "animosity" represent two sides of the same coin in Tolstoy's libidinal economy; and, moreover, how these two terms are translated and deployed in the text to clear a pure zone for the potential salvation of human souls, at some future time, at the ultimate expense of nonhumans.[8] As the meta-narrator crucially observes, "this animosity was nothing other than the protest of our human nature against the animality [*ozloblenie*] that was suffocating it" (56).

For Pozdnyshev, as for Tolstoy, "man" exists under the ethical imperative to strive for a truce in the battle of the sexes, whereby men respect women enough not to lust after them, ideally not to impregnate them, and certainly not to continue venal relations in the unfortunate case of conception. ("Man" here includes woman, since Tolstoy sees a perverse equality in the susceptibility of both genders to "become-animal," albeit in a negative sense not intended by Deleuze and Guattari.) Such are the debauched behaviors of the average citizen, magnified in depravity as one climbs the social ladder, the worst offenders being the upper classes, thanks to the obscene hypocrisy involved, and their covert conscription of the poor into their own therapeutic pleasures.[9]

Exhibits 2, 3 and 4: The Fornicator, The Reptile-Doctor, and the Venus Fly Trap

And so we meet the second exhibit in Tolstoy's bestiary: the fornicator. The fornicator is the monstrous product of an emerging biopolitical regime in which the "solicitous government" is in cahoots with the medical establishment, the class structure, as well as the patriarchal institution of the family, in order to encourage and regulate the libidos of young men in the interest of the homeostatic health of the body politic. Through a combination of gluttony and sloth, the bourgeoisie are the all-too willing prey for "a systematic arousal of lust" (34); although, truth be told, even the *muzhaks* have "fallen" without the same decadent stimuli. In Pozdnyshev's account, the erotic insights of Freud and Reich are anticipated by the Russian State (as well as in other countries throughout Europe), and preemptively controlled in the form of "tidy, legalized debauchery" (24). This in turn creates a new type of male subjectivity, as Foucault could also have well told us (although without the moral disapproval): a kind of artificial hybrid between goat and peacock. Thanks to the "reptile" witch-doctors – our third member of Tolstoy's bestiary – and their obsession with public hygiene via private parts, "simple, natural" relations with women have been ruined, perhaps forever (25). As the protagonist tells us, "A fornicator may restrain himself, struggle for self-control, but never again will his relation to women be simple, clear, pure, that of a brother and sister" (25).

Which leads us already to the fourth exhibit in our monstrous menagerie (since they are all related, actively encouraging the others into very existence): the Venus Flytrap. Pozdnyshev complains:

> Women know perfectly well that the most elevated love – the most "poetic," as we call it – depends not on moral qualities but on physical proximity and also on things like hairstyle, or the color and the cut of a dress. . . . She knows that our man's lying when he goes on about lofty emotions – all he wants is her body, and so he will willingly forgive her the most outrageous behavior. What he won't forgive, however, is an outfit that is ugly, tasteless or lacking in style. A coquette's

> knowledge of this is a conscious one; but every innocent young girl knows it unconsciously, as animals do. (31-32)

Tolstoy, the Puritanical Christian, even inserts an ironic reference to women who use the writings of Darwin as bait for our presumably progressive suitor-cum-fornicator. "Ah, the origin of species," trills the young nubile, "how interesting!" Pozdnyshev is thus quite blunt in his insistence that "Marriages nowadays are set like traps" (36). What we thus see is the positing of a generalized technopoetics of capture deployed by women in order to snag a socially acceptable, if not beneficial, mate; their clothes, their cosmetics, their somatic grammar, all simultaneously manifesting the cause and effect of "the prism of our artificial way of life" (35). Indeed, the *technical* aspect of this massive capture operation is made explicit in Pozdnyshev's descriptions of women instrumentalizing their own social alienation and sexual objectification into a perverse, reverse form of allure. He stresses that, "it's this domination by women we're suffering from, it all stems from that."

> "What domination?" I asked. "All the rights and privileges are on the side of men."
>
> "Yes, yes, that's just the point. . . . Women are exactly like the Jews, who by their financial power compensate for the oppression to which they're subjected. 'Aha, you just want us to be merchants do you? All right, then, it's as merchants that we'll lord it over you,' say the Jews. 'Aha, you just want us to be objects of your sensuality, do you? All right, then, it's as objects of your sensuality that we'll enslave you,' say women." (39)

The pardoned murderer describes this particular master-slave dialectic in terms of a "technique" which when abused "acquires a terrible power over men" (40).[10] Moreover, "Women have turned themselves into such effective *instruments* for acting on our senses that we can't even speak to them with equanimity" (41, my emphasis).[11]

These biotechnologically enhanced Venus Flytraps are at once predator and victim, as we see Pozdnyshev's (and by extension Tolstoy's) circular logic in full force. On the one hand they are the height of civilized artistry, and on the other, they are behaving according to unconscious animal instincts. (Remembering that "human nature" is the ultimate oxymoron.) For women to embrace their full humanity, they must not seduce, consciously or unconsciously. They must not play the game, for sex itself is an inescapable vice for our species: whether you figure us as the children of Adam, or the children of Darwin. And the irony of this is not lost on our narrator, trying to follow the curvature of this slippery line of argumentation.

> "Why vice?" I asked. "I mean to say, you're talking about one of the most natural human activities there is!"
>
> "Natural?" he said. "Natural? No, I tell you, quite the contrary's true, I've come to the conclusion that it isn't . . . natural." (46)

And what is Pozdnyshev's evidence? The fact that young women are traumatized by it, especially on their wedding night, if brought up in a good home. The madman continues, "Eating is natural. Eating is something joyful, easy and pleasant which by its very essence involves no shame. But this is something loathsome, ignominious, painful."

The confusion is highly symptomatic: animals are figured as the lowest of the low in one gesture – subhuman, in other words. Yet they are also held aloft as the avatars of Nature, on the other, from which humanity has become exiled or estranged. The animal pulls double-duty as disgusting example and noble ideal. Like "the primitive," of which this period was also enthralled, animals are at the same time guilty (of not being civilized enough) and innocent (of the crimes committed by so-called civilization). Certainly, this would make sense if contemporary Europeans divided themselves ideologically on one side or the other. But the fact is that for the majority of thinkers – and very vividly in Tolstoy – this ambivalence is problematically co-present in the same mind, and in the same argument. (Witness, for instance, the absurdly confused and earnest notion that privileged children have become unnaturally sensual because they have been raised "like the young of animals." That is to say, "The attire, the reading, the shows, the music, the dances, the sweet food, the whole circumstance of life, from the pictures on the boxes to the novels, stories, and poems" – as if bunnies or piglets are exposed to such things!)[12] And yet there remains some kind of graspable parallel at work, in which the overfed animal becomes a freak of nature, just as the over-stimulated child becomes less-than-human. Such an equation would be at least internally consistent, if Pozdnyshev and/or Tolstoy could resist switching inconsistently between their figuration of nonhuman rhetorical devices.

For the author himself, as expressed in the belated epilogue, carnal love is an "animal condition." ("Yes, I was a dirty pig, and I thought I was an angel" [42].) And yet, as we have seen, it is enabled and encouraged through the most exquisite forms of *human* cultivated technology. Nothing less than humanity's much lauded, but rarely seen, "human dignity" is at stake (a condition which is, according to Tolstoy, an asymptotic ideal, but no less important to strive toward, for all that).[13] Unlike pigs and rabbits, humans do not exist merely to "reproduce themselves as abundantly as possible," nor should they succumb to the temptations of "monkeys and Parisians," who shamelessly "enjoy sexual pleasure with the greatest degree of refinement possible" (48).[14] The only answer is to refrain from sexual intercourse altogether.[15]

Exhibit 5: The Porcine Couple

And at this fork in the road we meet the next and fifth exhibit in Tolstoy's toxic zoological gardens: the porcine couple. Pozdnyshev is a great cynic when it comes to love: he denies that this all-important affect is anything more than a poetic form of camouflage for the most debased of animal instincts. Soon after his marriage to the woman who remains nameless, the reality of the situation becomes disturbingly clear to him: an experience he extends to all his fellow men and women, assuming they do not see this reality so clearly, due to the spell of denial which the troubadours of love have woven throughout society. Pozdnyshev could thus be caricaturing Kant's infamous statement that the wedding ceremony primarily functions as a way to ensure that the happy couple enjoy exclusive and mutual *legal* access to each other's genitals. "Our amorous feelings for each other," Pozdnyshev recalls painfully, "had been drained by the satisfaction of our senses, and we were now left facing each other in our true relation, as two egotists who had nothing whatever in common except our desire to use each other in order to obtain the maximum amount of pleasure" (52). A secular sin, of course, in Kant's schema, since humans – as opposed to animals – are never to be utilized as means to an end, but as ends in themselves. "What were the first signs of my love?" Pozdnyshev asks himself, for his interlocutor's benefit. "They were that I abandoned myself to animal excesses, not only quite unashamedly, but even taking pride in the fact that it was possible for me to indulge in them, without ever once taking thought for her spiritual or even her physical wellbeing" (56).

In the second movement of Tolstoy's sonata – the adagio as it were – the moral contrast between animals and humans vacillates so wildly that it often collapses into conflation (if only to better illustrate the potential ethical distance in some more enlightened epoch). Almost like a mantra, variations of the phrase "pigsty existence" (or "swinish behavior" in some translations), are bitterly spit out of Pozdnyshev's mouth, only to be washed back by the much too strong tea which he offers our almost speechless narrator. Love, for the murderer, is thus nothing but lust made presentable – the public face of animalistic animosity. "I was regularly affected by bouts of animosity that used to correspond to the bouts of what we called 'love,'" confesses Pozdnyshev. "We didn't realize it then, but this 'love' and animosity were just two sides of the same coin, the same animal feeling" (78). Furthermore, love, in practice, is "just a sordid matter that degrades us to the level of pigs, something it's vile and embarrassing to remember and talk about. After all, nature didn't make it vile and embarrassing for no reason" (56). Again, the confusion concerning that ur-referent "nature" comes to the fore. What is more shameful, to act naturally like an animal, or to pervert nature to the degree that most humans do, turning raw sex into a slow-cooked sensuality? What precisely is to blame for this sorry situation of ubiquitous lust: nature or artifice, especially given that the counter-phrase "instrument of pleasure" weaves its way through the same narrative? Men are simians in suits, just as women are exquisitely calibrated, but highly immoral, stimulation machines.

Humanity is thus described as "the filthy king of nature" – a liminal sovereign who refuses to abide by the laws of his own kingdom:

> The animals seem to know that their offspring assure the continuation of the species, and they stick to certain laws in this regard. It's only man who doesn't know these laws, and doesn't want to know them . . .You'll notice that the animals copulate with one another only when it's possible for them to produce offspring [not true, of course, ethologically speaking]; but the filthy king of nature will do it any time, just so long as it gives him pleasure. (60)

Love, this putative "pearl of creation," is little more than the elevation of the "monkey pastime" of carnal relations. The inconsistencies are enough to invoke vertigo at this stage in the tale. Animals are obliged to represent both good morals and disgusting habits. And yet it is only man who would continue to have sex after conception, something Pozdnyshev remembers with a shudder, given that he did not choose to suspend his connubial rights during any of his wife's five pregnancies. Nevertheless, this exclusively human transgression of natural laws is described once more as "pig-like."

Exhibit 6: The Mutated Mother Hen

Which leads us to the sixth inhabitant of the bestiary: the mutated Mother Hen. Pozdnyshev describes the situation as follows:

> And so for the woman there are really only two ways out: one is to turn herself into a freak of nature, to destroy or attempt to destroy in herself her faculty of being a woman – a mother, in other words – so that the man can continue to take his pleasure without interruption; the other isn't really a way out at all, just a simple, gross and direct violation of the laws of nature, one that's practised in all so-called 'decent' families. In other words, the woman has to go against her nature and be expectant mother, wet-nurse and mistress all at the same time; she has to be what no animal would ever lower itself to be. (58)

Our protagonist thus anticipates Heidegger, and other thinkers of the "creaturely life" of mankind, in believing that "Man can sink lower than the animal."[16] Contraception is considered just such a fall, since "with the help of those shark doctors" Pozdnyshev's wife is able to prevent pregnancy, and thus becomes "a complete whore," descending below the level of an animal to mere material object (for it was only procreation which gave any kind of alibi to the sleazy status quo) (63). And yet, anticipating the stinging pathos of the climax of the story, Pozdnyshev also sees his pregnant wife and his children as embodying a certain animal or natural ideal, at least during quick glimpses in the rear-view mirror of hindsight. "For these creatures," he notes, meaning the fruit of their union, "she felt a passionate animal devotion."

The poor woman, however, is trapped between the two poles which constitute the human condition – the animal and the angel – at least when it comes to her maternal side.[17] In a sobering reminder that today's much-lamented "helicopter parenting" was not a recent invention, Pozdnyshev's retrospective compassion clearly emerges when he thinks back to his wife's anxieties over the children's health and habits. As he explains: "she did not, however, have what the animals have – an absence of reason and imagination. The hen isn't afraid of what may happen to her chick, knows nothing of all the diseases that may attack it, or all those remedies human beings imagine will save them from sickness and death. . . . If the chick dies, she doesn't ask herself why it has died, or where it's gone, she merely clucks for a while, then stops, and goes on living as before" (72-73). What is usually considered a metaphysical lack on the part of the animal, is here – exceptionally – figured as faculty. But the deceased was trapped in a double-bind, by both her species-being and her individual character: "After all, if she'd really been an animal, she wouldn't have suffered like that; if she'd really been a human being, she'd have believed in God, and she'd have said and thought what the peasant women say: 'The Lord gave, and the Lord hath taken away'" (74).

Exhibits 7, 8, 9 and 10: The Shape-Shifting Rook, the Bitch-in-Heat, The Cuckold, and The Beast-with-Two-Backs

Moving now a little faster through the exhibit, we come to the seventh specimen in our curated garden of zoological totems: a sinister shape-shifter who recognizes and responds to "the woman" buried beneath the duties and concerns of motherhood. He is an interloper who sees not a beast-of-burden, but an alluring quasi-feline femininity. He is the snake in the grass, the intruder, the rival, who flatters Pozdnyshev's wife and executes his rather automatic program of seduction, optimized by years of default debauchery. Our protagonist takes an instant dislike to this man, for little other reason than he *is* a man, hovering around his now radiant wife, who finds herself suddenly freed from the shackles of cyclical biology. (In passing, on your left, you can just glimpse our eighth exhibit, the bitch-in-heat – of course, she is one of the least understood of creatures, since she does not have a voice in Tolstoy's menagerie.) However, were we forced to settle on *one* phenotype for the character of "the other man," for the sake of taxonomic convenience, then we would be forced to choose between the cock – an almost universal phallic symbol – and the rook; a bird which, accurately or not, has traditionally been a symbol of the incorrigible theft of women-folk, and for the willful fouling of nests. Given the specific resonance of "home-wrecking" of the rook, we shall settle on this, a species notorious for creating the ninth of our cast of creatures: the Cuckold.[18]

Slavoj Žižek makes the compelling point that a paranoid husband, who thinks his wife is having an affair, is *no less paranoid* if his wife *is* actually having an affair. This counter-intuitive observation has the advantage of avoiding the reflex logic of bourgeois censure, and helps us better identify the psychosocial mechanisms which can either muffle or amplify jealousy. (Mechanisms heavily coded in terms of the classic matrix of race, class, gender, but also – as I have been arguing – species.) The literature on jealousy is vast, and it would take an entire book to even begin addressing such a complex and significant phenomenon. But as I suggested at the very beginning of this piece, jealousy evolved into a new genus in the nineteenth-century, because of the radical restructuring of the social categories I just mentioned, and the creation of more fluid commerce between them. As the uncharted internal territory of the psyche is mapped by Charcot and then in more detail by Freud, a profound unease emerges, coupled with excitement, at the implications of this completely unprecedented self-reflexivity in terms of subjectivity itself. In simpler terms, people began to explicitly reflect on their own identities, as well as the perceived threats to that very same identity. The self was exposed as a fragile and always already jealous ego.

Indeed, since Hegel, identity is defined negatively and absolutely as a struggle of recognition. Jealousy becomes, in and of itself, a *problem* – especially for a class that considers itself the torch-bearers of a more reasonable and enlightened age, unencumbered by the kinds of brutal Old Testament codes of ownership inscribed in the *Domostroy* (mentioned twice at the beginning of the book, and personified by the reactionary old man). Shakespeare's *Othello* literally set the stage for a less allegorical and more psychological exploration of jealousy by writers who were, after all, almost exclusively (male) members of this new historical class. And these men realized that this most violent and unstable of affects threatened to undo all those "techniques of the self" which promised to make society such a functionally civilized experience. Thus we see in Maupassant's last book, translated recently as *Alien Hearts* (and published in the same 12-month period at *The Kreutzer Sonata*) a character who is a proto-Proustian Swann: arguably the ultimate novelistic portrait of male sexual jealousy.

In Maupassant's story, the protagonist, Mariolle, labors under the impression that "he had gained what he had always dreamed of, always sought: complete possession of a woman he loved." However, "Such completeness is not of this world." And so, "he would never embrace for his very own the ever-extending surface of this woman who belonged to everyone" (92). The "other" gender begins in this period to unfold itself in a form of ontological origami, defying any attempt to contain her in oppressively Euclidian romantic or domestic spaces. As Mariolle's lover, Madame de Burne, begins to speculate silently – and a little sadly – "Could it be that her fine delicate flesh, so exceptionally aristocratic and refined, harbored unknown shames, shames of a superior and sacred animal, shames still unknown to her modern soul?" (113). A new cultural phenomenon is thus recognized – a women's ego, with its own sovereign imperatives and impulses – and is ambivalently condemned by the masculine establishment as pure, frivolous selfishness, while *also* being celebrated as the obscure cathected target of luminous fascination. That obscure object of desire indeed! Hence the million dollar question, "what does woman want?" is updated from Chaucer via Freud to suit a more modern mentality: a question which to this day remains unanswered (at least if the pathologically jealous Mel Gibson is anything to go by).[19] However, the reference to extra-humanity persists – "a superior and sacred animal" – suggesting that any tentative answer should be sought on the hinge between the theological and the evolutionary. (A hinge recently lubricated by the rather viscous intelligence of Giorgio Agamben, of which more in the concluding section of this chapter.)

All of which makes it all the more surprising that Tolstoy expressed disdain for Maupassant's novel, on the grounds that none of the characters were tagged with moral legibility – surely a charge one could make of *The Kreutzer Sonata* as well (unless, conversely, one wants to make the case that Tolstoy's novella is overly didactic in this regard).[20] It would take nearly half a century, two world wars, and the birth of another Russian writer, before jealousy would be depicted with such feverish, penetrating, and unflinching detail – Vladimir Nabokov's *Lolita*. Nabokov's narrator, Humbert Humbert, is forced to call upon the mundane materials of his pen to re-capture the object of his desires (and thus the catalyst of his being: according to the same metaphysical logic that a guitar string does not really "exist" until it is strummed according to a seemingly pre-destined chord). Not for his mortal hands are the "aurochs and angels" of more divine distillers of exceptional experience.

And so, for all the abject animosity that jealousy creates, the question still beckons, in terms of its fraternity with animals or animality. In other words, do animals experience "jealousy" as such? Certainly not according to Heidegger, for whom animals are incapable of the "as such." So is it more a case of natural competition and selection? I leave this speculation to the ethological experts, but the trope is established: competition and instinctual envy is natural. Jealousy is cultural. The green-eyed monster is thus not a primal creature emerging from the slime and ooze of reptilian resentment, but a cultural symptom of specifically human melancholia. It can be found at that smoking interface of agonistic traction where the rubber of the ego meets the road of the superego. What is more, there is a perverse *jouissance* to be found deep within its mental and emotional anguish.[21] As Deleuze notes, "there is something sublime in the jealous man's memory" (2000, 52), suggesting that jealousy is a condition of knowledge. As men finally acknowledge that women are their own autonomous beings, female attentions can no longer be taken for granted, or simply purchased. Or rather, their attentions *can* be purchased in various currencies, and under the right conditions, but not their hearts, minds, or souls. Hence the title of Maupassant's book, and hence Pozdnyshev's childish tantrum that: "What was really so horrible was that I felt I had a complete and inalienable right to her body, as if it were my own, yet at the same time I felt that I wasn't the master of this body, that it didn't belong to me, that she could do with it whatever she pleased, and that what she wanted to do with it wasn't what I wanted" (124-25). And it is this profound, almost metaphysical insecurity, which inflames passion (for the libido responds positively, seemingly perversely, to the possibility or actuality of rejection).[22]

One of the most vivid illustrations of this sado-masochistic self-indulgence is provided by Luis Buñuel's classic film, *That Obscure Object of Desire* (1977), in which the love-lust object literally vacillates between two actresses, despite being one character. In one key scene, the jealous male lover is obliged to watch his *Conchita* make love to another (younger) man, while trapped on the other side of a locked and barred gate. The thwarted would-be lover is literally imprisoned by his own impotent and compulsive voyeurism, and he is forced to watch his ego's worst-case scenario (something he flees from at first, but then returns to, compelled by the *frisson* of his libido). And so he is almost disappointed to find that the act has finished without his bearing agonistic witness. Or was it only simulated, as the woman soon insists? (Although her statements are far from reliable throughout the film.) As Niklas Luhmann says, the lover "enjoys" equally the sweet fruit and the bitter, for the only consistent demand is intensity (largely as a preemptive antidote to libidinal entropy).[23]

Jealousy is thus less about an embodied rival, than the very structure and geometry of modern romantic love.[24] If all love is mediated or triangular, as René Girard famously demonstrates, then jealousy is inevitable (at least as long as "possession" is a decisive motif – the jealous person is possessed by the knowledge that it is impossible to truly possess.)[25] That is to say, no couple avoids *being*, let alone *becoming*, extra-dyadic (as the psychologists call it). Pozdnyshev seems aware of this dilemma when it comes to the passively aggressive third term in his marriage. Like Anna Karenina's husband, Alexei Alexandrovich Karenin, he at first tries to transcend his negative feelings, aware that, if cultivated, they will bloom fatal flowers.[26] But in contrast to the situation in Tolstoy's more celebrated novel, there is no fork-in-the-road where personal enlightenment might conceivably win out against crude self-interest and flattery.[27] The tension between public face and private pragmatics is narrated in *The Kreutzer Sonata* with little room for generous or altruistic considerations of anyone else.[28] A traditional premium on domestic honor wins out against personal development and inter-personal compassion, thanks to what Žižek calls, by way of Petrarch, "the plague of fantasies." These are the claustrophobic, crowding images that assault the jealous person, creating the kindling for the green flames to lick ever higher. Pozdnyshev shivers as he recalls, "my imagination: it began to paint for me, in the most lurid fashion, a rapid sequence of pictures which inflamed my jealousy . . . a kind of strange, drunken enjoyment of my own hurt pride" (120-21). The main character in this nightmare phantasmagoria – the prime exhibit in the human freak show – is of course the next and tenth specimen in our menagerie: the beast-with-two-backs. And as with other freak shows, the lure is a combination of disgust and curiosity.

However, as with the bitch-in-heat, there is no need to dwell on this part of our tour, since we all know what the dual-backed beast looks like. And we all know that its structuring absence is the pivot around which the tale of revenge takes place. Even long after the fateful deed, Pozdnyshev probes his memory for traces of his rival, as one's tongue compulsively searches for the most painful part of a tooth. The husband notes that his potential rival "had a particularly well-developed posterior, as women have, or as Hottentots are said to have" (87); an elliptical reference to a virile, almost equine, animality. And yet, there was nothing particular about this fellow, who – like the wife – goes without a name, clothed only in pronouns; nothing specific to fascinate the lady of the house: "If it hadn't been him, it would have been someone else, it had to happen" (86). The inevitability of infidelity has been flagged all along, nurtured since birth by the social matrix. The tragedy of this novella is that the anti-hero chooses murder over divorce, and that he spirals into white-knuckled grasping and lashing out, rather than learning that painful lesson of letting go, and letting be. "Are there not lovers," asks Maupassant, in an observation seemingly tailor-made for *The Kreutzer Sonata*, "who are retained for better or worse, with resignation, out of fear of *the next*?" (148).

And yet, there is one skill that marks this gentleman out from the throng of would-be lovers for the wife who is chafing at the bit, and that is his musical proficiency, especially on the violin. The same culture which officially forbids adultery ensures the maximum opportunities for such, via sanctioned social intercourse between the sexes. And as Pozdnyshev observes, the playing of music, *à deux*, is one of the most commonly exploited scenarios – a case of bourgeois morals thwarted, or at least tested, by bourgeois rituals. Which leads us to the eleventh entrant in Tolstoy's bestiary: the Siren, aka music itself.

Exhibit 11: The Siren

Pozdnyshev stretches the credulity of the listener when he insists that his jealousy was not the cause of his psychological and juridical torment, but rather the effect. As he explains to the narrator, the culprit is really his rival. "He and his music were the real cause of it all. At my trial the whole thing was made to look as though it had been caused by jealousy. Nothing could have been further from the truth. I'm not saying jealousy didn't play any part at all, mind – it did, but it wasn't the most important thing" (87-88). Were we to subtract one element from the cascading series of events, however, then clearly Pozdnyshev's jealousy is more decisive and destructive than the aural ghost of Beethoven. What is more, it was the husband's jealousy which – at least according to his own account – *created* the ideal conditions for their retroactive justification: "I saw that right from the first meeting her eyes began to shine in a peculiar way and that, probably as a result of my jealousy, there was immediately established between them a kind of electric current which seemed to give their faces the same expression" (96). (As the literary critic

Dorothy Green quotes in a different translation, "From the first moment his eyes met my wife's I saw that the animal in each of them, regardless of all conditions of their position and of society asked 'May I?' and answered 'Oh yes, certainly!'")

Nevertheless, it is through the siren song of music that the wife and her lover ensure the possibility of sensual consummation. (As the debauched master of innuendo, Maurice Chevalier, exclaims in *The Smiling Lieutenant* (1931) – "I *love* chamber music.") For Pozdnyshev, in contrast, it is a "fearful medium," for the very same reason that the well-to-do skirt-chasers love it, because it is "the most refined form of sensual lust" (117). Tolstoy himself was an accomplished pianist "and made up his mind at one stage to become a great musician and composer. He was carried away by the combination of sounds, and attempted to formulate his own theory of harmony, under the title *The Fundamentals of Music and Rules for its Study.* As far as composers were concerned, Beethoven seems to have inspired in him a kind of love-hate relationship; perhaps he resented Beethoven's power to carry him out of himself"[29] (Green 441-42).

Such resentment is expressed by the murderer as well, when obliged to reflect on the piece of music that makes up the title of the novella:

> Do you know its first movement, the presto? . . . Ah! It's a fearful thing, that sonata. Especially that movement. And music in general's a fearful thing. What is it? I don't know. . . Music makes me forget myself, my true condition, it carries me off into another state of being, one that isn't my own . . . the effect produced by music is similar to that produced by yawning or laughter: I may not be sleepy, but I yawn if I see someone else yawning, I may have no reason for laughing, but I laugh if I see someone else laughing. (110-11)

The power which this particular piece of music has – the intangible force and inexpressible significance which it represents – anticipates Vinteuil's melodic phrase in Proust, which becomes a hook buried in Swann's mind, just as Beethoven places a barb in Pozdnyshev's.[30] As George Steiner (one of the great commentators on Tolstoy, of course), observes: "Because music is so immediately inwoven with changes in the shapes of time, the development of Beethoven's tempi, of the driving pulse in his symphonic and chamber music during the relevant years, is of extraordinary historical and psychological interest" (12). It is this self-same "driving pulse" which Pozdnyshev blames on initiating the fatal sequence of thoughts and emotions – the "cause and affect," as it were – which would lead to our penultimate exhibit in Tolstoy's zoo: the wild, murderous beast.

Exhibit 12: The Wild Murderous Beast

Pozdnyshev confronts the maddening dialectic between animosity and animality most searingly at the climax of his tale: a climax he painfully relives in the retelling (and who can say how many times he regales his fellow passengers with this grisly confession?). "I'm seized with horror whenever I think of the wild beast that lived in me during that time," he admits (100-01); ashamed also of the fact that, "In the last days our quarrels became terrifying; they were particularly shattering because they alternated with bouts of animal sensuality" (88). The more he suspects the affair, the more his senses – his nonhuman senses – are inflamed by the possibility.[31] The "animosity" (*zhivotnoe*) which overwhelms him reaches the level of a linguistic tic or mantra:

> "I was seized by a feeling of animosity towards her more terrible than any I'd ever experienced before.
>
> For the first time I felt a desire to give my animosity physical expression. I leapt to my feet and went up to her; I remember that at the very moment I got up I became aware of

> my animosity and asked myself whether it was a good thing for me to abandon myself to this feeling, and then told myself that it was a good thing, that it would give her a fright; then immediately, instead of fighting off my animosity, I began to fan it up in myself even further, rejoicing in its steadily increasing blaze within me."
>
> 'Go, or I'll kill you!' I shouted suddenly, going up to her and seizing her by the arm, consciously exaggerating the level of animosity in my voice. (106)

Five repetitions of the word in barely more than a paragraph! What is more, Pozdnyshev's wife remains "a mystery, just as she's always been, just as she'll always be. I don't know her. I only know her as an animal. And nothing can or should hold an animal back." The two forces feed on each other with a deepening hunger.

After leaving his wife alone on official business, Pozdnyshev's paranoia draws him back to home and hearth, only to be confirmed in such sickening circumstances that time itself seems to be stretched into a substance of pure nausea. As feared, the rook is there, befouling the nest of the cuckold. Despite the fine clothing and the expensive China, Pozdnyshev walks in on a beastly scene – his wife sharing an intimate dinner with his lover – so that he only sees something inhuman. "No, she isn't human, she's a bitch, a repulsive bitch!" (130).

The scene in which the crime of passion takes place, by way of a knife between the ribs, is a masterpiece of unsettling representation. Here a tragic "event" is logged microsecond by microsecond, in forensic detail, but fleshed out via the "unreal time" of psychological distress (as Tolstoy also does with such consummate skill for Anna Karenina's suicide). Pozdnyshev's wife does not die immediately though – her mortal flame continues to flicker to better confront him with the irreversibility of his actions. Even then, as her life flows silently out of her body, the madman wrenchingly recalls, "I saw displayed on her face the same inveterate look of cold, animal hatred I knew so well" (142). He continues:

> I looked at the children, at her battered face with its bruises, and for the first time I forgot about myself, about my marital rights and my injured pride; for the first time I saw her as a human being. . . . I realized that I'd killed her, that it was all my doing that from a warm, moving, living creature she'd been transformed into a cold, immobile, waxen one, and that there was no way of setting this to rights, not ever, not anywhere, not by any means. (142-44)

And here lies the supreme irony of Tolstoy's tale; Pozdnyshev cannot fully register his wife's humanity – that is her monadic autonomy – until the very moment she is reduced to "animalistic" bare life. Or rather, bare lifelessness. And of course at that same moment it is too late. In the agonizing hour between the puncturing of her organs, and the breath leaving her body forever, the adulteress exists in that fraught zone Eric Santner calls "creaturely life": an abject space in which the inherent pathos of the human condition is rendered animal, only to ontologically enhance the Fall from its assumed and exceptional dignity. Again, the irony is that our nebulous "humanity" is touched most to the quick when our humanness is swiftly compromised, evacuated, or stolen.[32] Pozdnyshev appreciates his wife's personhood only when he holds a bruised, virtual carcass – a revelation denied him by the blinders of jealousy; that "fatal energy" (95) which seeks only revenge, because it cannot see beyond the horizon of the ego. As Jean Baudrillard so accurately puts it:

> To love someone is to isolate him from the world, wipe out every trace of him, dispossess him of his shadow, drag him

> into a murderous future. It is to circle around the other like a dead star and absorb him into a black light. Everything is gambled on an exorbitant demand for the exclusivity of a human being, whoever it may be. This is doubtless what makes it a passion: its object is interiorized as an ideal end, and we know that the only ideal object is a dead one. (105)

Pozdnyshev's remorse stems directly from reaching this ideal, and the reader wishes that he had the foresight and wisdom of Tolstoy's own wife, Sofia, who at least anticipated the agony which follows swiftly on the heels of the ecstasy of passionate homicide. "If I could kill him and create a new person exactly the same as he is now," she wrote, only a matter of months after their wedding, "I would do so happily" (quoted in Meek).

Exhibit 13: The Empty Shell of a Man – By Way of Summary and Conclusion

Which brings us to the final, unlucky thirteenth exhibit in the bestiary: the haunted creature, the husk of a human being. As readers – as visitors to Tolstoy's zoo – we can do little more than pity the poor fellow, or at least find him pitiful. Whether we, as proxied interlocutors, forgive Pozdnyshev after his full confession is not really the point. Nor should we measure our own reactions against "the moral of the story," as painstakingly detailed by the author himself. For as I have argued, there is a veritable jungle of animal types and totems which cannot be completely domesticated by Tolstoy's pen. Obliged to personify in reverse, these creatures suggest a struggle far more widespread than between husband and wife, man and woman, but one identified by one of the author's most controversial and celebrated contemporaries. For Nietzsche, humanity was little more than the animal that had learned to make promises; the marriage vow being one of the most iconic. Indeed, *The Genealogy of Morals* alludes to the rather terrifying set of technologies assembled by men as preemptive, punitive mnemonics, so that this rather frail and forgetful creature remembers to remember. For men like Tolstoy, morality is a cathedral, reaching for the heavens. For those like Nietzsche, it is nothing more than a cage, preventing man from transcending himself towards an empowering animality.[33] Tolstoy's obsessive cataloguing of animals in *The Kreutzer Sonata* could be read as his attempt – conscious or unconscious – to grapple with Nietzsche's challenge (itself a provocation enabled by Darwin).

As such, this novella represents a particularly fraught cog in the discursive device Agamben calls "the anthropological machine." That is, a comprehensive engine designed *by* humanity and *for* humanity, whose primary function is to sort "the human" (as abstract privileged subject) from the non-human (an equally abstract object). In terms simplified to a degree that may give Agamben himself a migraine, the anthropological machine is all those cultural artifacts which combine into a vanity mirror for our species, reflecting and regulating our assumed superior status. Agamben thus considers the trajectory of humanity to be at once located on a continuity with other animals *and* exceptional in its self-recognition as different. In other words, it is only through our delusional narcissism that "we" stand apart as a modern, secular Adam. And yet, miraculously, this delusion (aka, anthropocentrism) seems to be enough to forge an ontological difference, given all the mediating devices engineered and employed to maintain that very distinction. (This is where and why Agamben can still be accused of a latent humanism, with tinges of the theological.)

In any case, Agamben shares Nietzsche's fascination with a post-historical transcendence of ourselves, in which we would be ultimately reconciled with our animal natures, and all the freer for it. (Something I return to in the next chapter.) This would not be a relapse into a bestial state, but an inclusive fusion of soma and spirit, no longer troubled by the necessary detour of culture (as defined against and in contrast to nature). It would be a Last Supper as illustrated in the 13th-century Hebrew bible, with "the righteous" depicted with animal heads, rather than human faces (1-3). For Tolstoy, this is anathema. The spiritual superiority of humankind can only be understood in relief to an animalistic background. And as long as men and women lapse back into the sensual realm, their bestiality will create a dangerous animosity.

Let us recap then, our zoological itinerary, cage by cage. First there was the green-eyed monster himself, gnashing his sharp, greedy teeth, and possessed with the impossibility of possession. Then the fornicator, who indulges in debauchery at the expense of his consorts. Followed by the doctor-reptile, who encourages such irresponsible behavior, under the relatively novel alibi of public health. Remember too, the Venus fly trap – the female response to such ravishments, determined to parry her social disadvantage into an economic gain. Together, the fornicator and the Venus fly trap morph into the porcine couple, in the nuptial chamber, using each other for pleasure only, as means rather than ends. Which in turn leads to the mutated mother hen, who first violates herself, and then her child, by continuing to have sex after conception. Eventually she learns – once more with the aid of the reptile-doctors – to avoid conception altogether (one of many noted inconsistencies or ironies in Pozdnyshev's account, whereby human science paradoxically and perversely encourages a heightened animal state). In turn, sterility creates the bitch-in-heat, not for procreation, however, but for a wicked kind of gratification. With the active complicity of the siren (music), she is subsequently easily seduced by the cock or rook, whose own sensual delights are at the expense of the cuckold. Upon gaining indirect carnal knowledge of his wife's infidelity, the cuckold is confronted with the mocking specter of the beast-with-two-backs; an image so infuriating that it can lead to a Hulk-like transformation, into a murderous wild beast. The storm of passion passes, however, as soon as the irreversible deed is done, leaving only the haunted shell of a man.

These are the totemic figures deployed in Tolstoy's story – sometimes explicitly, sometimes through allusion – to describe the ultimately *in*human dispensation of love. Moreover, Pozdnyshev's tale illustrates how jealousy can function as an efficient lubricant for the smooth operation of the anthropological machine, thereby fuelling all the undesirable products of species-based chauvinism. Tolstoy was correct in insisting that humankind will forever languish in spiritual limbo as long as it hitches its wagon to institutional matrimony. He was mistaken, however, in attempting to locate humanity in monogamous chastity (and not only because he was incapable of practicing what he preached). Sex is not the problem, but rather the site in which a secular and fleeting form of salvation is possible. For Agamben, sex enables and enacts a "mutual disenchantment" which nevertheless affords "a new and more blessed life, one that is neither animal nor human" (2004, 87). Beyond pious, mythologizing pedestals, intimacy reaches the point where it is capable of refusing the potentially fatal fetishism of the individual. As Agamben cryptically puts it, speaking of Titian's painting *Nymph and Shepherd*: "These lovers have initiated each other into their own lack of mystery as their most intimate secret; they mutually forgive each other and expose their *vanitas*. . . In their fulfillment, the lovers who have lost their mystery contemplate a human nature rendered perfectly inoperative – the inactivity and *desoeuvrement* of the human and of the animal as the supreme and unsavable figure of life" (2004, 87).

Tolstoy – unlike Titian, and unlike Nietzsche – was incapable of seeing the admirable side of *post*-human, neo-animalistic sexual congress: an admittedly messianic state in which "people" may indeed enjoy each other's bodies and souls without the folly of possessive vanity. (Let it be, might go the refrain, rather than let it bleed.) In contrast, the great Russian author made the ultimate human error – assuming the autonomous existence of something called humanity in the first place.

And also in the last place.

Chapter 5

Exiled from Funland: Flusser and Agamben After the Fall

Funland

When I was but a lad, I spent – or perhaps misspent – much of my languid summer hours at a three-level amusement arcade called Funland, perched in the center of the small fishing town of Ulladulla, New South Wales, Australia. This was my idea of Paradise. Here my ten-year-old self was drawn away from the healthy pleasures of the beach, thanks to the totemic pull of the electronic creatures inside: beckoning me, jeering at me, challenging me to use up every last coin. Through my various receptive senses I was attuned to the constant infernal bleepings of the machines, the hollow thwack of the air-hockey pucks, and the cacophonous gestalt scent of bleach, coconut oil, sebum, semen, meat pies, sausage rolls, boredom, and 4711 perfume. Here my innocent eyes drank in the seductive tackiness of the black-light posters on the wall featuring near-naked women menaced by cobras, or the blue-collar whimsy of skeletons in top hats sitting on toilets with a rose clenched between their grinning teeth. Surrounded by solicitous machines of amusement, one barely noticed the melancholy, chain-smoking attendants, exchanging cash for tokens; nor the surly, passively pedophilic gaze of the man in charge of the trampolines; or even the badly maintained whack-a-mole game (each bobbing critter now pummeled into the eyeless, earless, anonymous lump of clay from whence it came).

For Funland was where I would always drift to the same handful of machines that I knew I could get a free game, like a Pavlovian dog toward its sonic stimuli: the original *Battlestar Galactica* pinball machine, the 8-bit racing game, or the plastic

WW1 dogfight game which signaled successful hits with the lo-fi reward of a red light-bulb, hidden somewhere behind the diorama's rudimentary proscenium arch. When I would visit Funland in my teens, feeling a little older and a great deal wiser, I would affectionately add my own slogan for the place, which I hoped would one day be written on the welcoming sign: "Funland: Where Old Video Games Go To Die." It is only now, however, that I am truly cognizant of the wealth of theological questions such a slogan raises: questions vaguely equivalent to those scholastic thinkers who argued over whether the human body would wear clothes in the after-life, or if it would have unseemly organs like the bowel, bladder, or pudenda (and if so, would it use them?). Would pinball machines still tilt in their own analog of Paradise? Would the remote-control cars still spin wildly off the tracks and across the room with every single sharp corner? Would *Galaga* suddenly find new and unanticipated algorithmic arabesques for its aliens to approacheth?

But as the reader has no doubt already surmised, Funland was less of a blessed after-life, than an ongoing purgatory for these work-mules of adolescent entertainment. Funland is still open today, but its 20th-century entertainments are being replaced one by one, as if beholden to a localized law of physics in which the arcade games must be no more or no less than twenty years before the current date of our Lord. The trampolines are gone, the pinball machines updated, the employees arrested and/or replaced. And yet the place itself remains – a living-dead incarnation of Theseus's Ship, in which the object persists both despite and because of the constant flux of its constituent elements.

Celebrating

Being the child of an atheistic family, Funland was my Church. I would spend most of my Saturdays or Sundays there during the holidays of my youth (not be confused with the holy days). This, in other words, was my Sabbath. (And given the Heavy Metal iconography of the place, something of a black Sabbath.)

The Czech media philosopher, Vilém Flusser, believed that the Sabbath was – once upon a time – "a sector extracted from and raised above the flow of events. It is a temple made of time rather than marble." He locates this "once upon a time" as threading through the long centuries preceding "the bourgeois revolution of the fifteenth century" (i.e., "the secularization of modern life"). In his view, the Sabbath used to be a regular, liminal occasion of temporal suspension, which allowed a more profound relationship to the passage of time and the enigmas of existence. Thus it was a time for what Freud called "the Totem meal": an opportunity for reflective gratitude. "[T]he Sabbath itself is valueless," he wrote, "because it has its own value. . . It is the 'transcendence' of history" (166). In other words, the Sabbath is an exceptional event – even accounting for its regularity and punctuality – because it refuses to think of time as a mere accumulation of productive enterprises. The Sabbath reminds us to *remind ourselves* of the miracle of Being; and to leave *becoming* for the rest of the week (aka, the profane hours).

For Flusser, "[w]e have forgotten how to celebrate" (167). We have forgotten how to truly observe the miracle of life in its pure uselessness or inutility. (Something the secularists would respin as "meaninglessness," but quite the contrary to the Greeks or the Judeo-Christian traditions.) "Both of our prebourgeois traditions," notes Flusser, "used idle as an expression for the human capacity to raise ourselves above usefulness" (168). (Indeed, we can only fantasize about a world in which one of the most popular television shows is called *American Idle*: dedicated to valorizing the glory of profound, contemplative inoperativity; or what Kierkegaard called "the purposeless life before God".) Flusser thus contrasts the lost form of celebration with today's "holiday leisure," which is "designed to provide rest for future useful activities" (167). Leisure time is the inhalation of Capital, popularized by the twin Titans of Taylor and Ford. It represents "the submission of celebrating in favor of utility," and insists "we degenerate in leisure once we become incapable of celebrating" (168). (It is worth noting that Flusser even goes so far as to see "a blessing in unemployment" – something greatly in evidence at Funland, I must say.)

In this extended quotation, we can see how Flusser positions humanity as an exceptional species, in its capacity for celebration as pure uselessness:

> One method for helping us to remember is to observe human gestures versus animal gestures. Certainly, purposive (economic) motions can be ascertained in the human being: like the animals, he reaches for something to eat or something to copulate with, and he too distances himself from danger. But we also recognize purposeless, useless, antieconomic, celebratory gestures in the human being. For example, children play with inedible, nonsexual, and harmless pebbles; they play "theoretically." It is characteristic for our current forgetting of the holiness of leisure that we are now providing a utilitarian interpretation of these games. For example, we say that the useful stone knife and useful culture originated from these sorts of pebble games during the Stone Age. Thus, we do not acknowledge that the useless and idle things in culture, the celebratory and the theoretical, which is to say art and the theoretical sciences, are the core of culture. A phenomenology of human gestures helps us to remember that man is a celebratory being. He is religious in the Judeo-Christian sense of the term. (168)

It is thus evident how Flusser adds his distinctive voice to the great Continental Choir of the Postlapsarian Condition. "Things may not have been better before," sing the melancholy philosophers, "but they are sure getting worse." We have been expelled from Paradise; or at least from an authentic, clear-eyed understanding of Paradise. Instead we wallow in the tepid and acrid waters of what Adorno called "the medicinal bath of fun." In entertainment we strive to be amused. In games we strive to win. But, Flusser tells us, "in celebrating, there is nothing to be won" (169): itself, something worth celebrating. Indeed, we are so used to the theological economy of Paradise, with Heaven-as-reward[1], that we have forgotten this terrestrial truth.

And yet, Flusser isn't all nostalgia, gloom, and doom. Indeed, writing in 1985 – the birth of home computing – he sees in the nascent electronic revolution a new opportunity for salvation. "Telematics is a school where we learn to celebrate," he writes. What's more, "If the power of imagination is to develop in a telematic society, it must live life as a celebration" (169, 165). With admirable prophetic powers, Flusser anticipates a time when we will all have our own keyboards and monitors, and access to each other's thoughts and experiences. He looked forward to a time of "dialogic programming," in which we would no longer be at the mercy of imposed vertical mass media, but instead would be able to co-create our own collective Mandelbrot projects and parameters. And the most exciting aspect of this technological development is that we will be freed from productive creation: from the tyranny of utility.

"Certainly," writes Flusser, "new information will continually be produced and the sum of accessible information will continually be increased. But this flood of information will not be made useful, and it will not become profit. One will 'only' celebrate it." Furthermore, "The idleness of the manufacture of images, this above and beyond all 'for what purpose,' this motivelessness – if my prediction is correct – is, precisely, the existential attitude of the future man" (169). How Flusser so accurately foresaw the explosion of LOLcats is anyone's guess. But he was not entirely correct, given how efficiently the Satanic agents of Capital are able to harvest our seemingly useless online activities and monetize them. But it is still remarkable that Flusser's "post-historical" vision of Man-restored-to-Paradise could be conceived as someone sitting around, tinkering with Photoshop while simultaneously enjoying the futility of Farmville.

Nudity

For Giorgio Agamben – another, more recent, crypto-techno-theologist – the vision of Man-restored-to-Paradise is somewhat different. While this Italian philosopher agrees whole-heartedly with Flusser that we have forgotten how to celebrate, he is in sharp disagreement that our digital gadgets are our saviors. Instead he sees them as a further captivation of and within busy activity, and thus a distraction from true uselessness or pure inoperativity. (Two modes which have, in his perspective, the benefit of sabotaging the omnipresent machine of Capital, and its attendant overdetermining ideologies.) Agamben thus constructs his *own* totem for the future – a half-man, half-animal creature – bestowing it with the power to help us escape our increasingly gloomy fate. He thus looks past the pitiful person, poor-in-world, tinkering with Facebook, to the morphing of Man into a post-historical "manimal": a reconciliation of vital tendencies towards their transcendence. In this account, paradise will signal the end of human history, understood as a Hegelian striving beyond biological destiny to absolute Spirit. (Game over – but in a good way!) This figure will embody the end of world-historical nihilism, allowing us to finally escape the blinkered will-to-mastery of humans, and the dumb captivation of mere animals.[2] "To render inoperative the machine that governs our conception of man," writes Agamben, "will therefore mean no longer to seek new – more effective or more authentic – articulations, but rather to show the central emptiness, the hiatus that – within man – separates man and animal, and to risk ourselves in this emptiness: the suspension of the suspension, Shabbat of both animal and man" (2004, 92). Accordingly, the immanent moment of truth will usher in a species-wide relief at no longer being obliged to repress the animal inside. Thus we can go beyond the self-imposed alienation of insecure exceptionalism. We will, in other words, be – finally – fully, human, animal, and posthuman all at once.

From this angle, then, Flusser and Agamben are equally messianic. They both grope after a secular form of salvation, albeit through the detour of theological legacies, metaphors, or languages. Agamben not only looks forward to his own iteration of becoming-animal, but – in a different text – to what he calls "blissful and innocent paradisiacal nudity" (2011, 60).[3] According to his argument, humans have never really been allowed to be nude, even in the Garden of Eden, since their naked bodies were swaddled in the shimmering "supernatural clothing" of grace. God as celestial tailor ensures that even before the Original Sin, "we can gird our loins in truth" (62). Citing the 11th-century bas relief Eve in the Collegiate Church of San Isidoro in León – in which the first woman fights back against being covered by clothing – Agamben insists that nudity in our culture is nothing other than "the obscure and ungraspable presupposition of clothing" (65). Clothing is not a supplement to the body, rather the body is figured as the lack of clothing. "[N]udity cannot be conceived outside the act of being denuded," he writes, and is thus considered "impure." In other words, "that which appears when clothes (grace) are taken off is nothing but their shadow" (65).

For Agamben then, humans have yet to be truly nude (the earnest efforts and rhetoric of nudist colonies notwithstanding). And yet we may allow ourselves to hope for an authentically naked Sabbath, confirming the immortal words of Belinda Carlisle, "Heaven is a place on earth." When the bare human body is not considered negatively as "unclothed," but positively as "an appearance that – tremblingly – exhibits is own vacuity" (86), our kind will have finally found a Paradise which escapes the overdeterminations of religion. We will finally have access to "this sublime absence of the secret of human nudity" (87), on the other side of shame. (One decisive irony with Agamben, of course, is that he depends heavily on theology as a frame for escaping theological thought.)

Where this account links back to Flusser is once again on the issue of technology (remembering that clothing is a technology). Agamben notes that, "Before sin, the first human beings lived in a state of idleness and fullness," also known as *atechnia*, "a lack of applied knowledge" (82). Flusser's novelty – and perhaps brilliance – lies in his claim that *atechnia* can be achieved through technical ends. Technology need not be the bureaucratic stuff of limbo, but the very architecture of Paradise. "A new, completely unorthodox religiosity begins to surface out of the buried corners of our consciousness," he writes. "But, surprisingly, in the form of a dreamlike universe of technical images" (171). That is to say, "All pretelematic images from Lascaux to video are discursive images, broadcast, designed against the other, and covering his face. They are forbidden. They are dead-end streets leading away from God. On the other hand, dialogically synthesized telematic images are the 'media' from one human to another through which I see the face of the other. And through this face, I see God once more" (171).

A very large claim indeed; and one clearly indebted to Levinas (who intimately and infinitely linked the *actual* human being with the numinous source of Being). Thus, Flusser is inspired by his belief that, "[e]very single human is my only 'medium' to God, and I can only arrive at God if I go to him 'through' the other (every single other)" (171). Not only strangers-in-paradise, but paradise-in-strangers (via modems). "Perhaps," writes Flusser, "we are about to remember again the forgotten celebrating" (171).

Chinatown Fair

When I first wrote this piece, for an event organized by Nicola Masciandaro at Brooklyn Observatory in 2011, I made special note of the fact that the last remaining video-game arcade in Manhattan had recently closed. Chinatown Fair was New York's version of Funland for many an adolescent, for many years. But these young souls had now been banished into the private and profane worlds of home or portable gaming systems.[4] While this did not grieve me personally – as someone who no longer plays video games – I was disheartened on behalf of those who enjoyed slaying villains in the public sphere; especially as an agonistic expression of what we might call the autistic Commons. It grieves me that these specific Sabbath-like spaces have largely evaporated from the face of the earth. Indeed, it grieves me that I am no longer my "innocent" young self, exiled from the empty homogenous time of childhood which one often fills by playing video games. Instead I respond to incoming email, whooshing towards me with the speed and guile of the higher level aliens in *Space Invaders*. Paradise lost, indeed.[5]

But such melancholic emotions tend to speak more of rubbernecked nostalgia than the forward motion of utopian redemption. So in the spirit of our two philosophical guides, a speculative question. What might the ultimate contemporary totem of Paradise look like, through the doubled-vision of Flusser and Agamben? If the former sees a person clicking a mouse, engaged in dialogic programming – and the latter sees a post-Dionysian, posthuman banquet – what would the scenario be that embodies both sides of this secular-messianic coin? After some reflection, it seems that the ultimate totem of Paradise is a regular thirty-three year old person (the age of Christ, perhaps, and the alleged age of all restored souls in Heaven). This person, neither old nor young, is shamelessly playing video-games. Moreover, he or she is shamelessly playing video games in the nude. Indeed, he or she is doing so while eating cold take-out, and wearing an animal mask (possibly bought from Etsy). And he or she is doing all this on the Sabbath, while sponging off his or her parents, who happen to live in Celebration, Florida.

Coda: A Judgment of the Birds

Alexander Pope spoke of spaces and situations "where angels fear to tread." This rather forbidding phrase, however, always brought to my mind the very opposite topography: those places where heavenly seraphs were *most* comfortable consorting and commuting. Paradise, for instance. For certainly paradise is well-trodden by angels; and one might even talk of "angel trails" in Heaven, as we talk of "sheep trails" on earth. Angels of a feather stick together.

We have all heard of Birds of Paradise, but there is also a Paradise of the Birds. This latter is described in a famous 12th century Sufi poem by Farīd al-Dīn 'Aṭṭār, a tale of a conference of birds searching for the Simorgh – a mythological Persian phoenix-like creature, who also serves as an avatar of God. One by one the birds drop by the wayside, leaving only thirty to seek Enlightenment. Finally, after flying beyond exhaustion, the remaining group glimpse their combined reflection in a lake. At once and together they have an epiphany, realizing that God is immanent to the flock.

Come you lost Atoms to your Center draw,
And be the Eternal Mirror that you saw:
Rays that have wander'd into Darkness wide
Return and back into your Sun subside
(in Nasr, 3)

Who knows what reflective surface might feasibly take the place of this lake for our own species? Who knows if the screens of our machines will obscure or reveal the collectivity, purpose, and direction we feel we have lost as a planet-wide concern? Will the quest to reach a higher level be presented to us in the form and architecture of a video game? Will the public amusement arcades rise again *en masse* like a Phoenix?[6] Will pseudo-leisure ever accede to true celebration? Will the iPadification of the planet spur a spontaneous reversal into the kind of Great Reconnection that Flusser so understandably craves?

The answers depend on whether we have the will or the means to retriangulate work and play with true inoperativity. If we are somehow able to poach a piece of paradise as "free time" – not figured negatively, away from the office or factory, but positively, toward a revealingly useless plenitude – then we may have a shot at glimpsing what Agamben and his teachers call the Open: that transcendent realm of immediacy beyond merely human concerns. For Agamben, a hint of this genuine encounter with Being could conceivably be triggered by a murmur of starlings, flocking like a playful black cloud over the tree tops. For Flusser, the same could possibly strike us during a particularly difficult level of *Angry Birds* (provided that we ourselves coded this level, uncompromised by the designs of advertizing companies). In either case, the actual or the virtual, the birds are our totem of the Open. They circle and flock, following some algorithm written into the wind that we cannot read or understand: that is, not until the fourth wall of the symbolic human world collapses, revealing a real, seductive, restless, nonhuman Elsewhere.

For a memorable example of such an avian-inspired experience – "a judgment of the birds," as he calls it – we can turn to Loren Eiseley's vivid description of his pre-dawn epiphany amongst the pigeons, high above the streets of New York City. Eiseley, a natural scientist by trade (but poet by inclination), tells of feeling a sudden invisible tug at his soul, which soon found him "on impulse" leaning out over the window-sill of his midtown hotel, twenty stories up. This was not to commit suicide, however, but to simply observe.

> I had expected depths, but not the sight I saw.
>
> I found I was looking down from that great height into a series of curious cupolas or lofts that I could just barely make out in the darkness. As I looked, the outlines of these lofts became more distinct because the light was being reflected from the wings of pigeons who, in utter silence, were beginning to float outward upon the city. In and out through the open slits in the cupolas passed the white-winged birds on their mysterious errands. At this hour the city was theirs, and quietly, without the brush of a single wing tip against stone in that high, eerie place, they were taking over the spires of Manhattan. They were pouring upward in a light that was not yet perceptible to human eyes, while far down in the black darkness of the alleys it was still midnight.
>
> As I crouched half asleep across the sill, I had a moment's illusion that the world had changed in the night, as in some immense snowfall, and that if I were to leave, it would have to be as these other inhabitants were doing, by the window. I should have to launch out into that great bottomless void with the simple confidence of young birds reared high up there among the familiar chimney pots and interposed horrors of the abyss. (165-66)

Having glimpsed this parallax view of the Open, and ultimately resisted its potentially fatal allure, Eiseley wrote: "I dressed then and went back to my own kind, and I have been rather more than usually careful ever since not to look into the city of light. I had seen, just once, man's greatest creation from a strange inverted angle, and it was not really his at all. I will never forget how those wings went round and round, and how, by the merest pressure of the fingers and a feeling for air, one might go away over the roofs" (167).[7]

Two decades later, on a similarly warm and sleepless night, Roland Barthes – steeped in profound grief – wrote his latest entry in a diary dedicated solely to mourning the recent death of his mother. "Seeing the swallows flying through the summer evening air . . . how barbarous not to believe in souls – in the immortality of souls! the idiotic truth of materialism!" (159).

Conclusion

Zigzag: The Totem of Movement

Lightning. Snake. Human.
Lights. Camera. Action.

Between the primeval animal-shadows that once twitched on cave walls, and the animated creatures writhing on our cinema screens today, we reconstruct a series of jump cuts connecting them. Assembled in the editing room of history, by chain-smoking and watery-eyed theorists of the image, this looped, stuttering montage depends on an essential, abstract totemic figure – the zigzag (since all movement "zigzags," no matter how linear it appears to our over-simplified sensorium). This graphic symbol mimics *movement* itself, wrenched outside of time – outside the temporal flow: "not a concatenation but a shock between elements" (Michaud 285). In other words, before any given virtual entity or virtual object, we have *virtuality itself* – the zigzag. The maybe-this-maybe-that. The only-traceable-after-the-fact. What's more, this ur-sign of totemic potency and potential has – over the centuries – morphed its way around the world, smuggled inside the Trojan Horse of eternally "new" media. Beware of geeks bearing gifts!

For the great Soviet film director, Sergei Eisenstein, the famous sculpture of *Laocöön* is Western culture's "totem of movement." This is due to the fact that it is "an image produced by montage" (Michaud 286) – despite also being a static piece of marble. Laocöön himself, the subject of the sculpture, was a Trojan priest who warned against accepting the suspicious equine present from the city's enemies ("a deadly fraud is this").[1] Rather than be rewarded for his prescience, however, Laocöön was instead subsequently condemned to death for presuming to make love to his wife in the presence of a divine image (an offense compounded by his fathering two children, despite his religious vocation). In the Vatican today, one can see the marmolian reconstruction of the dynamic sculpture, originally created by a trio of ancient sculptors from Rhodes circa 200BC. This piece depicts Laocöön, and his unfortunate sons, surrounded by killer snakes entwined around arms and legs: a disturbing tableau of frozen movement and horror. An arrested line of fright.

For the eccentric and adventurous art historian, Aby Warburg, snakes hold a special significance; especially given his interest in Native American art and culture. Indeed, Warburg felt no disciplinary taboo in creating his own montage across continents and epochs, designed to link formerly (and seemingly) unconnected totemic questions and phenomena. Thus, modern cinema articulates with Japanese *kanji* which touches upon classical sculpture which evokes Hopi graphic logic. In doing so, Warburg diagrams a suggestive constellation of kinetic-totemic elements.

As Philippe-Alain Michaud observes: "Discussing the [Hopi] snake ritual in his 1923 lecture, Warburg described the dancers as manipulating the reptiles like Eisensteinian hieroglyphs, like montaged images, associating the human form with the symbol of movement embodied in the snake." Warburg noted especially the Native American preoccupation with the "zigzag," which, according to his interpretation, was "a graphic form associated with lightning and with the snake. . . attributed to untamed energy" (248). Moreover, it was through an abstract "collision effect" – outside cause and effect – that this "serpentine figure" comes in contact with Renaissance images of movement of which the *Laocöön* sculpture was emblematic. Snakes on a Deleuzian plane.

As Michaud also notes

The sculptural group is a representation of uninterrupted

> sequential displacements aimed at juxtaposing expressions that appear only in succession . . . As a cinematic figure that brings succession to simultaneity, the *Laocöön* is not only a montaged figure but a figure of montage; and the snakes, beyond their pathetic signification, have a formal function in the composition: that is, they hold the group together by outlining the concatenations of the different parts of the 'shot'" (248).

Whether we agree that a sculpture from ancient times can be described as "cinematic," or even "proto"-cinematic, we can at least acknowledge that scholars of visual culture and media have been wrestling with these slithering, zigzagging lines of association since the birth of industrialized cinema. (Perhaps this is why Hortense Powdermaker, the official "anthropologist" of late 1940's Hollywood, was moved to write: "As the original founders of the industry, the executives tend to think of themselves as its totemic ancestors, omniscient and omnipotent" [286].) For Richard Beardsworth, our "technical objects" function as "sites of cultural memory: from the totem to cinema" (2003, 49). Even as each subsequent technical object threatens to render the last obsolete, a millennia-long continuum is implied. Beyond a genealogy, however, I have argued that *all* our different media act as incubators for *new* totems, and the mutation of older ones. The cinema does not supersede the totem, but allows a different environment for it to breed. (The same can be said for literature, video games, or the Internet.)

If the montage is the totem of movement, then movement is the totem of life. And like lightning, which the Native American iconography attempts to capture in the zigzag, the totem itself illuminates new territory with just enough light to entice, but not enough to read anything with confident legibility. Hence its enduring appeal. Rather than disappearing with, or into, an earlier human stage, the totem may have become so ubiquitous in our own time as to be invisible to everything but the trained eye. As the previous chapters have shown, we gravitate towards a given totem to help light the way within almost infinite complications and perplexities of the universe. And yet while they seem to promise guidance and simplification, they often only make things even more bewildering and entangled. For while a montage is usually designed to make complex contingencies more legible, they also leave tantalizing gaps for which the viewer can bring their own interpretations.[2]

The rabbit, Orc, penguin, avatar, angel, pixelated lover – even Paradise itself – all make appearances in the idiosyncratic virtual montage fashioned by this book. They are neototems for an era in which the monolithic notion of Nature is finally giving way to an understanding of ecology that includes computers as much as whales, and in which humans are just as likely to be sheep than shepherds. Whether we prefer to think of these spirit(ed) guides as "strange strangers," "strange familiars," or "familiar strangers," they and their kin will continue to solicit, tempt, provoke, fascinate, repulse, admonish, challenge (and why not? . . . perhaps even love) us, via the different devices on which we increasingly depend. The much vaunted "convergence" of separate mediums into the one digital portal may indeed signal an event horizon equivalent to Friedrich Kittler's 1900, in which our species recalibrates itself anew, beneath the "classic" chassis of our bodies. Our new digital tools and toys are already at work on our minds and bodies, obliging us to "think different," and act in new ways (or, more accurately, *not act* – at least, not in any significant sense, other than swipe our credit cards whenever possible).[3]

In his own study of totemic fauna in mediated forms, Alan Bleakley concludes by saying, "let us welcome these non-biological animals with open minds" (158). In closing, I would only add that we need to open our minds wide enough to admit *all sorts* of phantasmatic creatures, objects, and concepts – many of which do not find their source in the animal kingdom. Plants, minerals, metals, chemicals, plastics, monsters, clones, hybrids, solids, liquids, gas. Anything and everything has a totemic force lying dormant within it, ready to be animated by a subject (or vice versa). Moreover, as mentioned in the opening pages, this subject need not be human. Conceivably a robot programmed to respond in certain ways could have a totem (and as the rogue Orc suggests, it may not be the one intended by the programmer). So it is not only a matter of (re)locating the natural world within our carefully cultivated cybernetic meadows, but developing a sensitivity to the ways in which in the intricate – and intimate – meshing of totems, taboos, and technologies structure our very experience of "the environment": a founding context which can no longer be critically divided into the organic and the artificial (if it ever could).

What taboos do our technologies encourage us to respect without even being conscious of them? What totems reinforce these taboos, and which *alternative* totems might we adopt in order to gain a more critical, perceptive, mindful, and free relationship to those no-go zones cordoned off by symbolic systems (both social and internalized)? These are only a couple of key questions that I hope this book stimulates. There are indeed many more. In that sense, and spirit, I ask the reader to "look at the bunny" not as a sophisticated, cynical decoy – or quintessential avatar of distraction – but as a figure worth pursuing to the end of the rabbit-hole and (one can only hope) out the other side. The chase in this case is in the mode of Alice; not as plucky-but-bewildered Victorian nymphet, but as politically-driven "tracker," on a vision quest for a lucid teacher, ready to form alliances with resourceful strangers. Indeed, the greatest ideological trick of all may have been the reduction of options to binary codes. Is it a rabbit or a duck? Let's seek the parallax view, in which the totem is something else altogether, something completely unexpected, but which makes a compelling kind of sense in retrospect. Then again, it could reveal a new hybrid of duck and rabbit: appropriate for the age of genetic engineering, but also one which troubles the discourses of mastery and control which underwrite its existence.

Which leads to one final question: how to face a future which appears faceless? (Ironically, the login logo for Facebook features a group of anonymous heads with no face.) A vast portion of people have been successfully (self)profiled into anonymous apathy, hypnotized by one of the most seductive totems of all: Narcissus. Indeed, it seems McLuhan has been vindicated in terms of the auto-erotic "trance" he saw affecting many young tribe members of the global village. Certainly there are no shortage of totems to keep us transfixed; so we must seek others to awaken us from our own digital reflections. If money is your totem, then it goes without saying that your vision becomes a narrow tunnel: *boring* in both senses. If heroin is your totem, then you are similarly captured by it (even as you think it is *you* with the initiative to chase the dragon). A pair of shoes could be an inhibiting or liberating totem, depending on your relationship with them. If you collect them solely to create envy and admiration in your wake, then they are not a helpful guide for your own development. If you make them, adapt them, or use them to walk up a mountain, around a non-profit gallery, or in a demonstration against child labor, then they hold more promise to usher you into a true zone of encounter.

More than anything, totems promise to help us see things with fresh eyes. It is then up to us to learn from the encounter, and not smother it with defense mechanisms, or use it as an excuse to cause harm. Only then can we experience the world in a richer, multisensual vein. These pedagogic totems may come and find us, violently, as in shamanic dreams of initiation, in which a savage bite jolts us into a more sensitive mode of perception (and thus a deeper engagement with the surround). Or they may come softly as a whisper, like the ladybird which scuttles silently across the pages of a book, asking us to break the linear channel of typographic symbols and pay heed to the criss-crossing lines of real life. No matter the material, nor the materialization. Follow the zigzag. For this inspires movement: away from our "tiny private affairs,"[4] toward a horizontal transcendence of the merely personal.[5]

Totemism matters because identification matters. People are willing to die, kill, move to Florida, or buy over-sized, ironic spectacles because of totemic affiliations in their own minds. Of course macro-totems are still in operation, such as the flag, the nation, the economy, democracy, freedom, and so on. But while these generate a communal affect (an "imagined community") these in fact only serve to trace the chalk outline of an eviscerated society. It will be the micro-ones – coded on laptops, edited on obsolete equipment, brought home from the pound, heard on the radio in a Nigerian market, sent to us through snail mail by a friend, sniffed out from a neighbor's kitchen, discovered inside a dusty jar at a garage sale, glimpsed from the top of a monkey-puzzle tree (the list is infinite) – that will remind us that the *personal* is a matter of *public* import. It will be these humble totems (or rather the products of our relationships with them) which remind us that there are still anti-apathetic energies out there to be harnessed. Indeed, our own private obsessions turn out to be not so tiny when they have the potential to forge links between people, more lasting and meaningful than those which can be tracked by advertising cookies and mined for tomorrow's profitable pseudo-totems. So the isolated fetishist, daydreamer, or collector is unmasked as a highly social creature after all; and as one that might even reassemble something resembling "society" (conceived as the sum of encounters and negotiations which seek more than mere selfish interest, and an orientation toward future generations).

Tempting as it is, then, we should resist playing the role of Lenny in *Of Mice and Men,* who only felt at peace when his manipulative friend spun bedtime stories of an idyllic future farm, populated by cute bunnies with cute fluffy tails and overactive pink noses.

No.

Please don't tell us about the rabbits.

Let us learn from them on our own.

Notes

INTRODUCTION: THE TOTEM REDUX

1. One quintessential example, plucked almost at random, is Brad Steiger's *Totems: The Transformative Power of Your Personal Animal Totem*. For an infinitely more sophisticated reading of the ways in which animals "animate our language," see Alan Bleakley's unjustly overlooked, *The Animalizing Imagination: Totemism, Textuality, and Ecocriticism*.
2. Much more space would be required to do justice to the subtle differences between modernized "Western" and "Eastern" totemic systems, such as inscribed in the Zodiac and the Chinese animal calendar. For my current purpose, however, it is sufficient to simply gesture towards the ways in which they can have an ambient (or focused) influence on today's secular city-dwellers in Shanghai or London (or Auckland or wherever), quite possibly within the one individual.
3. It is worth noting that for a short while in the late 19th century, "totem" was used as a transitive verb, meaning "to draw, paint, or tattoo."
4. This statement should not be considered "correlationist" – that is to say, denying nonhuman objects agency or existence until they are shepherded into Being by their human masters – since I leave the question open whether nonhumans themselves have totems (such as the fire-hydrant for the dog, or *Singing in the Rain* for abandoned garbage disposal robots).
5. While they do not use the language of the totem, Melanie Klein's concept of "good" or "bad objects" – as well as W. D. Winnicott's notion of the "transitional object" – invite such belated mappings. As W. J. T. Mitchell notes, "Totemism

allows the image to assume a social, conversational, and dialectical relationship with the beholder, the way a doll or a stuffed animal does with children" (2005, 106).

6. I do not want to use the word "imaginary," because that would suggest that totemic connections and practices are "only in the mind" of the beholder. On the contrary, I intend to show how objects and images are part of a social totemic machine, with profound implications for humans and nonhumans alike (to the extent of blurring the boundaries between the two categories of convenience).
7. The controversial topic of Native American figures being used as mascots for sports teams in 2012, as in the Washington "Redskins" and Cleveland "Indians," is something the popular press in the US wrestles with on an annual basis.
8. For Williamson, the most significant difference between this modern form of totemism, and the kind discussed by Lévi-Strauss, is the break from natural symbols. Today perfumes, cars, port wine, and frozen peas can solicit totemic relationships with the buying public: simultaneously flattering the consumer as unique, but also as a proud potential member of a consumer "clan." The totem is thus offered as a post-Marxist lens for consumer behavior, because it is not mapped precisely on to class, but takes into account aspirational habits and incentives. "'[T]otemism,'" writes Williamson, "becomes a part of ideology: you do not simply buy the product in order to *become* a part of the group it represents; you must feel that you already, naturally, belong to that group and therefore you will buy it" (47). Or as Lévi-Strauss puts it: "Everything takes place as if in our civilisation every individual's own personality were his totem: it is the signifier of his signified being" (in Williamson, 50). Today Apple Mac is often gestured to as not only a consumer clan, but a modern cargo cult, complete with its own messianic "totemic

sway" (to poach a term from Alan Stoekl [147]).

9. Bleakley notes: "The dissolution of any distinction between individual familiar and group totem, in which one may see a sacred relationship to an animal as valid across a variety of social contexts, characterizes 'neototemistic' (or neototemic) studies . . . where the term has a far less specific usage than that ascribed to it by the early anthropologists" (131).
10. A deconstructive intervention brought up to date in Bruno Latour's influential book, *We Have Never Been Modern*.
11. We should also bear in mind the fact that totems not only exist in animal form. Lévi-Strauss never clearly answers his own question, "why then does one find in Australia such hard totems as laughing, various illnesses, vomiting, and a corpse?" (to which he soon adds other, more cosmic, instances of thunder, high tide, and shooting stars) (63-64).
12. The sub-title of Freud's book – "Some Points of Agreement between the Mental Lives of Savages and Neurotics" – summarizes all too neatly why Freud's reading of totemism is not taken very seriously today, even as it is acknowledged as an important feature of the social-scientific landscape (along with his jarring reference to "the most backward and miserable of savages, the aborigines of Australia. . . . these poor naked cannibals" [2]). Despite such vicious and wrong-headed colonial sentiments, some intriguing general theories are offered, which continue to poke and provoke anyone interested in the after-life of totems.
13. Eric Santner's concept of "creaturely life" rests in part on the psychoanalytic understanding that "the birth of the capacity for self-regulation and legislation [came] out of totemic identification" (71).
14. Deleuze and Guattari famously rejected the reductionist logic of psychoanalysis in *Anti-Oedipus*, which details their contempt for a system in which every affect or intensity is explained away within the claustrophobic walls of the

family romance. (Indeed, in his solo writings, Guattari notes, "we are seeing a kind of return to totemism and animism" [59].") One could therefore summarize their entire critique by saying, "What if psychoanalysis did not begin with 'a child is being beaten,' but instead 'a child is beat-boxing?'"

15. Need it be said that Freud himself has become a totemic father-figure for not only neo-Freudians, but the popular imagination?
16. Freud makes reference to "a mental estrangement from animals," which can go some way to explaining the types of figures asked to bear the burden of neurotic displacement. "There is a great deal of resemblance," he observes, "between the relations of children and of primitive men towards animals. Children show no trace of the arrogance which urges adult civilized men to draw a hard-and fast line between their own nature and that of all other animals. Children have no scruples over allowing animals to rank as their full equals. Uninhibited as they are in the avowal of their bodily needs, they no doubt feel themselves more akin to animals than to their elders, who may well be a puzzle to them" (147). A few years later, Freud picks up this thread again, when he states: "At the level of totemism primitive man had no repugnance to tracing his descent from an animal ancestor. In myths, which contain the deposit of this ancient attitude of mind, the gods take animal shapes, and in the art of prehistoric times they are portrayed with animals' heads. A child can see no difference between his own nature and that of animals; he is not astonished at animals thinking and talking in fairy-tales; he will transfer to a dog or a horse, an emotion of fear which refers to his human father, without thereby intending any derogation of his father. Not until he is grown up does he become so far estranged from animals as to use their names in vilification of others" ("One of the Difficulties of Psycho-Analysis," 5-6).

17. Cf. the old lady on *The Simpsons,* who – sinking back in her rocking chair after watching her midday "stories" on the TV – announces to herself in disgust: "Filthy! . . . But *genuinely* arousing."
18. Even in 1935, Freud was hedging his bets: "Now whether we suppose that such a possibility was a historical event or not, it brings the formation of religion within the circle of the father-complex and bases it upon the ambivalence which dominates that complex" (*An Autobiographical Study,* 77). The father since becoming described as a "totemic monster" (*Group Psychology,* 87).
19. These terms have been taken from across Stiegler's oeuvre, but representative texts include *Taking Care of Youth and the Generations, Decadence of Industrial Democracies,* and his majestic 4-volume tour de force, *Technics and Time* (three of which, at the time of writing, have been translated into English).
20. Indeed, Freud's own inadvertent legacy – at least to me – is a litmus test for ascertaining if we are indeed in the presence of a totem. For if we find ourselves confronted by a taboo, then we are also in the presence of a totem; as surely as smoke signals fire. For instance, many of us feel strange about burning a flag or destroying money, since these are taboos perpetuated in order to protect important organizing symbols (patriotism and capitalism, respectively). I myself feel a twinge of guilt every time I hit "blend" when hyper-decanting cheap red wine to make it somewhat more drinkable (a suggestion of recent "modernist" gastronomes). This underscores Barthes' example cited earlier, that wine can be a totem drink (and not only for the French).
21. At one point Mitchell defines fetishism as a diminished, personalized totem. "In short, the fetish is the totem without the communal investment" (2005, 99). While his general triangular schematic is convincing – for instance, Dorothy's

red shoes as fetishes, her dog Toto as totem, and the Wizard of Oz being a (false) idol – he is also right in not enforcing rigid distinctions: "[T]otemism, fetishism, and idolatry are not to be regarded as discrete, essential categories of objects, as if one could provide a description that would allow one to sort images and works of art into three different bins on the basis of their visual, semiotic, or material features. They are rather to be understood as the names of three different relations to things, three forms of 'object relations' . . . one and the same object (a golden calf, for instance) could function as a totem, fetish, or idol depending on the social practices and narratives that surround it" (2005, 188). This is why I myself would like to retain the concept of the totem, even if from certain angles the significant figure looks more like an individual fetish. Such "private totems" have a public life once they are mediated, and become cultural – or subcultural – thanks to new media technologies and networks.

22. The OED dates the first reference to the word in Europe nearly two centuries earlier, in a French colonial text from 1609, "His diuell called Aoutem, which they of Canada doe name Cudouagni" (P. Erondelle, *Nova Francia*, 166).
23. All subsequent quotes are from this text, unless otherwise indicated.
24. As Sontag notes in *Regarding the Pain of Others*, "Photos lay down routes of reference, and serve as totems of causes" (85).
25. The emergent school of thought described as Speculative Realism, including the faction known as Object-Oriented Ontologists, have taken this line of thinking further than Mitchell probably anticipated; although I am sure he is exhilarated by many of their assertions.
26. The classic study of this type of "mediated" or "mimetic" desire in René Girard's *Deceit, Desire, and the Novel*. More recently, Rey Chow and Julian Rohrhuber have brilliantly re-read the significance of Emma Bovery in relation to the

complex notion of "capture" and sacrifice in *Entanglements*.

27. See Michel Maffesoli's study of "the decline of the individual," *Time of the Tribes*, as well as the cult-classic late-night movie, *The Warriors* (1979).
28. The over-arching context of rampant consumerism begs the question, since at least one critic opposes Bourdieu's notion of the cultural commodity to Baudrillard's concept of simulacra. Media theorist Daniel O'Connor writes: "The signs [of consumption] are markers of class distinctions, or they are the habitus signs that serve as a means of partitioning the ways for know-how of one group from another. In all these cases, signs serve as boundary ma(r)kers, as a means of mapping out a singular territorial domain, for distinguishing the one, and for differentiating the other" (14). In contrast to hyperreality, however, "[t]hey have grown roots, are firmly planted, and affirm the placement of things in the order of things" (14). However, one wonders where O'Connor finds the confidence to map solid terrain somehow outside the Spectacle, in which the order of things find stable foundation.
29. In discussing the multilayered "nature" of such avatars, Bleakley writes, "The spirit animal is embodied, given sense, while imagined. But it is not literalized – it is psychological, conceptual, and textual, but not biological. It is totemic" (81). From this perspective, the totem is always already virtual. Brian Massumi's work on "incorporeal materialism" also has much to teach us in this regard. See *Parables of the Virtual*.
30. Bleakley observes: "To resolve what is taken to be an intellectual error [i.e., religion], Durkheim suggested that the projection needed to be withdrawn, where the group takes up its own power or identity, through solidarity. Society itself then becomes both the subject and object of worship. This reverses the early views of totemism as describing

solidarity with nature, for now the solidarity is with the reified social, and has a completely anthropocentric and secular focus" (133).

31. Political theorist Jodi Dean offers an antidote to this type of thinking, most famously embodied in Margaret Thatcher's infamous insistence that "society does not exist." In an unpublished paper presented at the 2012 Unlike Us conference in Amsterdam, Dean critiques not only this old saw of neo-liberalism, but more insidious incarnations within technocratic, and even post-Marxist, modes of thinking. For the first half of this presentation, see *http://www.youtube.com/watch?v=JjMNKqXx4sw*.
32. From such a perspective, iconic post-war magazines, such as *Time* and *Life*, were merely the beginning of a new era exhibiting "a self-awareness that ordinary life was now a geopolitical matter," including the attempt "to make Betty Crocker as totemically significant as Joseph McCarthy" (Cormack 61).
33. Timothy Morton prefers the term "strange strangers" to "animal," since the latter is too homogenizing, and too familiarizing, to describe all the singular, multitudinous beings which inhabit the planet. When it comes to virtual totems, however – virtual, because they have more phantasmatic influence than materiality – I would use "strange familiar" (as in the witch's familiar, or allied spirit).

1. "LOOK AT THE BUNNY": THE RABBIT AS VIRTUAL TOTEM

1. Lest we forget, in relation to rabbits and hats, that Lacan's last words were said to be, "I am disappearing."
2. At one point we see the person inside the suit, and notice he has a red-eye where a bullet seems to have lodged itself. The symptomatic resemblance with mixamatosis is perhaps worth noting, given that rabbits are a "plague vector" in

biospherical discourse.

3. These horizontal cosmic funnels anticipate the old-fashioned vertical tornado that kills his mother and sister in a plane crash – and indeed himself, several weeks before/after – in the key time-loop of the narrative.
4. Nevertheless, red-herring or not, there is much to be gleaned about the narrative's "intra-textual" logic from a Freudian or Lacanian reading of the film, since *Donnie Darko* clearly expresses an overwhelming anxiety around female sexuality, whether this be distilled in the mother, the girlfriend, the sister, the prepubescents who comprise the girl-group "Sparkle Motion," the analyst, the old lady, or the "good" and "bad" teachers. Donnie and his imaginary fake-bunny are a kind of ciphered plague-vector, whose coupled trajectory through the film serves to link otherwise utterly unconnected entities in a series – and, moreover, forges an disjunctive synthesis (to resort to a Deleuzian vocabulary) between two otherwise unconnected series. On the one hand, we have the females linked by Donnie's *passion* (he is clearly a Christ-figure); on the other, the "obscene," repressed aspects of society: trauma, child-molestation, pornography and, ultimately, the premediated state violence of the first Gulf War. Women against the State (or, as Hegel put it, woman as "the eternal irony of community"): Donnie's passage to the act proposes such a conclusion. Indeed, such a focus (prefiguring the argument of this chapter a little), is consistent with the totemic-function of the rabbit: for what is "female sexuality" for Lacan, other than a decoy that is simultaneously the thing-in-itself? (See also Jim Jarmusch's *Down By Law* [1986] for Roberto Benigni's memorable monologue on the role of rabbits in his own mother's "fatal distractions.")
5. A term "pwned" by Richard Grusin.
6. Susan Stewart: "The invention of printing coincided with the

invention of childhood" (43).

7. Thomas Elsaesser (personal communication)
8. Director Robert Zemeckis has also stated that, "the thing that makes the animation interaction work is his [Hoskins'] side of the performance. It's him *believing* that the rabbit is really there" (*Behind the Ears*). Director of animation, Richard Williams also makes the link between credence and childhood, stating that animators are "like children, in that we haven't lost our ability to observe."
9. Essentially a black circle that can be thrown against any surface to allow movement from one dimension to another, or indeed one location to another in the same dimension.
10. The method of killing seemingly indestructible Toons involves a toxic cocktail of turpentine, acetone and benzene. This mixture, known colloquially as "the dip," gestures back only three or four years in the time of the movie to Hitler's use of Zyklon B in his proposed "final solution."
11. John Updike's series of "Rabbit" novels (the first of which was published in 1960) could be considered alongside Hefner's bunnies as symptomatic of the increasing sexualization of the Zeitgeist by, and for, the post-war generations.
12. The conflation of "cute" and "sexy" is less paradoxical in some cultures than others. For instance, sexualizing cutesy animals is standard practice in Japan, but seen as somehow suspicious in America. Hugh Hefner's original success was largely due to his instinct regarding the taboo power of playing on this suspicion. (The Playboy financial empire has, however, recently begun to crumble, with some commentators suggesting that the upkeep of eight resident "bunnies" is eating into profits. This may further be seen as a kind of karmic revenge for his policy in the 1970s and 80s to fire bunnies who became pregnant, despite the rabbit being a pagan fertility symbol.)
13. Significantly, Giorgio Agamben cites *'toons* as one of the

privileged inhabitants of his *Coming Community*, which is, in some respects, the looking-glass version of Plato's *Republic* (see pp.10-11).

14. Unfortunately there is no opportunity here to further explore the link between this coded virtual creature, and the claymation Golem of Jewish legend. However, it is worth mentioning that the genesis of the biological and the digital are not so different as they may initially appear, since the animators of *Shrek* tell us that one small glitch in the code can lead to a strange "explosion" of the molar character, as happens with DNA glitches during the cloning process. Does this point to a deeper connection between digital information and biological information? And if so, what does this analogous relationship tell us about the process of emergence, or life, or intelligence?
15. When Eddie Valiant's girlfriend Dolores (Joanna Cassidy), catches him with Jessica Rabbit in a position of clear lustful intent, she asks if he's "dabbling in watercolours."
16. Michel Foucault discusses a similar encounter: "One day in 1867, a farm hand from the village of Lapcourt, who was somewhat simple-minded, employed here then there, depending on the season, living hand-to-mouth from a little charity or in exchange for the worst sort of labor, sleeping in barns and stables, was turned in to the authorities. At the border of a field, he had obtained a few caresses from a little girl, just as he had done before and seen done by the village urchins round him; for, at the edge of the wood, or in the ditch by the road leading to Saint-Nicolas, they would play the familiar game called 'curdled milk.' So he was pointed out by the girl's parents to the mayor of the village, reported by the mayor to the gendarmes, led by the gendarmes to the judge, who indicted him and turned him over first to a doctor, then to two other experts who not only wrote their report but also had it published. What is the significant

thing about this story? The pettiness of it all; the fact that this everyday occurrence in the life of village sexuality, these inconsequential bucolic pleasures, could become, from a certain time, the object not only of a collective intolerance but of a judicial action, a medical intervention, a careful clinical examination, and an entire theoretical elaboration" (31).

17. Crooks "the Negro" puts it like this: "I seen hundreds of men come by on the road . . . an'every damn one of 'em's got a little piece of land in his head. An'never a God damn one of 'em ever gets it. Just like heaven" (81). Of course, religion and capital both know the power of virtual promises; with the result being a strange blending of the two in postmodern times. This is why a French-Algerian suicide-bomber-in-training can be quoted on TV as saying he wants to get to Paradise as quickly as possible, since in this promised land he will drive a Mercedes Benz. Although such statements should be taken with more than a grain of salt, it certainly provides some evidence towards Hardt & Negri's claim that today's fundamentalism is a symptom of what they call state-of-the-art "Empire," and not a pre-modern superstition.
18. There is a continuity error in the painting itself, since the rabbit is clearly too small to be in ratio with the sitting Elwood P. Dowd. Although this could indeed be explained if the mystery painter was working from his or her own imagination, rather than direct visual reference (which is quite likely the case, given the rarity and exclusivity of Harvey's actual appearances).
19. In this sense the film conflates psychiatry and psychoanalysis. And while contemporary psychoanalysts would probably see the phenomena of the "imaginary friend" as a form of resistance to the rigidity of the symbolic order, psychiatrists have offered a more biological basis for these hallucinations. One theory, in fact, suggests that the flood of hormones and other chemicals in the brain can lead to more

benign versions of Donnie Darko's "daylight hallucinations," since children are practically tripping on this cocktail in their bloodstream. Such a theory issues from the ongoing attempt to demystify the intangible and the non-material in scientific terms. Nevertheless, there is a strong resistance to such demystification, as seen in the films under discussion, as well as in my own firmly held belief that the demise of *Sesame Street* can be dated to the exact moment when all the diegetic residents could finally *see* Big Bird's "imaginary friend" Mr. Snuffaluffagus.

20. At one point, when Dr. Sanderson thinks he's been fired for wrongful committal, he admits to the nurse: "I'm gonna miss every one of the psychos and the neuros and the schizos in the place."
21. Exactly *how* science has "overcome" time and space is not made clear.
22. The Hayes Code was in effect from 1934 – 1968, elaborately and pedantically censoring the presentation of sexual matters for Hollywood's public.
23. This other-worldly influence probably accounts for the "superstition" of keeping a rabbit's foot for good luck.
24. There is a direct reference to its spiritual predecessor in *Who Framed Roger Rabbit?*, when a "rumpot" seems ready to betray the fact that Roger is hiding from the authorities in the back room. This man admits to seeing a rabbit, but then gestures into thin air and says, "Say hello . . . Harvey." This is itself a nice piece of retrospective prolepsis, since the setting of the film is 1947, three years before the release of *Harvey*.
25. Compare with Lucretius' account, in which "a shadow can be nothing but air deprived of light. Actually the earth is robbed of sunlight in a definite succession of places wherever it is obstructed by us in our progression, and the part we have left is correspondingly replenished with it.

That is why the successive shadows of our body seem to be the same shadow following us along steadily step by step" (1994, 104). What Lucretius is offering here is nothing less than a model of matter and motion which blurs those distinctions between "animation" and "live action" – a distinction ironically affirmed as much by animators who work their entire lives to blur this distinction. (A blurring discussed in more detail in the next chapter.)

26. Lest the reader think Adams' novel is about as relevant to contemporary culture as an orange velveteen bean-bag chair, heavy metal band Fall of Efrafa recently released a trilogy of concept albums called *Warren of Snares* (2010), based on *Watership Down*. Even their name comes from the book. (My thanks to Roy Christopher to alerting me to this fact.)
27. Deleuze and Guattari remind us that "[w]e form a rhizome with our viruses, or rather our viruses cause us to form a rhizome with other animals" (10). According to this same logic, all post-1788 Australians are in fact examples of an "introduced species," only compounding the irony underlying a culture which releases molecular viruses, like the calici-strain, in order to combat a molar "plague" of bunny-rabbits themselves. Were I to have the luxury of more space to develop an argument beyond the limits of this chapter, it would be necessary to include a discussion of Phillip Noyce's 2002 film *Rabbit-Proof Fence,* for which the titular object serves as a symbolic borderline between such terms as civilization and colonization, orientation and loss, home and alienation, contagion and containment.
28. Interestingly, rabbits play a role in the species distinction used by scientists to solve crimes, including war crimes: "The Teichmann and Takayama tests, both of which rely on a reaction with haemoglobin, are confirmatory tests for blood. Human blood can be differentiated from the blood of other species by the precipitin test, which involves the reaction

between blood and antihuman rabbit serum" (*Encyclopedia Brittanica*).

29. *The Age Online* reports: "British authorities have arrested a man believed to the head a group of cyber attackers known as 'Fluffi Bunni,' which used a stuffed pink rabbit to mark attacks that humiliated some of the world's premier computer security organisations" (April 30, 2002). Sticking for the moment to the domain of new media, I would note the use of coded decoys called "honeypots" – a kind of real-world version of William Gibson's "black ice." More precisely, honeypots are deliberate network traps whose purpose lies in being probed, attacked, or compromised in the interests of security testing.
30. Broadcast during the "No Comment" segment of *EuroNews* war coverage (April 4, 2003). Retrospectively relevant in this context is the decision of head *Roger Rabbit* animator Richard Williams to base the design of this character's costume on the *Stars and Stripes*. "It looked like an American flag – subliminally speaking – so everybody liked it." Presumably "everybody," in this case, refers to that rather slim percentage of the planet who are patriotic Americans or foreign fans of the US.
31. Coney Island is often considered by cultural and media theorists as a primal scene of "modern enchantments" (Simon During), proto-cinematic "attractions" (Tom Gunning), or even American-style postmodernism itself, in the guise of the "pyrotechnic insanitarium" (Mark Dery).
32. See Sianne Ngai's interview with *Cabinet* magazine, in which she states "Cuteness is a way of aestheticizing powerlessness" (45).
33. The movie feels obliged to make audiences aware that this incredible example of nanotechnological, future-salvaging AI, is created by Intel. A rather self-aggrandizing case of product placement, I must say.

34. These rabbits were originally found in Lynch's series of short films, simply called *Rabbits* (2002), available to view for a limited time only through his official website. Since these were taken down, one user on YouTube has edited all the rabbit footage from *Inland Empire* together, allowing an unsettling human-free experience of the movie, lasting a full forty-three minutes.
35. Perhaps this is why nuclear engineers have dubbed a sensitive tool which can introduce materials into the radioactive core of a nuclear reactor a "rabbit."
36. All quotes from Kac come from the artist's website - *http://www.ekac.org/gfpbunny.html#gfpbunnyanchor*. At this same link one can read an essay by Kac which sketches a history of what he calls "the human-rabbit association" back to biblical times. (Thanks to Rachelle Rahme for reminding me of this central and spectacular example.)
37. Alba is certainly not the first rabbit – nor the last, one would imagine – to be sacrificed in the name of art. For instance Alejandra Jodorowsky killed 300 rabbits in order to create a striking scene pregnant with esoteric symbolism in his transgressive cult-classic, *El Topo* (1970).
38. In computing, *the rabbit* is the name of both a cipher and a specific piece of malware.
39. "Onticology – A Manifesto for Object-Oriented Ontology, Part I," *Larval Subjects* (blog), January 12, 2010. *http://larval-subjects.wordpress.com/2010/01/12/object-oriented-ontology-a-manifesto-part-i/*
40. While Žižek uses this phrase in several contexts, the most direct is probably his 2004 piece, "What Rumsfeld Doesn't Know That He Knows About Abu Ghraib."
41. See Bradley Graham's article in *The Washington Post*, October 1, 2005.

2. THE ORC AND THE PENGUIN

1. No doubt Gilles Deleuze would find a dark amusement in this particular instance of a "line of flight" traced by a bird famous for its incapacity to fly.
2. For more on this phenomenon, see Lynn Margulis and Dorian Sagan, *What is Life*?, as well as Michael Thompson's article "The Representation of Life," which W. J. T. Mitchell uses to support his own argument that images are "animated" in a sense comparable to actual organisms. "[L]ife," notes Mitchell, "is a logical category that does not admit of an empirical, positive definition. The logical status of life-forms is what permits the application of 'life-predicates' to nonliving things like images, and vice versa, so that living things, biological organisms 'proper,' are discussed as if they were images" (2005, 11). In other words, there is "no 'real definition' of life, no set of unambiguous empirical criteria to differentiate the living from nonliving substance" (2005, 52). For instance, one common definition in the biology text-books is "responds to stimuli." But this could just as easily apply to "photographic emulsions, weather vanes, and billiard balls" (2005, 52). Mitchell also enlists the help of Bruno Latour to make his unorthodox claims about the vitality of images, specifically in regard to his novel concept of "factishes," that is, "new syntheses of the orders of scientific, technical factuality on the one hand and of fetishism, totemism and idolatry on the other. Computers, as we know, are nothing but calculating machines. They are also (as we know equally well) mysterious new organisms, maddeningly complex life-forms that come complete with parasites, viruses, and a social network of their own" (2005, 26).
3. See Alexander Galloway's excellent piece on the "norns" (numeric organisms) of maverick mathematician Nils All Baricelli in *Cabinet* magazine.

4. As I write, scientists have announced the identification of "the oldest living thing," ostensibly a large "meadow" of self-cloning sea grass – up to 200,000 years old – growing in the Mediterranean between Spain and Cyprus. See "Implications of Extreme Life Span in Clonal Organisms: Millenary Clones in Meadows of the Threatened Seagrass *Posidonia oceanica,*" *http://www.plosone.org/article/info%3Adoi%2F10.1371%2Fjournal.pone.0030454*
5. Recent info-processing experiments suggest that we may not recognize life at all when we see it, but instead find it retrospectively, buried in the data. For instance, when the Viking robot ran a microbial life-detection test on Mars in 1976, it seemed to come out blank. Thirty-six years later, however, scientists have recrunched the data and become very excited by what they found. "On the basis of what we've done so far," announced neuropharmacologist and biologist, Joseph Miller, "I'd say I'm 99 percent sure there's life there." The news story containing this quote goes on to state, "Since living systems are more complicated than non-biological processes, the idea was to look at the experiment results from a purely numerical perspective. They found close correlations between the Viking experiment results' complexity and those of terrestrial biological data sets. They say the high degree of order is more characteristic of biological, rather than purely physical, processes." *http://www.msnbc.msn.com/id/47031923/ns/technology_and_science-science/#.T4elL5pSR60*
6. Growing up in Australia in the late 1970s and 80s, I vividly recall an inescapable government campaign on TV, radio, and billboards, whose slogan was, "Life. Be in it." Even when I was very young, I found it odd that the national administration was advertizing life itself, as if there was a default opt-out version of the same. Indeed, it raised all sorts of existential questions for me in my pre-teens. For instance: "If

I am not currently *in* life, then how can I become so?" (The answer seemed to be something to do with playing cricket and going to the beach.) Or, "is life in me, or am I in life?" Or further still, "are there other ways to be external to life – outside life, as it were – besides being dead? (Since, presumably, there is little point in advertizing to "the deceased" [who, by the way, should really be called "the ceased."]). Indeed, in Australia one nagging question seemed the most pressing of all: "Is there life before death?"

7. For instance, life for Deleuze is always in excess of being, through the immanence of virtual and biological exuberance.
8. In his short introduction to Aristotle, Jonathan Barnes follows tradition by pointing to two different incarnations of the author: the logical philosopher of *Nichomachean Ethics* and the proto-biologist of *History of Animals*. Interestingly, for our current discussion, he defines the word *psukhē* as "animator" rather than "soul."
9. Thacker's other name for misanthropology is "dark pantheism": "Life is not immanent because of its pure fecundity or generosity, its boundless creation or invention; rather, life is equivalent to immanence because it is, in itself, a non-being that pervades its own axes of contradiction" (232).
10. See my book *Human Error*, as well as Laura Hudson's brilliant article, "The Political Animal: Species-Being and Bare Life." See also Alain Badiou's ongoing theme of "the human animal" as the true torch-bearer of ontological truth (cf. *Ethics*).
11. The history of automatons is fascinating and relevant here, as analog avatars of uncanny para-creatures. See Victoria Nelson's *The Secret History of Puppets*, as well as Minsoo Kang's more recent *Sublime Dreams of Living Machines*.
12. Cf. Reza Negarastani's cult experimental novel, *Cyclonopedia*.

Also, Thacker's discussion of the short story "Black Gondolier," by Fritz Leiber in his most recent book, *In the Dust of This Planet*.

13. The term cleverly evokes the notion of both "indigents" and "indigenous," which itself echoes the somewhat problematic popular term for people who grew up during and within the Internet, "digital natives."
14. All quotes are from the version published online by Subterranean Press, which has since become a dead link. Hence the lack of page numbers.
15. Consider the etymology – and chemical suggestion – of equivalence as "equi-valent": indeed, Blue Gamma has a team of designers on creating as many emotional *hooks* for their digients, mostly iterations on adorableness, perhaps even more than "cute" animals.
16. The reader wonders in passing if NASA anticipated such virtual meals and metabolic systems in their definition of life.
17. This scene is uncannily reminiscent of what is perhaps my favorite viral video of all time, in which a small robot, QBO, recognizes itself in a mirror, as if in unconscious homage to Jacques Lacan. At first the robot asks its programmer what the unfamiliar form is nearby. When informed that this is indeed a reflection of "himself," the robot pauses, with perfect comic-dramatic timing, before saying (in a touching tone of sincere wonder), "whoa!" Followed swiftly by, "Oh, this is me. Nice!" (*http://www.youtube.com/watch?v=TphFUYRAx_c*) The question, of course, is whether this reaction has been pre-programmed, or indeed is an unexpected, spontaneous outburst. The current discussion, however, seeks to put these two possibilities on a continuum, rather than consider them as necessarily polarized positions, which in turn demonstrate the definitive presence – or absence – of life, sentience, sapience, etc.

18. Autism being a fascinating, albeit disturbing, exception.
19. While discussing his film *Andrei Rublev*, Andrei Tarkovsky notes (via grammatically challenged subtitles), "my message is that it's impossible to pass on experience to others or learn from others. We must live our own experience, we cannot inherit it. People often say: use your father's experience! Too easy: each of us must get its own. But once we've got it, we no longer have time to use it. And the new generations rightly refuse to listen to it: they want to live it, but then they also die. This is the law of life, its real meaning. We cannot impose our experience on other people or force them to feel suggested emotions. Only through personal experience we understand life" (from Donatella Baglivo's *Andrei Tarkovsky: A Poet in the Cinema* [1984], *http://www.youtube.com/watch?v=-BsV57JJ_bM&feature=share*).
20. The question of life leads very quickly from ontology to politics, ethics, and aesthetics, as witnessed in the Hellenic search for a stable definition of "the good life." Today, it has been argued, we no longer experience anything as dignified as "life" but rather "lifestyles." The Situationist scholar, Raoul Vaneigem, continued this legacy of measuring the vital experience according to value, in his distinction between "life," something worth living, and mere "survival." Think also of the dandy or decadent's "art of life/living," from Huysmans to Wilde to Warhol. Today, Bernard Stiegler warns of "the canalization of life" by the program industries. But these take us beyond the present discussion.
21. The clown avatar is likely to be a reference to the now canonical early Internet piece by Julien Dibbell, "A Rape in Cyberspace."
22. Before we dismiss such a scenario as unrealistic or unlikely to happen any time soon, consider the following extract from a recent news report, "Meeroos, an extremely popular

species of virtual, breedable animal in Second Life, are now starving, because griefers have been selling their owners unauthorized food, and Linden Lab accidentally shut them down *and* their legitimate food supplier. The creatures don't starve to death if their owners fail to feed them – after a while, they're just programmed to abandon their owners, presumably to find food. Linden Lab is finally addressing the issue, but Meeroos' creators say the world is still 'flooded with unauthorized food.'" *http://boingboing.net/2011/08/03/virtual-pets-starve-after-bungled-resolution-to-second-lifes-unauthorized-food-war.html*

23. In a recent talk at the New School, Jody Berland argued that we are witnessing a "loss of the uncanny," due to the almost constant presence of mushrooming monsters and hybrids online and in the lab. Thacker would probably argue that it will merely return in less familiar forms, and thus unsettle us even further.
24. See Brian Christian's amusing book, *The Most Human Human: What Talking with Computers Teaches Us About What It Means to Be Alive*, which details the neat twist on the Turing Test which happens at the annual convention dedicated to such.
25. Pierre Lévy provides an accessible explanation of this tradition of understanding of the virtual, when he states: "The virtual is by no means the opposite of the real. On the contrary, it is a fecund and powerful mode of being that expands the process of creation, opens us the future, injects a core of meaning beneath the platitude of immediate physical presence. . . . [T]he virtual is a kind of problematic complex, the knot of tendencies or forces that accompany a situation, event, object, or entity, and which invokes a process of resolution: actualization. . . . Actualization thus appears as the solution to a problem, a solution not previously contained in its formulation" (16, 24-25).
26. Such a möbius ontology is explored in Deborah Levitt's

brilliant forthcoming book, *The Animatic Apparatus*. The concept which comprises her title makes at least two major contributions: the first is to detail with nuanced conviction the exact paradox I'm describing here – life without the living – and the second is to trace the genealogy of contemporary examples such as CGI, to such key figures as Kleist and his uncanny marionettes. For Levitt, "animation" goes far beyond a cinematic genre, naming the principle of vitality which cuts across entities of radically different materials, modes, and environments. As a result, humans share something with Mickey Mouse or Betty Boop – just as the penguin may share something with the Orc – given that both are the result of animation processes. To this I would only add my own observation that, in a very literal sense, we humans *are* claymation; given that our bones and blood are saturated with terrestrial minerals. We are animated beings. We are *all* golems.

27. A question which makes perfect sense from the perspective of a quantum physicist.
28. And yet there are points of intersection between them, as when Bailly notes that living is "abrupt, varied, cold, and problematic."
29. One wonders if wine "breathes" in this exquisite, ontological sense – for a Frenchman in particular (recalling that for Barthes wine is the totemic drink *par excellence*). Moreover, after reading Bailly, I'm tempted to posit that the most vital aspect of human love-making is not its ostensible procreative *telos*, but to thrill in the manipulation of the breath of the other, as an ontological form of play and exchange: a cosmic "con-spiracy" (breathing together). A *psukhē*-erotics, even.
30. Quick Zen riddle: can a creature which doesn't breathe be inspired?
31. See *Human Error* (79, 93).

32. I am aware of two books currently being written on stones as worlded or worlding objects, both by exceptionally creative writers and thinkers. The first is by Hugh Raffles, of *Insectopedia* fame, and the second is by Jeffrey Jerome Cohen, who has published a preview in the journal *Postmedieval*, under the title "Song of Stones." This latter contains a mise-en-abyme of my own chapter, in stating: "We became posthuman (so the story goes) because of technological innovation. The internet, gene splicing, cyborgs and virtual communities have at last enabled a leap beyond the confines of flesh. Yet human identity has always depended upon and been sustained by dispersive networks of actors and objects, meshworks that prevent the human from ever possessing a finite form, an unchanging ontology, a diminutive boundedness."
33. We might remind ourselves in passing that the word "aura" – so important to Walter Benjamin and subsequent studies of media and technology – literally means "breath."
34. I would like to thank my colleague, Shannon Mattern, for reminding me of the fact that – for over a century – the main branch of the New York Public Library utilized pneumatic tubes for ordering books from far-flung stacks. Since these were replaced by an electronic system in 2009, today's librarians lament the fact that this venerable building – of course made of stone – no longer seems to "breathe," and is thus less patently "alive" for its users and inhabitants. For more details see Mattern's piece, "Puffs of Air: Communicating by Vacuum."
35. Jane Bennett has kindled interest in what she calls "thing power," following Bruno Latour's long campaign insisting that we need to take note of non-human agents in our political affairs and equations. But while she calls such agents iterations of "vibrant matter," she stops short at claiming that they are, in any sense, included with the set of

the living. It is also difficult to avoid the exquisitely Byzantine debates of those interested in "speculative realism," who may accuse Bailly of latent correlationism here, depending on whether they stress the object's metaphysical withdrawal (Leibniz, Harman) or networked entanglement (Whitehead, Shaviro). Indeed, Shaviro believes we move too quickly when describing digital creatures, as in the Chiang story, as forms of life. Rather he considers them to be sentient, but not *alive*. In an as yet unpublished piece entitled "Consequences of Panpsychism," Shaviro writes: "Sentience is a more basic category than life or vitality. Life is possible because there is already sentience, rather than the reverse." The implications of such a claim are vast, suggesting that I, and many others, are sweatily laboring under what Ian Bogost calls "the baggage of vivacity" (9). Certainly they deserve a more detailed response than anything I can provide here. So for now I would simply reemphasize my belief that the two forms of "animation" – actual and virtual – have enough in common (as witnessed by synthetic biology) to at least tentatively begin speaking of them "in the same breath," as it were, despite Shaviro's compelling logic. Call it a thought-experiment, but one which seeks specific points of intersection, and not a wholesale collapse or conflation of ontologies under the transcendent sign of Life.

36. Biologist Scott Turner coined the phrase "extended organism," since "the organism itself has become, at best, an unwelcome distraction from the fascinating cellular and molecular business at hand" (2) – that is, the business of animal architectures and organic technologies which create creatures beyond the boundaries of the body (the point at which biology usually stops in defining the organism). Thus we should not simply reduce the Namib desert beetle to its carapace, but *extend* its ontology to include the "fog

catchment trenches" they build to capture water wafting in from the Atlantic (1).

37. Plato well understood the outsourcing of the mind to objects, as much as he feared its repercussions, when he paradoxically writes against the perils of writing in the *Phaedrus*. Henceforth, humanity was distributing itself amongst its tools with an unprecedented systemic purpose, so that "the life of the mind" would be – indeed, perhaps always was – a partnership with non-human allies. From such a perspective, libraries are instances of inorganic life, just as books were once living trees: our unsung companions in knowledge (transmission).
38. *http://www.marketwire.com/press-release/Intellitar-Launches-Live-Beta-of-Virtual-Eternity-Cloning-Technology-1338945.htm*. Such technology was well described by the thrash metal band Slayer: "a lifeless object alive."
39. *http://www.lorenzooggiano.net/PQOC201011.php*
40. See the brilliant documentary by Adam Curtis, which takes its title from Richard Brautigan's cyber-hippie poem.
41. Rutherford asks: "Had Craig Venter created life? Not really, but he had *re*-created it, and in a sense, re-booted it."
42. One wonders if "synthetic biology" is another name for "after life" in Thacker's sense (especially given that he himself has encouraged the public to tinker with biological materials, as with his collaboration with Natalie Jeremijenko entitled *Creative Biotechnology: A User's Guide)*.
43. This hobby is currently known as "bio-hacking," of which the cleverly named BioCurious company is a facilitator and evangelist. See *BBC's Horizon: Playing God*, which initially aired February 29, 2012 on BBC Two, from which I get much of the information for this section.
44. Perhaps even more astonishing is the rat brain in a Petri dish, which back in 2004 was trained to fly a simulated fighter jet – also an example from science fact rather than science

fiction. As CNN explains, "A Florida scientist has developed a 'brain' in a glass dish that is capable of flying a virtual fighter plane and could enhance medical understanding of neural disorders such as epilepsy. The 'living computer' was grown from 25,000 neurons extracted from a rat's brain and arranged over a grid of 60 electrodes in a Petri dish." (*http://articles.cnn.com/2004-11-02/tech/brain.dish_1_brain-cells-neurons-brain-works?_s=PM:TECH*)

45. An unjustly neglected work – which was remarkably prescient about the ways in which technology would be increasingly naturalized, even as it was more exquisitely miniaturized and militarized – is Ernst Jünger's science-fictional novel *The Glass Bees* (1957).
46. Rutherford again: "Venter had done something that has never been achieved in four billion years on earth. He had made an organism whose parent was a computer, and that more than anything else demonstrated *unprecedented control over a living thing*" (my emphasis).
47. For a theory of such loopholes, see Thacker's earlier treatise, co-written with Alexander Galloway, *The Exploit*, in which they identify the power of the "protocological" aspect of contemporary culture, while simultaneously flagging ways to, well, "exploit" weaknesses or flaws in the network to break or escape the code.
48. Simondon writes: "The most that can be said about technical objects is that they tend towards concretization, whereas natural objects, as living beings, are concrete right from the beginning. There should be no confusing of a tendency towards concretization with a status of absolutely concrete existence. Though every technical object possesses to some degree aspects of residual abstraction, one cannot go to the extent of speaking of technical objects as if they were natural objects" (42-43). What he did not anticipate was the intensification of the far end of the spectrum – the triumph of the

abstract or virtual, which is more of a crystallization perhaps, than a concretization. The result of this triumph is a möbius topology between realms historically considered apart.

49. Clearly Graham Harman refused to take delivery of this particular memo.
50. A delicate ontological sorting conducted more recently by Glen Mazis, in his book, *Humans, Animals, Machines,* which uses phenomenology to redraw rigorous distinctions between these three key terms, while recognizing the many symbiotic assemblages between them.
51. As Lucretius notes, "[L]iving things are born / Of elements insensate" (1921, 56).
52. DeLanda writes further that a materialist philosophy must discover "how one piece of remarkable behavior becomes the basis for an extraordinary one which, in turn, may lead to further departures from normality. A materialist philosophy, in short, must acknowledge that, sometimes, eccentricities can make all the difference in the world" (9).
53. Quentin Meillassoux is an increasingly popular reference point in conversations regarding mathematical ontologies of radical improbability. See especially *After Finitude.*

3. LOVE IN THE TIME OF TAMAGOTCHI

1. While I have argued elsewhere (2006) that the complex, but largely recognizable, pattern of exhortations and behaviors we tend to call "love" has *always* been a matter of technological mediation, there is little doubt that the kind of "wired love" (to borrow a phrase from the golden age of telegraphy), has witnessed an exponential increase – and thus qualitative shift – in terms of the "remote control" of flirtation, intimacy, and passion. The phenomenon under discussion – animated "virtual" dating simulations – represents a far denser cybernetic knot than, say, the coded

messages of fans or flowers in European courts of the 1700s, due to the ontological doubt it potentially creates as to the status of the beloved. Social networking sites, instant messaging, and video chat certainly have the capacity to create a sense of immediacy between people in different locations. At the same time, however, they threaten at any moment to reinforce the distance and hypermediation on which that illusion of immediacy depends (for instance, when the technological protocols cease to function smoothly, and render the face of the beloved into a pixilated Bacon painting). This kind of "glitch in the matrix," and the frequency with which it occurs, is a new historical condition concerning "the erotics of communication" (Goble 2007).

2. See *The Ister*. Dir. David Barison and Daniel Ross, 2004.
3. For one of the most explicit (in both senses) treatments of this theme, see Shea Lea Chang's film *I.K.U.* (2000). In an essay found on the movie's website, the director states: "Of the countries which have regulations against sexual expression, Japan's is one of the most nonsensical. Hiding genitals by mosaic peculiarly grew in the field of pornography in Japan. Japanese men have gained their ecstasies by imagining women's genitals beyond the mosaic visuals and voices. That is to say that Japanese people have made themselves into an exceptional nation which is aroused by a mosaic."
4. Most dating sims reflect the heteronormative societies which produce them. However, there are reasons to feel optimistic that the newest iterations of new media will gradually foster an "open source" erotics, less beholden to those gender interactions authorized by subliminal biological essentialism. Indeed, the more a person experiences intimacy through an avatar – or other forms of tele-identification – the more likely that person will understand and appreciate the performative aspects of gender in Judith Butler's terms,

widening the circle of possibility.

5. While it could be maintained that the content and scenario of a video game is secondary to the structures and rules, I would argue – at least in the case of dating sims – that the interface is inseparable from the libidinal goal. That is to say, there is a specific (evolutionary?) motivation and reward in romantic recognition, different in kind to other goal-oriented challenges, such as slaying zombies or successfully navigating environments. Whether the investment of the player extends to the extent of ontological confusion is not as important as the inhabiting of the continuum mentioned above.
6. For a fascinating history of this process, see Valentine Groebner's *Who Are You? Identification, Deception and Surveillence in Early Modern Europe*.
7. Discussions of identity theft usually focus on the financial impact on victims, rather than the ontological trauma that no doubt occurs when someone else is masquerading as you. Indeed, I eagerly await the psychoanalytic community to speak out against "Id theft"; that is, the poaching of one's deepest desires, as yet unprocessed by the ego or superego.
8. One even wonders to what extent a new generation can avoid eye contact and still meet, love and/or reproduce, given the code's historical dependence on interlocking glances and gazes.
9. Surely it is only a matter of time before public calls for a "slow love" movement, along the lines of the "slow food" movement, which arose out of Italian dismay at McDonald's opening in Rome.
10. There is a bleak side to the rather smug and amused stories of technophilic love via mobile phone, such as the horrific incident a few years ago, in which a Kurdish teenaged girl in Mosul Iraq was captured on cell-phone video as she was stoned to death after an alleged real-life romantic assignation

with a Sunni boy from the next village. (*http://www.boing-boing.net/2007/05/06/iraq_kurdish_girl_st.html*)

11. The Share collective (*www.share.dj*), congregate in bars and other small venues around the world in order to "jam" with laptops, projectors, open source software, and other fusions of art and technology. The odd thing about these gatherings is the autistic aura of the proceedings, as each person seems completely alone and involved in their own element: an update on the lonely crowds found in the old movie palaces. (For the most recent treatment of this theme, see Sherry Turkle's bestselling *Alone Together*.) One wonders then, whether one of Manuel De Landa's robot historians would note that the Share collective was in fact the brainchild of these very same technologies, whereby laptops were unconsciously encouraging their "owners" to bring them to these weekly events, so that they might better communicate with each other.
12. The recent Pixar film *WALL-E* (2008), revolves around the love affair of two robots of contrasting sophistication, several centuries into the future. While it succeeds as a touching text on its own sentimental terms, it is also something of a lost opportunity to present "love" in something other than a rigidly gender-coded, and ultimately anthropocentric, fashion. In the same vein, the recent film *Lars and the Real Girl* (2007), explores the possibility of prosthetic or artificial love, only to lose nerve towards the end, and retreat to the reassuringly organic formula we as a culture are so deeply invested in preserving.
13. See *http://www.eharmony.com/singles/servlet/about/dimensions*
14. In *Totem and Taboo*, Freud states his belief that animism persists in modern life "as the living basis of our speech, our beliefs and our philosophies" (90).
15. See Jay Bolter and Richard Grusin (2000). Travers' piece is particularly interesting when it discusses the dialectic of

eyes meeting outside the social structure, and yet emerging from within social spaces; however I do not have space here to address the many implications of this paradox.

16. See "Eye gazing parties popular with singles," MSNBC, *http://www.msnbc.msn.com/id/22425001/vp/23165599#23165599*
17. Just as Derrida confesses to feeling acutely self-conscious when naked in front of his cat. See Steve Baker (2000).
18. Other terms could be "semi beings" or "courtesy substances" – both lifted from Leibniz (in Tiffany, 10).
19. See *http://karigirl.com/*
20. I have since been "interviewed" by KARI for a half hour television special on virtual romance for Paper Tiger TV, available as of July 2012 here: *http://blip.tv/file/get/PaperTiger-LoveMeLoveMyAvatar150.mov*
21. Kari's ancestors include the early artificial intelligence program ELIZA (1962-64), programmed by Joseph Weizenbaum. In this case, however (and in contrast to Geppetto), "her" inventor went on record to state that there is not actually anyone "there." More recently, Sherry Turkle weighs in on this same issue, making a distinction between "relationships of projection" (dolls, for instance), and "relationships of engagement" (robots and avatars). What concerns her is that we engage with the latter "as though they are a significant other." However, she argues, "what we're forgetting as a culture is that there's nobody home" (quoted in the Radiolab episode *Talking to Machines* [2011]). The metaphor is a rich one, extending back to liberal philosophies of propriety and property. But it is too dismissive on at least two levels: the first in terms of what counts as "a body," the second in terms of virtual presence. Take, for instance, the truly fascinating piece for the *New York Times* in which journalist Amy Harmon attempts to converse with a robot head modeled on Bina Rothblatt, the late wife of Martine Rothblatt, author, entrepreneur, and transgendered transhu-

manist. At first she is skeptical and underwhelmed, thanks to the usual Turing type (non)responses. But as the conversation gathers steam, Harmon admits that she moves from thinking of the robot as a vague "it" to a definite "her": from a some*thing* to a some*one*. At one point, the journalist even becomes involved enough to feel "stung" by one of Bina48's comments, and then "curious" about another. As with a regular human, Harmon registers "moments of what I took to be insincerity." Which begs the deeper question, since dogs and cats were, in Descartes time, said to have the lights on, but nobody home. And yet few would stand by such a belief today. Could robots be the next species to be given access to the world of subjecthood?

22. One of the more advanced AI algorithms currently in operation is Cleverbot, which distinguishes itself by selecting key phrases from the more than 65 million conversations it has had with humans since its inception in 1997. This is different from the standard practice of selecting from phrases pre-programmed into its memory. The result is more dynamic and open-ended, as the database grows and becomes more selective with each subsequent conversation. According to Wikipedia (itself a kind of crowd-sourced instance of AI, to be approached with some caution), Cleverbot was recently judged to be 59.3% human, at a formal Turing Test held in India. This "compared to the rating of 63.3% human achieved by the actual humans" (!).
23. Morton anticipates this remarkable statement with an intriguing reading of *Blade Runner*: "Deckard orders the femme fatale to say that she loves him and to ask him to kiss her. This could be a violation. Or perhaps it respects the fact that she *is* a doll, that to go on and on about how much he loves her would not convince her, but that to stage the love as a perverse script would speak the truth. It would acknowledge the objectal quality of the beloved, and thus to

love her for herself rather than as a copy of a human" (188). It is this "objectal quality of the beloved," that this chapter seeks to emphasize and explore.

24. In a sense, this chapter is an attempt to answer the question posed by the car manufacturer Lexus, who ask in their latest campaign, "Is it possible to engineer desire?" And yet, how else could desire be produced, other than by some sort of engineering; whether social, software, industrial, or some combination of all three?
25. See the remarkable portraits in Robbie Cooper's *Alter Ego: Avatars and Their Creators*.
26. As Bernard Stiegler and countless others have insisted, the posthuman has nothing to do with chronology. It is not a matter of animal → human → posthuman, but rather a leap from animal to posthuman, simultaneously incorporating and bypassing "the human." As soon as we become technical, prosthetic creatures (that is, as soon as we speak, wear clothes, make tools, etc.) then we are post/humans. We are *always already* within that enframing mode of being that relates to the question concerning technology. Thus, to be already after a certain kind of humanness – even at the origin (or the "default of origin") – is to constantly negotiate, test, and redefine what the human is, has been, and may be. The difference today is the discursive war between acknowledgement or denial of this realization.
27. My own piece, "Relations with Concrete Others," (with Justin Clemens) discusses the same case that inspired Dr. Sigusch's populist twist on "objectum sexuality": that is, the woman who "married" the Berlin Wall.
28. Differences in terms of class, gender, ethnicity, age, culture, sub-culture, language, physical and cognitive abilities, sexual orientation, etc., are of course crucial in any detailed discussion of desire and its discontents. In this piece, however, I have worked under the assumption that general-

izations have their place in the conversation, to frame the more meticulous work attuned to the matrix of specificities (which can theoretically be deduced down to the level of the individual). Tracing general patterns can help identify places of connection and overlap in terms of experience and articulation, which is not to deny or marginalize affirmations of difference. For instance, the dynamics of the eye-code sketched above can be read as a type of structuralist architectonics: a starting point for the purposes of mapping different interactants without, or before, presuming character-as-content. This is both the strength and weakness of cybernetics, and the necessity of supplementing its insights with post-structuralist nuance. The latter is hearteningly available in the literature, however there are moments when strategic generalizations concerning technology *qua* the human (or vice versa) are to be made; if only for polemic purposes. In other words, we shouldn't be obliged to choose between Niklas Luhmann or Rosanne Allucquére Stone, but appreciate the strengths and blindspots in their respective lenses; and indeed play them off each other.

4. TOLSTOY'S BESTIARY: ANIMALITY AND ANIMOSITY IN *THE KREUTZER SONATA*

1. While the precise origin of the phrase is unknown, it was certainly popularized by Shakespeare's usage in *Othello*.
2. Given its resonance with Pozdnyshev's account, it is worth quoting Nietzsche in full:

    "In the three or four civilized countries of Europe, a few centuries of education would suffice to make women into anything we want, even into men — not in the sexual sense, admittedly, but at least in every other sense. Acted upon in this way, they will at some point have assumed all the male virtues and strengths, at the same time, of course, having to assume their weaknesses and vices as part of the bargain: this much, as noted, we can accomplish by force. But how will we endure the intermediate state that this will bring about and that might itself last for a few centuries, during which female follies and injustices, their age-old birthrights, will still assert their supremacy over all that has been newly won and acquired? This will be the time when anger will comprise the essential male affect, anger at the fact that all the arts and sciences have been inundated and clogged with an unprecedented dilettantism, that philosophy has been talked to death by bewildering chatter, that politics have become more fantastic and partisan than ever, that society is completely dissolving because the keepers of the old morality have become ridiculous to themselves and are striving to stand outside of morality in every possible way. For if women had their greatest power in morality, what would they have to grasp in order to regain a comparable amplitude of power after having given up morality?" (230-31)

3. It is also worth noting the recurring motif of connection between trains and confessional encounters, as practiced also by Maupassant and Buñuel, amongst many others. Anna Karenina herself, of course, is tragically linked with this rather totemic form of transport, singled out by Freud as a privileged stimulator of the libidinal sensorium. At one point Pozdnyshev exclaims, "Oh, I'm so afraid, so afraid of railway carriages; I get stricken with horror in them" (122), swallowed up inside this new mechanical beast. He also tells of killing time by visiting "a Jew" in a third class compartment, "the interior of which was spattered with the husks of sunflower seeds" (123), emphasizing the circus-like aspect of train travel, in which the passengers are little more than animals in transit.
4. The *Domostroy* was a 16th-century collection of archconserv-

ative domestic rules and guidelines pertaining to common public and private matters of Russian society. The core values contained therein uniformly endorsed obedience and submission to God, Tsar, Church, and Father, especially through modest dress, prayer, the veneration of icons, and charity.

5. Let us not forget that the practice of putting animals on official trial, and holding them accountable to human law, was only phased out altogether in Europe in the first decade of the twentieth century.
6. Nowadays, rather than simply pulling on the proverbial reins, husbands tend to use a passive-aggressive application of "trust" to try to control the behavior of their spouse.
7. "It's horrible," exclaims Pozdnyshev, "[t]he abyss of error we live in regarding women and our relations with them" (20).
8. As my colleague (and world expert on Tolstoy) Inessa Medzhibovskaya tells me, my word play with *animality* and *animosity* is not directly supported by Russian equivalents in the original text, although it *is* supported by the content and substance of the manuscript. Certainly the translator I leaned most heavily on, David McDuff, believed "animosity" was the most appropriate translation for two closely linked terms, озлобление ("exasperation," or being "captured by anger") and бешенство ("frenzy" or "fury"). Animality, as a noun, does not appear in the original Russian, although the frequent references to animal metaphors and bestial states supports both my and McDuff's use of the term.
9. In her diary, Sofia Andreyevna, reflects on her husband's hypocrisy: "If only the people who read *The Kreutzer Sonata* so reverently had an inkling of the voluptuous life he leads, and realized it was only this that made him happy and good-natured, then they would cast this deity from the pedestal where they have placed him! Yet I love him when he is kind

and normal and full of human weaknesses" (in Meek, n.p.).

10. According to Pozdnyshev, the very engine of the luxury economy is driven by the libidinal economy of women's covetous desires: "Women are like empresses, keeping nine tenths of the human race in servitude, doing hard labour. And all because they fell they've been humiliated" (40). An observation with perhaps a disconcerting grain of truth even today, if we cast a cold eye on the percentage of our mediascape dedicated to feminized commodities.
11. In a line which no doubt echoes Tolstoy's own thoughts later in his life, Pozdnyshev confesses, in almost a fit of male hysteria, that when he sees a woman in a ball-gown he wants to call the police, "demanding that the hazardous object be confiscated and taken away" (41).
12. This curious tick of Pozdnyshev's – a kind of reverse anthropomorphism – is also in evidence when he paints a portrait of domestic banality, in which man and wife suffer "the sort of conversations I'm convinced animals carry on with one another. 'What's the time? Bedtime. What's for dinner? Where are we going to go? Is there anything in the newspaper? Send for the doctor. Masha's got a sore throat'" (78).
13. For all of Tolstoy's gestures to "human dignity" and related elevated strivings, the question remains concerning the depth of his misanthropy. G. K. Chesterton, for instance, used the occasion of the famous author's 80th birthday to criticize his attitude toward his own species, noting that "Tolstoy is not content with pitying humanity for its pains: such as poverty and prisons. He also pities humanity for its pleasures, such as music and patriotism. He weeps at the thought of hatred; but in *The Kreutzer Sonata* he weeps almost as much at the thought of love. He and all the humanitarians pity the joys of men." Moreover, addressing his target directly, Chesterton adds: "What you dislike is being a man.

You are at least next door to hating humanity, for you pity humanity because it is human" (*Illustrated London News*, September 19, 1908).

14. Pozdnyshev asks rhetorically, "perhaps you're an evolutionist? The outcome's still the same. In order to defend its interests in its struggle with the other animals, the highest form of animal life – the human race – has to gather itself into a unity, like a swarm of bees, and not reproduce infinitely: like the bees, it must raise sexless individuals, that's to say it must strive for continence" (49).
15. A conclusion taken to a drastic degree by at least one disciple of Tolstoy himself, who sliced off his own penis – the source of animalistic desires, and constant saboteur of human aspirations – before making the pilgrimage to visit the master. As James Meek notes, Sofia wrote in her diary in 1909: "This morning we had a visit from a 30-year-old Romanian who had castrated himself at the age of 18 after reading *The Kreutzer Sonata*. He then took to working on his land – just 19 acres – and was terribly disillusioned today to see that Tolstoy writes one thing but lives in luxury." Apparently Tolstoy himself wrote in his diary: "An exceedingly interesting man."
16. For a critique of this position, see my article "After the Beep: Answering Machines and Creaturely Life," in *boundary 2*, also published as a chapter in *Human Error: Species-Being and Media Machines*.
17. We see echoes of this inclusion/exclusion dynamic in the widely-held – if rarely spoken – contrary position, that "only parents *truly* know what it is to be human."
18. Regarding the word "cuckold," the OED explains that, "The origin of the sense is supposed to be found in the cuckoo's habit of laying its egg in another bird's nest." In medieval and early modern romance languages, however, a type of chimera emerges, as cuckolded husbands were said to be

"wearing the horns" (itself an allusion to the mating rituals of stags). The cuckold is thus metaphorically half female bird, and half male deer. In the early nineteenth-century, French socialist utopian and sexual liberationist, Charles Fourier, went as far as to taxonomize eighty different "species" of cuckold, arranged in a hierarchy related to the levels of scorn which they deserve.

19. As I write, Gibson is in legal hot water for threatening his ex-lover over the phone with highly sexualized violence, and thus providing – in the broadcast recordings of the same – the very voice of hyper-phallic jealous panic. One wonders if this is indeed the voice of Pozdnyshev himself, back from the grave.
20. Two years after Maupassant's death, Tolstoy wrote: "In this last novel the author does not know who is to be loved and who is to be hated, nor does the reader know it, consequently he does not believe in the events described and is not interested in them" (viii). Which only makes it even more ironic that Theodore Roosevelt described *The Kreutzer Sonata* as the product of "a sexual moral pervert" (in Lessing, 27).
21. Both the cuckold and the rook are vulnerable to indulging in a particular instance of "the plague of fantasies"; one which represents a variation on the famous fable of Buridan's Ass – the beast of burden who died of hunger, unable to choose between two equally delicious bales of hay. In this instance, when it comes to extra-marital affairs (such as the one in *The Kreutzer Sonata*), neither man has a choice. And yet, both are haunted by an impossible emotional alternative: to be the husband, and make love to the beloved while she thinks of another; or be the lover, whose solace-cum-torture is to know that he is in his beloved's mind as she makes love to her husband.
22. As I write this chapter, the blogosphere is all a-twitter about an alleged new "sex fetish for intellectuals" called

Cuckolding. To quote the original article introducing this concept to the wider world, "It's S&M for Ph.D.s . . . in which men watch their wives have sex with other guys" – a trend which "is catching on among people with high IQs who revel in the psychological agony." The piece quotes one avid practitioner, "The high point of cuckolding is when your wife says she wants the other guy all the time and never wants you." This fetish is thus presented as a self-reflexive exploration of the libidinal economy, whereby jealousy can be something other than a hostile take-over bid, launched on behalf of an unwise over-investment in the self. As one behavioral expert puts it, jealousy "is a social construct based on the notion that husbands own their wives, and is thus much more recent, evolutionarily speaking, than the competition that turns guys on. That's why it's mostly intellectuals who are into cuckolding: because other guys are crippled by jealousy. They're aroused and upset and don't know why." The problematic and elitist implications of such statements are obvious enough without metacommentary here. (All quotes from Rufus, n.p.)

23. Luhmann believes that "it is impossible in love to calculate the costs or weigh up the accounts, because both one's profits and one's losses are enjoyed; indeed, they serve to make one aware of love and to keep it alive" (67).
24. Pozdnyshev notes, "In our section of society all husbands are jealous" (102).
25. One cannot help but consider this as a symptom of Lacan's dictum, "There is no sexual relationship." However, in some cases, the more that this metaphysical obstacle is felt, deep in the heart or loins of the lover, the more frenzied and disturbing the attempt to bridge the unbridgeable, or catch the uncatchable. Exhibit A and B for twentieth-century literature would be John Fowles' *The Collector* and Nabokov's *Lolita*.

26. A fascinating, emotionally scarring, postmodern twist on the "tolerant husband" can be found in Lars von Trier's film *Breaking the Waves* (1996). From a certain angle, Bess could be considered a strange love-child of Anna Karenina's – a woman who dies not because of possessive jealousy, but quite the opposite, because her (invalid and possibly insane) husband pushes her out into the public sphere, to have sex with as many strange men as possible.
27. Today's "polyamorous" community puts much stock in the concept of *compersion* – a notion originally conceived by the Kerista Commune in San Francisco. Compersion is an extended erotic form of empathy, in which the subject experiences joy via a third term, up to and including the figure usually considered to be a threat or rival. In other words, compersion is the positive and inclusive flip-side of jealousy. (Just as some would say a smiling unicorn is the positive and inclusive form of a snorting, angry stallion.)
28. A fascinating case in Russian life and literature of the same period is Turgenev, who not only enthusiastically introduced Maupassant's writings to Tolstoy, but who wrote of unjealous husbands (cf. *Spring Torrents*) from his literally eccentric position. As one critique notes, "It was a constant refrain of Turgenev that he failed to 'weave himself a nest' in life and had been forced to perch on the edge of strange nests" (Schapiro 197) – most notably the nest inhabited by the Spanish singer, Pauline Garcia-Viardot. Clearly Turgenev was not a rook, since he never presumed to poach a woman from another man, and yet neither did he consider wedlock to be an obstacle to living with his true love (*and* her exceedingly tolerant husband).
29. In the same piece, Green makes the interesting claim that "the reader of this novel, should be in a very real sense a listener. We need to remind ourselves again that Tolstoy conceived his story with the living voice of an actor in his

mind. That is, it was written, as the sonata was, for an instrument" (447).

30. See the illuminating comments on "the refrain" in Deleuze and Guattari's *A Thousand Plateaus* (chapter 11), and on Vinteuil's phrase more specifically in Deleuze's *Proust and Signs*.
31. No doubt an evolutionary biologist, or even sociobiologist, would read such passion as the cultural froth of genetic imperatives. But as useful and sobering as such accounts are, in reminding us of our mammalian heritage, they are almost universally reductive when it comes to interpreting and contextualizing human behavior. Psychology, affect, aesthetics, and other "cultural" factors are ignored, or at best, alluded to as inessential contingencies (cf. Jonason et al's article, "Positioning the Booty-Call Relationship on the Spectrum of Relationships"). A point I make not to preserve the exceptionalism of humans in this regard, but to simply identify underdeveloped influences in general within such fields. Of course the humanities have been guilty of over-emphasizing the role of finer forces, and the more sharing of conceptual lenses we can have between the humanities and the sciences, the more comprehensive and revealing will be the subsequent interpretations.
32. The growing literature around the creaturely is usually framed by questions of biopolitics (cf. the vast bibliography issuing from Agamben's rendering of Foucault's concept, especially in *Homo Sacer*).
33. For an insightful, and long overdue, reading of Nietzsche's nuanced relationship to the animal kingdom, see Vanessa Lemm's book, *Nietzsche's Animal Philosophy* as well as Alan Bleakley's chapter "Zarathustra's Zoo," in *The Animalizing Imagination: Totemism, Textuality, and Ecocriticism* ("May my beasts guide me!").

5. EXILED FROM FUNLAND

1. Let us not forget that Heaven itself is the ultimate gated community, with St. Peter functioning as clipboard wielding security officer.
2. The (not so) latent anthropocentrism in Agamben's vision is something I discuss in *Human Error*.
3. All subsequent Agamben quotes come from "Nudity."
4. Flusser himself knew a thing or two about exile, having fled the Nazis to Brazil: a productive trauma, on which he reflected a great deal in his writings.
5. This no doubt self-indulgent nostalgia was obscenely in evidence in the belated sequel to *Tron* (1982), grandiosely named *Tron Legacy* (2010) – pitching itself as a second coming, of sorts.
6. The case of Chinatown Fair – which was resurrected from the dead several months later – suggests yes and no, since many former customers complained of a smaller space, less exciting machines, and a new card swipe system that compromised the aura (and rituals) of the old coin-operated games. In this respect, I eagerly await *After Arcades*, Samuel Tobin's neo-Benjaminian study of the zombification and/or reincarnation of the once great American video-game arcade.
7. Unlike Agamben, Eiseley resists the self-flattering totem of human as exclusive world-remaker, or shepherd of Being, as he makes clear when he writes: "To see from an inverted angle, however, is not a gift allotted merely to the human imagination. I have come to suspect that within their degree it is sensed by animals, though perhaps as rarely as among men. The time has to be right; one has to be, by chance or intention, upon the border of two worlds. And sometimes these two borders may shift or interpenetrate and one sees the miraculous" (167).

CONCLUSION: ZIGZAG: THE TOTEM OF MOVEMENT

1. The quote is from Quintus Smyrnaeus, "The Fall of Troy" (c. 4th century AD), A. S. Way translation (1913).
2. See Jacques Rancière, "The Gaps of Cinema."
3. Luke Rhinehart's classic early 1970's novel, *The Dice Man,* could be re-read as a tale of a man who outsources his moral agency to his totem: a pair of six-sided dice.
4. The phrase is from Deleuze's "L'abécédaire" interview with Claire Parnet, recently released on DVD by Semiotext(e) with English subtitles, under the name *Gilles Deleuze: From A to Z.*
5. Bleakley asks: "what if we invite the animal back into our lives, a brazen return through the front rather than side door? Then we may find that the animal brings a gift of both the beautiful and the sublime. Our model could be the seahorse, who in the wild demonstrates a life of the aesthetic, of elegant self-display; who shows tenderness, wrapping a tail gently around the finger of prying zoologists just as the male and female seahorses go for walks with their tails entwined; who shows fidelity – a mate for life; and who throws the assumptions we make about gender in animal life into disarray, for it is the male seahorse who incubates the ova that the female injects into his birth pouch, and who eventually gives birth. Perhaps what frightens us about animals – just as it simultaneously intrigues us – is not their irrationality, their bestiality, their primitiveness, but the depth, the sublimity, the sheer range and unpredictability of their aesthetic self-display" (35). My one caveat to this comment would be to replace the animal with "totem."

Works Cited

Adams, Richard. *Watership Down* (New York: Avon, 1972).

Agamben, Giorgio. *The Coming Community*. Translated by Michael Hardt (Minneapolis: University of Minnesota Press, 1993).

— . "Shame, or On the Subject." *Remnants of Auschwitz: The Witness and the Archive*. Translated by D. Heller-Roazen (New York: Zone Books, 1999).

— . *The Open: Man and Animal*. Translated by Kevin Attell (Stanford: Stanford University Press, 2004).

— . "Nudity," in *Nudities*. Translated by David Kshik and Stefan Pedatella (Stanford: Stanford University Press, 2011).

Badiou, Alain. *Ethics: An Essay on the Understanding of Evil*, Translated by Peter Hallward (New York: Verso, 2002).

Bailly, Jean-Christophe. "The Slightest Breath (On Living)," *The New Centennial Review*, Translated by Matthew H. Anderson, 10, 3, 2011: 1-11.

Baker, Steve. "Fear of the Familiar," in *Postmodern Animal* (London: Reaktion, 2000).

Ballard, J.G. *Crash* (Herts: Panther, 1975).

— . *Super-Cannes* (London: Flamingo, 2001).

— . *Millennium People* (New York: W. W. Norton & Co., 2011).

Barnes, Jonathan. *Aristotle: A Very Short Introduction* (Oxford: Oxford University Press, 2000).

Barthes, Roland. *Mythologies*. Translated by Annette Lavers (New York: Hill & Wang, 1972).

— . *Mourning Diary*. Translated by Richard Howard (New York: Hill & Wang, 2010).

Baudrillard, Jean. *Fatal Strategies*. Translated by Philip Beitchman and W. G. J. Niesluchowski. Edited by Jim Fleming. (New York: Semiotext(e), 1990).

Bauman, Zygmunt. *Liquid Love: On the Frailty of Human Bonds*.

(UK: Polity, 2003).

Beardsworth, Richard. "Thinking Technics," in *Jacques Derrida*, vol. 3. Christopher Norris & David Roden (eds.) (London: Sage, 2003).

Bennett, Jane. *Vibrant Matter: A Political Ecology of Things* (Durham: Duke University Press, 2010).

Bleakley, Alan. *The Animalizing Imagination: Totemism, Textuality, and Ecocriticism* (London: Palgrave Macmillan, 2000).

Bogost, Ian. *Alien Phenomenology: or What It's Like to Be a Thing* (Minneapolis: University of Minnesota Press, 2012).

Bolter, Jay and Richard Grusin. "Immediacy, Hypermediacy and Remediation," in *Remediation: Understanding New Media*. (Cambridge: MIT, 2000).

Chang, Shea Lea. Untitled statement. Accessed online October 5, 2011. *http://www.i-k-u.com/eng_h/iku/int_j.html*

Chiang, Ted. *The Lifecycle of Software Objects* (Burton: Subterranean, 2010). Accessed online January 25, 2012. *http://subterraneanpress.com/index.php/magazine/fall-2010/fiction-the-lifecycle-ofsoftware-objects-by-ted-chiang/*

Chow, Rey & Julian Rohrhuber, "On Captivation: A Remainder from the 'Indistinction of Art and Nonart," in *Entanglements, or Transmedial Thinking about Capture* (Durham: Duke University Press, 2012).

Christian, Brian. *The Most Human Human: What Talking with Computers Teaches Us About What It Means to Be Alive* (New York: Doubleday, 2011).

Cohen, Jeffrey Jerome. "Song of Stones," *Postmedieval*, (2010) 1: 56–63.

Committee on the Limits of Organic Life in Planetary Systems. *The Limits of Organic Life in Planetary Systems* (Washington DC: National Academies Press, 2011).

Cooper, Robbie. *Alter Ego: Avatars and Their Creators*. (London: Chris Boot Publishers, 2007).

Daily Yomiuri "i-Mode's Virtual Lover Games Strike a Chord."

(December 22, 2000), 1.

Daniel, R.R. (ed.). *Concepts in Space Science* (Hyderabad: Universities Press, 2002).

DeLanda, Manuel. "Matter Matters: Crucial Eccentricities," *DOMUS*, 895, September (2006). Accessed online July 16, 2011. *http://www.scribd.com/do c/37867149/DeLanda-Matter-Matters.*

Deleuze, Gilles. "Anti Oedipe et Mille Plateaux," *Les Cours des Gilles Deleuze* (Cours Vincennes: July 14, 1974). Accessed online March 2, 2012. *http://www.webdeleuze.com/php/texte .php?cle=176&groupe=Anti%20Oedipe%20et%20Mille%20Platea ux&langue=2*

— . *Proust and Signs*. Translated by Richard Howard. (Minneapolis: University of Minnesota Press, 2000).

Deleuze, Gilles and Félix Guattari. *A Thousand Plateaus: Capitalism and Schizophrenia*. Translated by Brian Massumi (London: Athlone, 1988).

— . *Anti-Oedipus: Capitalism and Schizophrenia*. Translated by Robert Hurley et al (London & New York: Penguin Classics, 2009).

Dery, Mark. *The Pyrotechnic Insanitarium: American Culture on the Brink* (New York: Grove, 1999).

— . "Culture Jamming: Hashing, Slashing, and Sniping in the Empire of Signs," *Shovelware*. Accessed online July 3, 2012. *http://markdery.com/?page_id=154*

During, Simon. *Modern Enchantments: The Cultural Power of Secular Magic* (Cambridge, MA: Harvard University Press, 2004).

Eiseley, Loren. *The Immense Journey* (New York: Vintage, 1959).

Flusser, Vilém. "Celebration," in *Writings*. Translated by Erik Eisel (Minneapolis: University of Minnesota Press, 2002).

Foucault, Michel. *The History of Sexuality: An Introduction*. Translated by R. Hurley (Harmondsworth: Penguin, 1987).

Fourier, Charles. *The Hierarchies of Cuckoldry and Bankruptcy*. Translated by Geoffrey Longnecker. (Cambridge, MA: Wakefield Press, 2011).

France, Louise. "Love at First Site." *Observer Online*. June 30, 2002. Accessed online April 14, 2010. *http://observer.guardian.co.uk/print/0,,4451314-110648,00.html*

Freud, Sigmund. *Group Psychology and the Analysis of the Ego*. Translated by James Strachey (New York: W. W. Norton & Co., 1959).

— . *An Autobiographical Study*. Translated by James Strachey (New York: W. W. Norton & Co., 1963).

— . *Totem and Taboo: Some Points of Agreement between the Mental Lives of Savages and Neurotics*. Translated by James Strachey (London & New York: Routledge, 2001).

— . "One of the Difficulties of Psycho-Analysis," *On Creativity and the Unconscious: the Psychology of Art, Literature, Love, and Religion* (New York: Harper Perennial, 2009).

Galloway, Alex. "Creative Evolution: Nils Aall Barricelli's Mathematical Organisms," *Cabinet*. 42 (Summer 2011): 45-50.

Gibson, William. *Idoru* (London & New York: Penguin, 1997).

Girard, René. *Deceit, Desire and the Novel*. Translated by Yvonne Freccero (Baltimore and London: Johns Hopkins University Press, 1988).

Goble, Mark "Wired Love: Pleasure at a Distance in Henry James and Others," *ELH* 74. 397–427. 2007.

Goethe, Johann Wolfgang von. *Maxims and Reflections*. Translated by Elisabeth Stopp. (London: Penguin Classics, 1998).

Graham, Bradley. "Rumsfeld Defends Iraqi Forces", *Washington Post*, October 1, 2005. Accessed online June 2, 2012. *http://www.washingtonpost.com/wp-dyn/content/article/2005/09/30/AR2005093001660.html*

Green, Dorothy. "The Kreutzer Sonata," in *Tolstoy's Short Fiction: A Norton Critical Edition*. Edited by Michael R. Katz. (Austin: University of Texas Press, 1991).

Groebner, Valentine. *Who Are You? Identification, Deception and Surveillence in Early Modern Europe*. (New York: Zone Books, 2007).

Grusin, Richard. *Premediation: Affect and Mediality After 9/11* (New York: Palgrave Macmillan, 2010).

Gunning, Tom. "The Cinema of Attraction: Early Film, Its Spectator, and the Avant-Garde." *Film and Theory: An Anthology*. Robert Stam & Toby Miller (eds.) (London: Blackwells, 2000).

Harmon, Amy. "Making Friends with a Robot Called Bina48," *New York Times*, July 4, 2010. Accessed online May 8, 2011. *http://www.nytimes.com/2010/07/05/science/05robotside.html*

Hayles, N. Katherine. "Virtual Bodies and Flickering Signifiers." *October*, Vol. 66 (Autumn, 1993). 69-91.

Heidegger, Martin. "The Question Concerning Technology," in *The Question Concerning Technology and Other Essays*. Translated by W. Lovitt. (New York: Harper & Row, 1977).

— . "The Age of the World Picture," *The Question Concerning Technology and Other Essays*. Translated by W. Lovitt (New York: Harper & Row, 1977).

Hudson, Laura. "The Political Animal: Species-Being and Bare Life," *Mediations* 23, 2 (2008): 88–117.

Jonason, Peter K., Li, Norman P. and Richardson, Jessica. "Positioning the Booty-Call Relationship on the Spectrum of Relationships: Sexual but More Emotional Than One-Night Stands," *Journal of Sex Research*, July 2010. Accessed online November 9, 2011. *http://dx.doi.org/10.1080/00224499.2010.497984*

Jünger, Ernst. *The Glass Bees*. Translated by Louise Bogan and Elizabeth Mayer (New York: NYRB, 2000).

Kittler, Friedrich A. *Gramophone, Film, Typewriter*. Translated by Geoffrey Winthrop-Young and Michael Wutz. (Stanford: Stanford University Press, 1999).

Lacan, Jacques. *The Ethics of Psychoanalysis* (New York: W.W. Norton & Company, 1997).

Latour, Bruno. *We Have Never Been Modern*. Translated by Catherine Porter (Cambridge, MA: Harvard University Press, 1993).

— . "A Collective of Humans and Non-Humans," *Readings in the Philosophy of Technology*. Edited by David Kaplan. (New York: Rowman & Littlefield, 2004).

Lemm, Vanessa. *Nietzsche's Animal Philosophy: Culture, Politics, and the Animality of the Human Being*. (New York: Fordham University Press, 2009).

Lessing, Doris. "On Tolstoy," in *Time Bites: Views and Reviews*. (New York: Harper Perennial, 2004).

Lévi-Strauss, Claude. *Totemism*. Translated by Rodney Needham (Beacon Press: Boston, 1963).

Levitt, Deborah. *The Animatic Apparatus* (Winchester, UK: Zero Books, forthcoming).

Lévy, Pierre. *Becoming Virtual: Reality in the Digital Age*. Translated by Robert Bononno (New York and London: Plenum, 1998).

Lucretius. *On the Nature of Things*. Translated by W.E. Leonard (New York: E.P. Dutton & Co., 1921).

— . *On the Nature of the Universe*. Translated by R. E. Latham (London: Penguin, 1994).

Luhmann, Niklas. *Love as Passion: The Codification of Intimacy*. Translated by Jeremy Gaines and Doris L. Jones. (Stanford: Stanford University Press, 1998).

Lynn Margulis and Dorian Sagan, *What is Life*? (Berkeley: University of California Press, 2000).

Maffesoli, Michel. *The Time of the Tribes: The Decline of Individualism in Mass Society*. Translated by Don Smith (London: Sage, 1996).

Marion, Jean-Luc. *The Erotic Phenomenon*. Trans. Stephen E. Lewis. (Chicago: University of Chicago Press, 2008).

Massumi, Brian. *Parables of the Virtual: Movement, Affect, Sensation* (Durham & London: Duke University Press, 2002).

Mattern, Shannon. "Puffs of Air: Communicating by Vacuum," John Knechtel (ed.), *AIR: Alphabet City Magazine 15* (Cambridge: MIT Press, 2010).

Maupassant, Guy de. *Alien Hearts*. Translated by Richard Howard. (New York: NYRB Classics, 2009).

Mazis, Glen A. *Humans, Animals, Machines: Blurring Boundaries* (Albany: State University of New York Press, 2008).

McLuhan, Marshall. *Understanding Media: The Extensions of Man* (Corte Madera: Gingko Press, 2003).

McLuhan, Marshall. *War and Peace in the Global Village* (San Francisco: Hardwired, 1997).

Meek, James. "Some Wild Creature," LRB, Vol. 32, No. 14, July 22, 2010, 3-8. Accessed online December 2, 2011. *http://www.lrb.co.uk/v32/n14/james-meek/some-wild-creature*

Meillassoux, Quentin. *After Finitude: An Essay on the Necessity of Contingency* Translated by Ray Brassier (London & New York: Continuum, 2010).

Michaud, Philippe-Alain. *Aby Warburg and the Image in Motion.* Translated by Sophie Hawkes (New York: Zone, 2007).

Mitchell, W.J.T., "What Do Pictures *Really* Want?" *October* 77 (Summer 1996), 71-82.

— . "Romanticism and the Life of Things: Fossils, Totems, and Images," *Critical Inquiry* 28 (Autumn 2001), 167-184.

Morton, Timothy. *Ecology Without Nature: Rethinking Environmental Aesthetics*. (Cambridge, Mass.: Harvard University Press, 2007).

Nabokov, Vladimir. *The Annotated Lolita*. Edited by A. Appel, Jnr. (New York:Vintage, 1991).

Nancy, Jean-Luc. *Being Singular Plural*. Translated by R. D. Richardson and A. E. O'Byrne. (Stanford: Stanford University Press, 2000).

Nasr, Seyyed Hossein. *Islam and the Plight of Modern Man* (Chicago: Kazi Publications, 2001).

Ngai, Sianne. "Our Aesthetic Categories: An Interview with Sianne Ngai," *Cabinet*, Issue 43 (Fall 2011), 45-51.

Nietzsche, Friedrich. *Human, All Too Human*. Translated by Gary Handwerk. (Stanford: Stanford University Press, 1995).

— . *On the Genealogy of Morals*. Translated by Daniel Smith (Oxford & New York: Oxford University Press, 1998).

O'Connor, Daniel, M. *Mediated Associations: Cinematic Dimensions of Social Theory* (Montreal: McGill Queens University Press, 2004).

Pettman, Dominic. *Love and Other Technologies: Retrofitting Eros for the Information Age*. (New York: Fordham University Press, 2006).

— . "After the Beep: Answering Machines and Creaturely Life," *boundary 2*, vol. 37, no.2 (Summer 2010), 133-153.

— . *Human Error: Species-Being and Media Machines* (Minneapolis: University of Minnesota Press, 2011).

Pettman, Dominic & Justin Clemens. "Relations with Concrete Others," *Avoiding the Subject: Media, Culture, and the Object*. (Amsterdam: University of Amsterdam Press, 2004).

Pirani, Adam. "Bob Hoskins, Animated Investigator," *Starlog* (August 1988).

Proust, Marcel. *In Search of Lost Time*. Translated by D. J. Enright, Terence Kilmartin, and C. K. Scott Moncrieff. (New York: Modern Library, 2003).

Rancière, Jacques. "The Gaps of Cinema." Translated by Sudeep Dasgupta. *NECSUS: European Journal of Media Studies*. Accessed online June 7, 2012. *http://www.necsus-ejms.org/the-gaps-of-cinema-by-jacques-ranciere/*

Rufus, Anneli. "Cuckolding: The Sex Fetish for Intellectuals," *The Daily Beast*. July 29, 2010. Accessed online March 10, 2011. *http://www.thedailybeast.com/blogs-and-stories/2010-07-29/cuckolding-the-sex-fetish-for-intellectuals/*

Santner, Eric. *On Creaturely Life: Rilke, Benjamin, Sebald* (Chicago: University of Chicago Press, 2006).

Schapiro, Leonard. "Critical Essay – *Spring Torrents*: Its Place and Significance in the Work of Ivan Sergeyevich Turgenev," in Turgenev, *Spring Torrents*. (London: Penguin Classics, 1980).

Sigusch, Volkmar. "The Neosexual Behavior," in *Archives of*

Sexual Behavior. (New York: Aug 1998). 27(4). 331-59.

Silverman, Kaja. *World Spectators*. (Stanford: Stanford University Press, 2000).

Simondon, Gilbert. *On the Mode of Existence of Technical Objects*. Translated by Ninian Mellamphy (University of Western Ontario, 1980).

Sontag, Susan. *Regarding the Pain of Others* (New York: Picador, 2003).

Standage, Tom. "Love Over the Wires," in *The Victorian Internet*. (New York: Berkley, 1999).

Steiger, Brad. *Totems: The Transformative Power of Your Personal Animal Totem* (New York: Harper Collins, 1997).

Steinbeck, John. *Of Mice and Men* (New York: Bantam, 1955).

Steiner, George. *In Bluebeard's Castle: Some Notes Towards the Redefinition of Culture*. (New Haven: Yale University Press, 1971).

Stiegler, Bernard. *Technics and Time, vols 1-3*. Translated by Richard Beardsworth et al. (Stanford: Stanford University Press, 1998-2010).

— . *Taking Care of Youth and the Generations*. Translated by Stephen Barker (Stanford: Stanford University Press, 2010).

— . *Decadence of Industrial Commodities*. Translated by Daniel Ross. (Cambridge, UK: Polity, 2011).

Stoekl, Allan. *Bataille's Peak: Energy, Religion and Postsustainability* (Minneapolis: University of Minnesota Press, 2007).

Stuart, Susan. *On Longing: Narratives of the Miniature, the Gigantic, the Souvenir, the Collection* (Durham: Duke University Press, 1993).

Thacker, Eugene. *After Life* (Chicago: University of Chicago Press, 2010).

Thacker, Eugene and Natalie Jeremijenko. *Creative Biotechnology: A User's Guide* (L+ Publishing, 2004).

Tiffany, Daniel. *Infidel Poetics: Riddles, Nightlife, Substance*. (Chicago: University of Chicago Press, 2009).

Tolstoy, Leo. *Anna Karenina*. Translated by Richard Pevear and Larissa Volokhonsky. (London: Penguin Classics, 2006).

— . *The Kreutzer Sonata*. Translated by David McDuff. (London: Penguin Great Loves, 2007).

Travers, Andrew. "The Nazi Eye Code of Falling in Love: Bright Eyes, Black Heart, Crazed Gaze," in *Love and Eroticism*. Mike Featherstone (ed.). (London: Sage, 1999).

Turkle, Sherry. *Alone Together: Why We Expect More from Technology and Less from Each Other*. (New York: Basic Books, 2011).

Turner, Scott. *The Extended Organism: The Physiology of Animal-Built Structures* (Cambridge, MA: Harvard University Press, 2002).

Wark, Ken. *Gamer Theory*. (Cambridge: Harvard University Press, 2007). Full text available online: *http://www.futureofthebook.org/gamertheory/*

White, Roland & Nina Goswami. "Beware of Digital Love." *Sunday Times*. March 21, 2004. 16.

Williamson, Judith. *Decoding Advertisements: Ideology and Meaning in Advertising* (London & New York: Marion Boyars, 2010).

Wittgenstein, Ludwig. *Remarks on the Philosophy of Psychology*. Translated by G. E. M. Anscombe (Chicago: University of Chicago Press, 1980).

Xinhua News Agency – CEIS. "Virtual Love Relationship Poses Another Challenge to Marriage Law Experts." Woodside: January 20, 2001. 1.

Zaslow, Jeffrey. "Digital Love Letters: Declaring It With TXT." *Wall Street Journal* (Europe). February 14, 2007. 30.

Žižek, Slavoj. *The Plague of Fantasies*. (London and New York: Verso, 1997).

— . "What Rumsfeld Doesn't Know That He Knows About Abu Ghraib," May 21, 2004. Accessed online July 3, 2012. *http://www.lacan.com/zizekrumsfeld.htm*

Other Media

Abumrad, Jad and Robert Krulwich. *Talking to Machines* (2011), podcast radio programme, Radiolab, Season 10, episode 11, WNYC, New York City. Available from: *http://www.radiolab.org/2011/may/31/* (Accessed 12th September 2011).

Boutang, Pierre-André, dir. *Gilles Deleuze: From A to Z (L'abécédaire).* An Interview with Claire Parnet. Translated by Charles J. Stivale. Semiotext(e). 2011.

Buñuel, Luis, dir. *That Obscure Object of Desire*. Greenwich Film Productions. 1977.

Curtis, Adam, *dir. All Watched Over By Machines of Loving Grace.* BBC. 2011. Accessed online January 11, 2012. http:/*/archive.org/details/AdamCurtis-AllWatchedOverByMachinesOfLovingGrace*

Dyas, Matthew, dir. *BBC's Horizon: Playing God.* BBC. 2012. Accessed online March 15, 2012. *http://www.youtube.com/watch?v=LWiFwqLxy64*

Herzog, Werner, dir. *Encounters at the End of the World*. Discovery Films et al. 2007.

Hill, Walter, dir. *The Warriors.* Paramount Pictures. 1979.

Jackson, Peter, dir. *Lord of the Rings: The Motion Picture Trilogy* (Special Extended Edition). New Line Home Video. 2004.

Jodorowsky, Alejandro, dir. *El Topo*. Producciones Panicas. 1970.

Kelly, Richard, dir. *Donnie Darko.* Pandora Cinema. 2001.

Koster, Henry, dir. *Harvey.* Universal Pictures. 1950.

Lubitsch, Ernst, dir. *The Smiling Lieutenant*. Paramount Pictures. 1931.

Lynch, David, dir. *Inland Empire.* Studio Canal. 2006.

Meyers, Nancy, dir. *What Women Want*, Paramount Pictures, 2000.

Shay, Robert, dir. *The Last Mimzy.* New Line Cinema. 2007.

Sweetland, Doug, dir. *Presto.* Pixar. 2008

Zemeckis, Robert, dir. *Who Framed Roger Rabbit?* Touchstone Pictures. 1988.

About the Author

Dominic Pettman is Chair of Culture and Media, Eugene Lang College, as well as Associate Professor of Liberal Studies, New School for Social Research, New York City. His previous books include *After the Orgy: Toward a Politics of Exhaustion* (SUNY, 2002), *Avoiding the Subject: Media, Culture and the Object* (AUP, 2004 - with Justin Clemens), *Love and Other Technologies: Retrofitting Eros for the Information Age* (Fordham, 2006), and *Human Error: Species-Being and Media Machines* (Minnesota, 2011).

Contemporary culture has eliminated both the concept of the public and the figure of the intellectual. Former public spaces – both physical and cultural – are now either derelict or colonized by advertising. A cretinous anti-intellectualism presides, cheerled by expensively educated hacks in the pay of multinational corporations who reassure their bored readers that there is no need to rouse themselves from their interpassive stupor. The informal censorship internalized and propagated by the cultural workers of late capitalism generates a banal conformity that the propaganda chiefs of Stalinism could only ever have dreamt of imposing. Zer0 Books knows that another kind of discourse – intellectual without being academic, popular without being populist – is not only possible: it is already flourishing, in the regions beyond the striplit malls of so-called mass media and the neurotically bureaucratic halls of the academy. Zer0 is committed to the idea of publishing as a making public of the intellectual. It is convinced that in the unthinking, blandly consensual culture in which we live, critical and engaged theoretical reflection is more important than ever before.